The Easy Listening Catalog

The
Easy Listening Catalog

by
Todd Frye

Published by

Todd Frye
Harrogate, Tennessee

The Easy Listening Catalog

Published by:
Todd Frye
PO Box 577
Harrogate TN 37752
toddfrye@yahoo.com

ISBN-10: 0-9979420-0-2
ISBN-13: 978-0-9979420-0-2

That Other Music:
A Brief, Poorly Sourced, and Probably Wildly Inaccurate History of Easy Listening, Exotica, and Other Neglected Genres

Writing a history of musical genres, no matter how modest or brief one attempts to be, is a complicated undertaking. Genres are fluid, with poorly-defined boundaries, and tend to shift and melt into one another as time goes forward. Looking back from the future we can see certain trends take shape, as certain styles rise and fall in popularity; but this is really a perspective only available with hindsight. Such a perspective also gives us the opportunity to look at social and historical trends that reflect themselves within the music, allowing certain forms to rise up and take shape, while other trends are downplayed, intentionally or otherwise.

It certainly doesn't help the matter when the types of music one wants to talk about are generally overlooked by the modern listening public, as well as by scholars and critics. Jazz, rock and roll, rhythm and blues – these are all important musical trends, and certainly deserve the bulk of listeners' attention; but does that mean that other forms should be completely ignored? To look within histories of popular music, or even at album collectors' price guides, one would be tempted to think that these other genres didn't even exist – like Communist officials who have fallen out of favor, and are therefore removed from paintings and history books.

This is not to suggest that there's some sort of organized conspiracy to never speak of Easy Listening or other previous styles of music; rather, the attitude seems to be more one of contempt: why would anybody want to listen to, much less talk about, such old-fashioned stuff? It's all mostly white people's music anyway, from back when the boys wore a jacket and slacks, and the girls wore dresses, even to a casual get-together. Squaresville, man – strictly squaresville.

Given the current political climate, one might be tempted to think that such a backlash might be so racially motivated – if Black Lives Matter, does White Music Matter? But, it's not quite that simple. If anything, it's not Black Vs. White, but Youth Vs. Squares – i.e., Mom and Dad. The 1950's saw a definite break between music meant for teenagers, and music meant for a somewhat older and more settled audience. What we are looking at in this book is primarily the latter.

Easy Listening

The genre we tend to refer to now as Easy Listening had its origins in the late 1940's when different orchestras began recording music that was softer, lighter, and usually offered no overt vocals or harsh instrumental sections that might tend to break the mood. It was meant, theoretically, to be played in the background, during dinner or pleasant conversation, without intruding or imposing itself on the listener. Rather, it could enhance moments of romance or relaxation, if necessary, but without overwhelming the given situation. In the commercial world, this took the form of Muzak, which was music licensed by companies to play unobtrusively in the background, soothing and mellow.

Composer and arranger Paul Weston began recording albums starting in about 1945 that were slower and smoother than what most other bandleaders were doing – this seemed to be part of a larger musical trend where audiences were going to hear bands just to listen, and not to dance. 'Hot' bands and faster songs were also still popular, and always would be, but there was also a desire (probably more from the female audience members) for music that was slower and softer. Weston's *Music For Dreaming*, released at first as a 10" disc, fit the bill perfectly. Calling the style Mood Music, Weston had a hit, and knew he was onto something.

Easy Listening (or Mood Music, or Beautiful Music, as it was also called) might have been okay with the younger female audience members, but it was certainly palatable to older listeners – the parents, but also young marrieds who were settling into domestic life. The adults generally didn't want to be confronted by the more abrasive aspects of much popular music; Easy Listening strode somewhere between Classical and Pop music; not harsh, but lively and interesting enough to make for a pleasant listening experience.

In time, arrangers found that they could do Easy Listening versions of popular tunes that were never meant for such treatment. The results were ultra-smooth concoctions with all of the jagged edges ground down, and naturally musical purists hated them – but nevertheless, a certain portion of the record-buying public preferred these versions to the originals. The songwriters, of course, still got their royalty payments regardless of the interpretation; and besides, if one preferred, one could always go back to the source material. But the fact that – for example – the Hollyridge Strings could offer their *Beatles Song Book* albums and get respectable sales, *while the original Beatles recordings were still in the charts*, proves that there were two distinct audiences, each of whom had very different wants and expectations.

This sort of thing, of course, further convinced the kids and the hardcore fans that Easy Listening was the music of squares – watered-down, milquetoast versions of popular songs cranked out for Mom and Dad who couldn't handle the originals. In essence, this was correct. Not that Mom and Dad 'couldn't handle' the more raucous musical styles that came along during the 1950's & 60's, but they generally didn't want to: Easy Listening gave them a certain aural satisfaction without demanding much from them. The kids might go buy a Jimi Hendrix album and bring it home to listen to over and over, staring at the cover and trying to grok every note, but generally their parents just wanted something nice playing in the background while they ate dinner. Certainly, from a more purist point of view, the kids' motivations are more laudable; but does that completely invalidate Mom and Dad's desires?

Given its softer and romantic nature, Easy Listening was also deemed perfect music for *affaires d'amour*, whether it was a young bachelor trying to seduce his date for the evening, or a couple in love hoping to get each other in the mood. These days this aspect of Easy Listening is usually referred to as **Bachelor Pad Music**, or some variation thereof. Indeed, the 1950's and 60's were certainly the Age of the Bachelor, when that lifestyle was essentially defined by the men's magazines and other aspects of the popular culture: not for nothing did so many album covers from that period feature lovely, buxom young women in glorious *dishabille*. Most were in fact quite tame – like those of, say, Jackie Gleason or Ray Conniff, which featured young women in the throes of romantic love, often embracing the male of their desire. Others featured women in quite a different mood, the look in their eyes unmistakably one of lust and animal passion (or so it was supposed to appear to the common male record purchaser).

Another aspect of Easy Listening that may strike modern listeners is that... well... it's really, really *white*. Not that black people could not, or did not, participate; but the vast majority of the genre's progenitors were not only white, but *seriously* white dudes. Percy Faith and Henry Mancini may have been giants of popular music during the 1960's, but God love 'em, they tended to resemble high school shop teachers more than rock stars. Black record buyers tended to stick with the shifting landscape of rhythm and blues, jazz, gospel, and popular music during the time period covered in this book. This isn't to say that their tastes were superior, nor inferior; but much of it didn't seem to resonate with black listeners. Who can blame them? It's really *not* very funky; in fact, it's practically anti-funky. But, by definition, that's what Easy Listening is.

Easy Listening began to fade somewhat in the late 1960's. Why this is, is probably a complex topic of study, but the changes in popular music that were taking place, first in 1964 with the Beatles, then with groups like the Tijuana Brass and Brazil '66, then toward the end of the decade with the hippie movement when things tended to get looser and harsher at the same time – all of this resulted in a radically altered listening landscape. Even the music that the grownups enjoyed was changing. Post-*Whipped Cream and Other Delights*, softened versions of popular songs were still around, but tended to take a more modern approach, doing away with the heavy use of strings and multi-piece orchestras. This was **The Now Sound**, which had the same basic goals as Easy Listening, but used different methods to achieve its aims.

By the early 70's, Easy Listening was still around, but was barely hanging on. A lot of popular music seemed to be about excess, but there were also a few trends with a softer and more relaxed approach. Singer-songwriters like Carole King were coming more often to the forefront, offering a nice alternative to the harsher radio offerings. Songs from the 40's and 50's became less and less in demand, and when the more modern (i.e., post-Beatles) songs were desired, more listeners wanted to hear the original artists rather than some orchestra's interpretation – so, the decades-old habit of doing 'standards' (that is, songs that existed in many different versions) gradually began disappearing. (*Name That Tune* notwithstanding.)

It wasn't until 1979 that the *Billboard* Easy Listening chart was renamed Adult Contemporary; it had held its previous name since 1961. But those two dates are each a bit late to the party; the trend had started several years before 1961, but certainly ended long before 1979.

Exotica

Men and women have probably always dreamed of faraway lands, exotic and tempting, seeking either adventure or abject comfort, away from the grinding indignities that exemplify modern civilized life. For those of us in the Western world, that generally means the lands to the East: spicy Asia; dense Africa; the remote South Pacific. We daydream of remote beaches populated by tawny, attractive people welcoming us with tart fruits and little clothing; and in the tall grass outside the village there just might be some clawed animal waiting to pounce, which just adds a pinch of danger to the proceedings.

The musical genre of Exotica plays upon this fantasy, offering us an aural glimpse of what such far-flung places might be like... well, a watered-down white man's version, anyway. For, let's not beat around the poison-fruited bush: this is largely the music of the white man imitating the sounds of his darker-skinned (and presumably more ethnically authentic) brothers. There were certainly a handful of Exotica musicians who really did come from foreign shores (especially within the Hawaiian Music genre), but the vast majority of these guys were, again, pasty white fellows creating a type of ostensibly exotic music that was palatable to their postwar, workaday listening audience.

Speaking of the war, that was apparently how a number of Exotica fans got their taste for such foreign delights, at least apocryphally. Imagine a nice young Kansas farmboy, 19 years old and hardly ever left his hometown, suddenly sent off by the Navy to some hot port on the other side of the world. Everything from the food to the weather is vastly different from what he's always known, and *golly!* – the ladies are dark-skinned and doe-eyed beauties who aren't at all like the ones back home. He gets a taste of another land, another culture, a bit of danger – then just as suddenly he's back in Kansas working in a factory, living in a quiet subdivision and married to Ida Jean who's nice enough and pretty but not terribly exciting. One can hardly blame him for reminiscing about his war years and wishing he could get back to that tropical paradise.

Exotica music definitely had a godfather, and that was Les Baxter. Baxter had an eclectic musical education, and was skilled enough as a singer to work regularly until he could gain a reputation for his songwriting and arranging, which is where his real genius lay. Baxter began mixing more exotic themes into his music, evoking faraway places with his compositions, so that he became known for that type of spiced-up orchestral sound. Over time he drifted more and more into writing film scores, which proved a fine showplace for his talents.

In 1957, bandleader Martin Denny, who had a regular gig at the Hawaiian Village hotel in Oahu, Hawaii, released the album *Exotica*, which featured several Baxter compositions including "Quiet Village." The album featured Denny's band using authentic ethnic instruments as well as bird calls and other jungle sound effects to create a total aural package. *Exotica* eventually went all the way to #1 and the song to #2 in the *Billboard* charts, and as a result the album title gave its name to a new genre of music. Exotica, the musical style, lasted well into the 1960's, as it offered an alternative to the more mundane Easy Listening format.

For some, just visiting the other side of the world wasn't enough – they wanted to travel to other planets. The Space Race was in full force in the late 1950's and early 60's, and this cultural push was felt in American music as well. Thus was born **Space Age Pop**, in which an album tries to make the listener think that he or she is, well, in outer space, or visiting another planet, or somesuch. This was usually achieved by the use of the otherworldly-sounding theremin, as well as whatever electronic and studio sound effects could be shoehorned into the mix. Again, Les Baxter was one of the pioneers of this musical style as well, his album *Space Escapade* being one of the absolute classics of this sub-genre.

Another sort-of subgenre of Exotica is **Hawaiian Music**, which has long existed in the public consciousness – it was extremely popular in the first few decades of the 20th century, with a few revivals of interest now and then. For the purposes of this book, it's counted as a sub-genre of Exotica because that format also embraces other formats from that part of the world. The entirety of Hawaiian music, however, is vast; this book only lists a select number of recordings, in the general 1952-1972 timeframe. Listeners interested in hearing more are encouraged to do their own research.

That Other Stuff

There are other genres included in this book as well. **Latin music** is a vast category, encompassing a wide range of styles and eras. Naturally we can only cover a certain small number of them that fall within the book's timeframe. Actually, the only reason it is included at all is because it is often covered by so many musicians and groups in this book: there are several albums with titles like _______ *Goes Latin*, where the given performers do their own twist on that scene; nevertheless, such personalities as Perez Prado and Xavier Cugat are included. The Brazil/bossa nova stuff which started in the early-to-mid 1960's with Astrud Gilberto singing "The Girl From Ipanema" and leading to Sergio Mendes and Brazil '66 was an important component to what would become the Now Sound.

Spy and Crime Jazz are basically components of the world of film and TV soundtrack music, but a few examples are included, especially ones dating from the early part of the Spy Craze in the early-mid 1960's.

Herb Alpert and the Tijuana Brass practically created their own genre when the album *Whipped Cream and Other Delights* kept selling and selling, staying in the charts for months at a time; this wasn't really a genre (although the blandness of it did contribute somewhat to the Now Sound) but there was an unusually large number of cheap imitators that sprung up, with even some big names trying to get in on the act.

There's a good deal of music that is really difficult to classify. Is it jazz? Is it pop? What would one call Mel Henke's near-comedic arrangements? Or Buddy Cole's organ-ic offerings? Russ Garcia's *Fantastica* is self-consciously Space Age Pop, but what about his more fanciful efforts like his version of "I Get a Kick Out of You" from his *Songs in the Night*? The point is, there's a lot of music listed in this book that doesn't really fit into any neat classification.

But whatever you call it, the point is, much of this music is being completely overlooked by modern listeners, critics, and historians. And that's a terrible shame, because so much of it is just incredible. Sure, modern kids who like hip-hop and the latest pitch-shifted diva's hits won't be interested; but everybody knew that going in. If you're holding this book in your hands, you're already interested, or at least intrigued enough to look into the subject.

And, thanks to modern technologies, one can do so without having to buy a significant number of the albums listed in this volume. Youtube will yield up a surprisingly vast amount of great forgotten music, thanks to other people with similar interests, who have done the work of sharing their own vinyl LP's.

Nothing is a substitute, however, for owning a turntable and hunting down the original albums listed here – after all, that's what this book is: readers are encouraged to go and seek out the original vinyl versions of this music. Record stores may be difficult to locate in modern America, especially in small towns, but there's always Ebay – and in the warmer months, garage and yard sales. The local Goodwill, modest as it may be, is often a good place to check, as is the local junk or second-hand store. The thrill of finding a highly-desired or even rare item while lurking in some modest corner of one's own hometown is one that collectors of any sort can relate to – it's one of the best parts of the whole endeavor; and finding such a gem at a modest price is just the icing on the cake.

If this book has any value, therefore, it's to act as a rough guide to what's out there, waiting to be explored and enjoyed. Collectors and enthusiasts can use it to seek out new artists, new items that they've never heard of before. There are literally hundreds and hundreds of albums, largely unexplored by 99.999% of the population, a whole uncharted territory of great tunes waiting to be (re)discovered.

Who knows? Through the efforts of enthusiasts like us, maybe word will spread about all this cool music from the past, and a more fitting recognition of its value can finally be realized; and those of us who were already here can say, "I told you so."

Todd Frye
Harrogate, Tennessee
June, 2016

The Record Listing

This guide attempts to be comprehensive; but the author doesn't claim to have covered every single eligible work or artist. Ultimately, it behooves collectors to use this book as a guide to the breadth and depth of this collecting field. But ultimately, it falls to individual collectors – should they wish to do so – to track down every item released for a given artist. Half of the fun is in the hunt anyway, so unearthing rare releases or uncatalogued variations is better left to hardcore collectors, and happily so.

The era covered by this volume encompasses the years from about 1952 to 1972. While making that year a soft cutoff point is a bit of a personal decision by the author, it just seems that music from after that time (and perhaps a bit before) no longer encompasses any of the relevant genres, but falls under the later term 'Adult Contemporary.' Also, while 1952 might seem arbitrary, the widespread proliferation of 12", 33-rpm LP's started around that date, so we are beginning there.

This volume lists only full-sized 12" LP's; no EP's, 10" discs, or 45's; no quadraphonic records.

American releases only.

Mono and stereo catalog numbers included where known. If not indicated, usually before 1958 everything was monophonic, and after 1967 the market was almost completely devoted to only stereophonic. Some record companies may have lagged behind others in changing over.

What's not included: Greatest hits collections (for the most part); mainstream jazz; blues, folk, classical, opera, march, Dixieland, Big Band, pre-1950's (mostly), or waltz music (although it is sometimes difficult to separate some of these out from 'straight' Easy Listening); country & Western or folk music, for the most part; Christmas music; hymns or other religious music; some material released after of the artist's main period of creativity, e.g., a 'comeback' album. Pop music and similar material also is not included, although again it is often difficult to distinguish between that and some of the genres covered here. Exceptions to this are when artists would do albums devoted to then-current popular music from other genres – e.g., an album full of Beatles songs.

Not every album of each artist may be listed. Nor is every release of every album listed; this is unnecessary and burdensome. Where possible, the catalog number of the original release is given priority.

Soundtrack and other film music albums are largely de-emphasized in this volume, so not too many are included.

Not every album of Hawaiian, Latin jazz, or similar 'foreign' or 'ethnic' musical styles is included, else this book would probably be about three times its current size. The author has tried to include many of the most important artists, however. For that matter, there may have been artists of other genres who have slipped through the cracks also. The primary focus of the book is on Easy Listening and Exotica, so the most emphasis has been placed on these.

Solo singers are largely excluded, with a very few notable exceptions. (It greatly pained the author to take out the completed Frank Sinatra section.) Solo singers, even if backed by a top orchestra, fall more solidly into the Pop category than any of these other genres, so… no.

Specific works of some artists may be included while the majority of their output isn't; this is usually because they may do one or more albums which are of relevant interest while the rest of their catalog isn't. For example, Count Basie's *Basie Meets Bond* is included (falling into the Spy Jazz category), while the majority of his work, being straight jazz, doesn't belong in this volume.

Album titles in italics are considered either historically important, or are (in the author's opinion) classics of their respective genres.

Note: 'Compilations' don't always refer to albums featuring multiple artists, but may occasionally refer to albums where the artist (a) isn't listed on the front cover, (b) isn't listed at all, or (c) appears under a pseudonym. Certain compilations may be listed in that section because they are part of a series, such as RCA Custom's Volume For Hi-Fi Living albums from 1957. This section really only scratches the surface of what's available, as producing a more comprehensive listing is a feat beyond the scope of this volume.

50 Guitars of Tommy Garrett, The

Although Tommy 'Snuff' Garrett was a successful record producer, the Tommy who actually played guitar on these albums was Tommy Tedesco, the versatile Los Angeles session musician.

- 50 Guitars Around the World (1970?, Liberty L2S-5108/SCR-2) This was an exclusive release for the Columbia Record Club.
- 50 Guitars for Midnight Lovers (1970, Liberty LSS-14047)
- 50 Guitars Go Italiano (1964, Liberty LMM-13028 (mono), LSS-14028 (stereo))
- 50 Guitars Go South of the Border (1961, Liberty LMM-13005 (mono), LSS-14005 (stereo)
- 50 Guitars Go South of the Border, Vol. 2 (1962, Liberty LMM-13016 (mono), LSS-14016 (stereo))
- The 50 Guitars In Love (1966, Liberty LMM-13037 (mono), LSS-14037 (stereo))
- 50 Guitars Visit Hawaii (1962, Liberty LMM-13022 (mono), LSS-14022 (stereo))
- Bordertown Bandido (1964, Liberty LMM-13031 (mono), LSS-14031 (stereo))
- El Hombre (1968, Liberty LSS-14042)
- Espana (1965, Liberty LMM-13032 (mono), LSS-14032 (stereo))
- In A Brazilian Mood (1967, Liberty LMM-13038 (mono), LSS-14038 (stereo))

- Love Songs From South of the Border (1966, Liberty LMM-13035 (mono), LSS-14035 (stereo))
- Maria Elena (1963, Liberty LMM-13030 (mono), LSS-14030 (stereo))
- Mexican Leather and Spanish Lace (1969, Liberty LSS-14046)
- More 50 Guitars In Love (1967, Liberty LMM-13039 (mono), LSS-14039 (stereo))
- Our Love Affair (1969, Liberty LSS-14041)
- Return to Paradise (1965, Liberty LMM-13033 (mono), LSS-14033 (stereo))
- Six Flags Over Texas (1962, Liberty LMM-13040 (mono), LSS-14040 (stereo))
- The Sound of Love (1969, Liberty LSS-14044)
- Viva Mexico! (1966, Liberty LMM-13036 (mono), LSS-14036 (stereo))

101 Strings (see also **Les Baxter**; **Nelson Riddle**)

The collection of various studio musicians collectively called 101 Strings played on over 100 albums over a 30-year career.

- 25 Years of Show Hits (1961, Somerset P-13700; Stereo-Fidelity SF-13700)
- 101 Strings Plays Hit Songs for Girls (1967, Alshire S-5064)
- 101 Strings Play Hits Written by the Beatles (1968, Alshire S-5111)
- 101 Strings Play Love is Blue (1967, Alshire S-5086)
- 101 Strings Play Million Selling Hits, Vol. 1 (1967, Alshire S-5087)
- 101 Strings Play Million Selling Hits, Vol. 2 (1967, Alshire S-5089)
- 101 Strings Play Songs for Lovers on a Summer Night (1969, Alshire S-5143)
- 101 Strings Play the World's Great Standards (1957, Somerset P-4300; Stereo-Fidelity SF-4300; re-released in 1966 on Alshire S-5020)
- 101 Strings Play Three O'Clock in the Morning, etc. (1972, Alshire S-5265)
- Astro-Sounds from Beyond the Year 2000 (1968, Alshire S-5119)
- Award Winning Scores from the Silver Screen (1958, Somerset P-7000; Stereo-Fidelity SF-7000)
- Best of the Soul Series (1967, Alshire S-5069)
- A Bridal Bouquet (1958, Somerset P-6400; Stereo-Fidelity SF-6400)

- Broadway Cocktail Party (1960, Somerset P-12100; Stereo-Fidelity SF-12100)
- Cole Porter (1966, Alshire M-5007 (mono), S-5007 (stereo))
- East of Suez (1959, Somerset P-11200; Stereo-Fidelity SF-11200)
- Exodus and Other Great Movie Themes... (1966, Alshire ST-5075)
- The 'Exotic' Sounds of Love (1970, A/S Records AS-201)
- Fire and Romance of South America (1965, Stereo-Fidelity SF-22200; Alshire S-5040)
- Fly Me to the Moon (1963, Somerset P-19600; Stereo-Fidelity SF-19600; also 1964, Alshire ST-5033)
- Gold Award Hits (1969, Alshire S-5161)
- Guitars Galore (1966, Alshire S-5065)
- Guitars Galore, Vol. 2 (1969, Alshire S-5141)
- Here Come the Birds (1968, Alshire S-5148)
- I Love Paris (1960, Somerset P-13000; Stereo-Fidelity SF-13000)
- In a Hawaiian Paradise (1961, Somerset P-12800; Stereo-Fidelity SF-12800)
- Irving Berlin (1966?, Alshire S-5005)
- Lullabies For Baby (1969, Alshire S-5138)
- Million Seller Hits (1972, Alshire S-5251)
- Million Seller Hits Arranged and Conducted by Les Baxter (1970, Alshire S-5188)
- Million Seller Hits from Italy (1968, Alshire S-5113)
- Million Seller Hits from Mexico (1967, Alshire S-5099)
- Million Seller Hits of 1966 (1966, Alshire S-5050)
- Million Seller Hits of Today (1968, Alshire S-5112)
- A Night in the Tropics (1957, Somerset P-4400; Stereo-Fidelity SF-4400; also released on Trans-World)
- On A Summer Night (1969, Alshire S-5143)
- Quiet Hours (1960, Somerset P-10200; Stereo-Fidelity SF-10200)
- Rhapsody (1961, Somerset P-13600; Stereo-Fidelity SF-13600)
- The Romance of Hawaii (1970, Alshire S-5177)
- The Romance of Magic Island (1967, Alshire S-5063)
- Romantic Piano at Cocktail Time (1972, Alshire S-5139; with **Pietro Dero**)
- S.R.O. Broadway Hits (1967, Alshire S-5061)
- Songs of Love (1967, Alshire S-5072)
- The Soul of Mexico (1963, Somerset P-17000; Stereo-Fidelity SF-17000; Alshire S-5032)
- Sounds and Songs of the Jet Set (1965, Alshire S-5043)

- The Sounds of Love (1969, A/S Records AS-199)
- Sounds of Today (1967, Alshire S-5078)
- Spanish Eyes and Other Romantic Songs (1967, Alshire S-5051)
- Spectacular Brass!!! Fantastic Reeds!!! (1971, Alshire S-5229; with **Nelson Riddle**)
- Swingin' Things from 101 Strings (1967, Alshire S-5055)
- The Tijuana Sound (1967, Alshire S-5091)

Acquaviva and His Orchestra

Tony Acquaviva was an American composer and conductor who was married to singer Joni James.

- The Exciting Sound of Acquaviva and His Orchestra (1963, Decca DL 4465 (mono), DL 74465 (stereo))
- Music for Your Midnight Mood (1955, MGM E3226)

Addeo, Leo and His Orchestra

Leo Addeo was a skilled orchestra leader and became a longtime producer for RCA.

- Blue Hawaii (1973, RCA Camden CXS-9035) Two-disc set.
- Calypso and Other Island Favorites (1964, RCA Camden CAL 807 (mono), CAS 807 (stereo))
- Far Away Places (1965, RCA Camden CAS-901)
- Great Standards with a Hawaiian Touch (1963, RCA Camden CAL-672 (mono), CAS-672 (stereo))
- Hawaii in Hi-Fi (1958, Vik LX-1107; 1959, RCA Camden CAL-510 (mono), CAS-510 (stereo))
- Hawaii's Greatest Hits (1972, RCA Camden CAS-2506)
- Hawaiian Paradise (1965, RCA Camden CAL-853 (mono), CAS-853 (stereo))
- Hello Dolly! and Other Favorites (1964, RCA Camden CAL-828 (mono), CAL-828 (stereo))
- Love is a Hurtin' Thing (1967, RCA Camden CAS-2134)
- The Magic of Hawaii (1968, RCA Camden CAS-2211)
- More Hawaii in Hi-Fi (1960, RCA Camden CAL-594 (mono), CAS-594 (stereo))
- The Music Goes 'Round and 'Round (1961, RCA Victor LSA-2353) (Stereo Action)
- Musical Orchids from Hawaii (1966, RCA Camden CAS-977)
- On the Sunny Side of the Street (1963, RCA Camden CAL-758 (mono), CAS-758 (stereo))
- Paradise Regained (1961, RCA Victor LSA-2414) (Stereo Action)

- Songs of Hawaii (1963, RCA Camden CAL-759 (mono), CAS-759 (stereo))

Adler, Larry

- Again! (1968, Audio Fidelity AFSD 6193)
- An Evening with Larry Adler (1959, Decca DL 8908)
- Larry Adler and Quartet (1959, Audio Fidelity AFLP 1916 (mono), AFSD 5916 (stereo))

Ahbez, Eden

The man known as Eden Ahbez must have been quite a character. The composer of "Nature Boy" and other tunes during the 1940's and 50's, Ahbez at one point became an important L.A.-based proto-hippie when he elected to live his life in as simple and primitive a manner as possible, sleeping outdoors and living off the land while going dressed like an island castaway. *Eden's Island* is a classic of exotica, and his only album.

- *Eden's Island* (1960, Del-Fi DFLP-1211 (mono), DFST-1211 (stereo))

Albam, Manny and His Orchestra

- I Had the Craziest Dream (1962, RCA Victor LSA-2508) (Stereo Action)
- More Double Exposure (1962, RCA Victor LSA-2432) (Stereo Action)

Alberto, Xavier and His Orchestra

Given the album's title, this was almost certainly a studio group put together to cash in on the popularity of **Sergio Mendes and Brazil '66**.

- Brazil Today featuring Guantanamera (1968, Crown CLP-5570 (mono), CST-570 (stereo))

Aldrich, Ronnie (and His Two Pianos)

Aldrich was a British pianist and composer who was known for playing two pianos during recording sessions.

- All-Time Piano Hits (1966, London SP 44081)
- Close To You (1970, London SP 44156)
- Destination Love (1969, London SP 44135; with The London Festival Orchestra)
- For Young Lovers (1968, London SP 44108)
- Here Come the Hits! (1970, London SP 44143; with The London Festival Orchestra)
- The Magic Moods of Ronnie Aldrich (1965, London SP 44062; with The London Festival Orchestra)

- The Magnificent Pianos of Ronnie Aldrich (1963, London SP 44029)

- Melody and Percussion For Two Pianos (1962, London SP 44007)

- Ronnie Aldrich and His Two Pianos (1962, London SP 44018)

- That Aldrich Feeling (1965, London SP 44070)

- This Way "In" (1968, London SP 44116; with The London Festival Orchestra)

- Two Pianos in Hollywood (1967, London SP 44092)

- Two Pianos Today! (1967, London SP 44100; with The London Festival Orchestra)

All Stars

- Persistent Percussion (1960, Kent KLP 3000 (mono), KST 500 (stereo); black and red vinyl) This little gem brought together a number of talented people like arranger **Maxwell Davis**, saxophonist **Buddy Collette**, and percussionist **Irv Cottler**.

Almeida, Laurindo (and the Bossa Nova All Stars)

Almeida was a Brazilian guitarist with a very far-ranging career including hundreds of film and television soundtracks.

- Acapulco '22 (1963, Tower T 5060 (mono), DT 5060 (stereo); re-released in 1967 with different cover?)

- Broadway Solo Guitar (1964, Capitol T 2063 (mono), DT 2063 (stereo))

- Concert Creations For Guitar (1950, Capitol H-193)

- Guitar from Ipanema (1964, Capitol T 2197 (mono), ST 2197 (stereo))

- It's a Bossa Nova World (1963, Capitol ST-01946)

- The Look of Love and the Sounds of Laurindo Almeida (1968, Capitol ST 2866)

- A Man and a Woman (1967, Capitol T 2701 (mono), ST 2701 (stereo); re-released in 1976)

- Maracaibo (1958, Decca DL 8756)

- New Broadway-Hollywood Hits (1960, Capitol T 2419 (mono), ST 2419 (stereo))

- Suenos (Dreams) (1965, Capitol T 2345; only available in Mono?)

Aloma, Hal (and His Hawaiians; and His Hawaiian Orchestra)

- Hal Aloma Sings Island Songs (1962, Dot DLP 3451 (mono), DLP 25451 (stereo))

- Hal Aloma Takes Your Favorite Tunes on a Trip to Hawaii (1960, Dot DLP 3287 (mono), DLP 25287 (stereo))

- Hawaiian Holiday (1953, Columbia CL 538; apparently a re-release of *A Musical Portrait of Hawaii*)
- Island Serenade (1966, Hamilton HLP 12174)
- Lure of the Islands (1965, Dot DLP 3057 (mono), DLP 25057 (stereo))
- A Musical Portrait of Hawaii (1953, Columbia CL 538; re-released as *Hawaiian Holiday*)
- On Paradise Isle (1963, Dot DLP 3514 (mono), DLP 25514 (stereo))
- Songs of the Islands (Pickwick SPC-3099)
- Sweet Leilani (1959, Dot DLP 3228 (mono), DLP 25228 (stereo))

Alpert, Herb and the Tijuana Brass

This entry isn't quite the place to adequately document the popularity of trumpeter Alpert and his backing band, much less their brief-but-intense impact upon popular music. Suffice it to say that *Whipped Cream and Other Delights* sold untold millions of copies, stayed in the Billboard charts for a couple of years, and is now as common at yard sales and thrift shops as World's Fair Beer. Dozens of imitators and knockoff albums were created (some, like **The Baja Marimba Band**, with Alpert's blessing), and the softening of popular music in the post-Beatles-debut era was able to continue for a few more years.

- The Beat of the Brass (1968, A&M SP 4146)
- The Brass Are Comin' (1969, A&M SP 4228)
- Going Places!! (1965, A&M LP 112 (mono), SP 4112 (stereo)) Re-released in several editions.
- Herb Alpert's Ninth (1967, A&M SP 4134)
- The Lonely Bull (1962, A&M 101) Released in both mono and stereo, with several re-releases and international versions.
- S.R.O. (1966, A&M LP 119 (mono), SP 4119 (stereo))
- Sounds Like... (1967, A&M SP 4124)
- South of the Border (1964, A&M LP 108 (mono), SP 108 (stereo)) Re-released in several editions.
- Volume 2 (1963, A&M LP 103 (mono), SP 103 (stereo)) Re-released in several editions.
- Warm (1969, A&M SP 4190)
- What Now My Love (1966, A&M SP 4114)
- *Whipped Cream and Other Delights* (1965, A&M LP 110 (mono), SP 4110 (stereo)) Many, many re-releases, record club editions, and foreign releases.

Alunuai, Willie and His Band

- Hawaiian Holiday (1957, Parade SP-315) This was apparently re-released (or was a re-release itself!) under such titles as *Aloha*

Hawaii/Hawaiian Holiday by **Harry Kaapuni and His Royal Polynesians**; *Lure of Hawaii* (in the Compilations section); *Hawaiian Holiday/Passport to Romance* by **Luke Leilani and His Hawaiian Rhythm**; and certainly others as well.

Andre, Pierre (aka **Pierre Andre and The Golden Leaves**)

- Here Comes Love Again (1969, Challenge 2003)
- Romantic Organ Moods (Masterseal MS-91)

Anthony, Ray

Ray Anthony is a trumpeter whose career goes back all the way to the 1940's, when he plaed with Glenn Miller's orchestra. He's still with us today at the age of 94.

- Dancers in Love (1957, Capitol T-768)
- Dream Dancing (1956, Capitol T-723)
- Dream Dancing Medley (1961, Capitol T-1608 (mono), ST-1608 (stereo))
- Dream Dancing Today (1966, Capitol T-2457 (mono), ST-2457 (stereo))
- Golden Horn (1955, Capitol T-563)
- Hit Songs to Remember (1966, Capitol T-2530 (mono), ST-2530 (stereo); later reissued)
- Houseparty Hop (1956, Capitol T-292)
- I Almost Lost My Mind (1962, Capitol T-1783 (mono), ST-1783 (stereo))
- Like Wild! (1959, Capitol T-1304 (mono), ST-1304 (stereo))
- More Dream Dancing (1959, Capitol T-1252 (mono), ST-1252 (stereo))
- The New Ray Anthony Show (1960, Capitol T-1421 (mono), ST-1421 (stereo))
- Smash Hits of '63! (1963, Capitol T-1917 (mono), ST-1917 (stereo))
- Sound Spectacular (1959, Capitol T-1200 (mono), ST-1200 (stereo))
- Standards (1956, Capitol T-663)
- Swim Swim C'Mon and Swim (1964, Capitol T-2188 (mono), ST-2188 (stereo))
- Swingin' On Campus! (1956, Capitol T-645)
- That's Show Biz (1961, Capitol T-1496 (mono), ST-1496 (stereo))
- The Young Man With the Horn (1951, Capitol T-373)

Antoine, Michael and His Orchestra

- And So To Bed (1956, RCA Victor LPM-1285)

Applebaum, Stan and His Orchestra

- Hollywood's Bad but Beautiful Girls (1962, Warner Brothers W 1502)

Appleyard, Peter and His Orchestra

- Percussive Jazz: Doctored for Super-Sound (1960, Audo Fidelity DFM 3002 (mono), DFS 7002 (stereo))

Arnaud, Leo (**and His Orchestra**)

- Marimbita (1957, Liberty LRP-3088)
- Spectra Sonic Sounds (1956, Liberty LRP-3009)

Ashby, Dorothy

Not many musicians could blend the sound of the harp into popular and jazz music, but Dorothy Ashby made it look easy.

- Afro-Harping (1968, Cadet LPS-809)
- Dorothy Ashby (1962, Argo LP 690 (mono), LPS 690 (stereo))
- Dorothy's Harp (1969, Cadet LPS-825)
- The Fantastic Jazz Harp of Dorothy Ashby (1965, Atlantic 1447 (mono), SD 1447 (stereo))
- The Jazz Harpist (1957, Regent MG 6039; Savoy 12212)
- Soft Winds (1961, Jazzland JLP 61 (mono), JLP 961 (stereo))

August, Jan and His Orchestra

- Accent! (1959, Mercury MG-20618 (mono), SR-60618 (stereo))
- Cha-Cha Charm (1959, Mercury MG-20408 (mono), SR-60082 (stereo))
- Cocktails and Conversation (1957, Mercury MG-20272)
- Jan August Plays Songs to Remember (1955, Mercury MG-20072)
- Jan August Styles Great International Hits (1962, Mercury SR-60667)
- Latin Rhythms (Mercury MG-20274)
- Music for the Quiet Hour (1955, Mercury MG-20078; Mercury Wing MGW 12129 (with different cover))

Auld, Georgie and His Hula-Gans

- Hawaii on the Rocks (1959, Jaro International JAM-5003 (mono), JAS-8003 (stereo))

Auletta, Ted

Ted Auletta would be part of the history of Exotica music even if he had only recorded one album – his classic album which takes helped cement the name of the genre, *Exotica*.

- *Exotica* (1962, Cameo C 4008 (mono), SC 4008 (stereo))
- For the Young At Heart: Hawaii (1964, 20th Century Fox TFS 4120)
- Hawaiian Shores (Mount Vernon MVM 103; as Ted Auletta and His Beachboys)

Bacal, Dave

- The Latin Touch of Dave Bacal (1960, Crown CLP 5146 (mono), CST 176 (stereo); released in both black and red vinyl)

Bacharach, Burt

Although Bacharach's work usually belongs more in the Pop camp, this soundtrack album needs to be included for its contribution as part of both the Now Sound and Spy genres.

- Casino Royale (1967, Colgems COMO-5005 (mono), COSO-5005 (stereo)) Soundtrack to the James Bond (sort of) film.

Backus, Earl

- Haunted Guitar (1957, Dot DLP 3026)

Baden – see **Baden Powell**

Bain, Bob

- Guitar de Amor (1960, Capitol T-1500 (mono), ST-1500 (stereo))
- Latin Love (1960, Capitol T-1201 (mono), ST-1201 (stereo))

Baja Marimba Band (aka **Julius Wechter and The Baja Marimba Band**)

Julius Wechter had done some work with Herb Alpert on his **Tijuana Brass** albums, including writing the hit "Spanish Flea." Alpert convinced him to start his own faux-Mexican band, similar to the Brass, to take further advantage for that group's style which was extremely popular at the time.

- As Time Goes By (1971, A&M SP-4298)
- Baja Marimba Band (1964, A&M LP-104 (mono), SP-104 (stereo))
- Baja Marimba Band Rides Again (1965, A&M LP-109 (mono), SP-4109 (stereo))
- The Baja Marimba Band's Back (1973, A&M Bell 1124)
- Do You Know the Way to San Jose? (1968, A&M SP-4150)
- For Animals Only (1965, A&M LP-113 (mono), SP-4113 (stereo))
- Fowl Play (1968, A&M SP-4136)
- Fresh Air (1969, A&M SP-4200)

- Heads Up! (1967, A&M LP-123 (mono), SP-4123 (stereo))
- Those Were the Days (1968, A&M SP-4167)
- Watch Out! (1966, A&M LP-118 (mono), SP-4118 (stereo))

Banana, Milton and The Oscar Castro Neves Orchestra

- The Rhythm and Sound of Bossa Nova (1963, Audio Fidelity AFLP-1984 (mono), AFSD-5984 (stereo))

Barclay, Eddie and His Orchestra

- Americans in Paris (1959, United Artists UAL-3023)
- Film Festival at Cannes (1957, Mercury MG 20188)
- Twilight Time (1960, Mercury MG 20488 (mono), SR 60167 (stereo))

Barclay, Peter and His Orchestra – see the Compilations section, 'Music for Gracious Living'

Barker, Warren and His Orchestra (see also **Tommy Morgan**)

- 77 Sunset Strip (1959, Warner Brothers W 1289 (mono), WS 1289 (stereo)) Music from the TV series.
- Music of Desire (1960, Warren Brothers W 1364 (mono), WS 1364 (stereo))
- TV Guide Top Television Themes (1959, Warner Brothers W 1290 (mono), WS 1290 (stereo))
- Warren Barker Is In (1959, Warner Brothers W 1331 (mono), WS 1331 (stereo))

Barlow, Dick and His Orchestra

- Music to Make You Feel That Certain Way (1956, Mercury MG 20168)

Barnes, George

- Guitar Galaxies (1962, Mercury MG-20956; re-released at least twice)
- Guitar in Velvet (1957, Grand Award 33-358)
- Guitars Galore (1962, Mercury PPS 2020 (mono), PPS 6020 (stereo))

Barnes, George and Carl Kress

- Guitars Anyone? Why Not Start at the Top? (1963, Carney LPM 202)
- Ten Duets For Two Guitars (Music Minus One MMO 4011) This album was primarily for those who wanted to learn to play the guitar;

each track had a second version which the user could play along with. The album came with an instructional booklet.

Barry, John

Though he orchestrated the music for dozens of movies, Barry is remembered best for his association with the James Bond film series.

- From Russia With Love (1963, United Artists UAL 4114 (mono), UAS 5114 (stereo)) Soundtrack to the James Bond film.

- Goldfinger (1964, United Artists UAL 4117 (mono), UAS 5117 (stereo)) Soundtrack to the James Bond film.

- The Ipcress File (1965, Decca DL 9124 (mono), DL 79124 (stereo)) Soundtrack to the film.

- The Knack... And How to Get It (1965, United Artists UAL 4129 (mono), UAS 5129 (stereo)) Soundtrack to the film.

- Thunderball (1965, United Artists UAL 4132 (mono), UAS 5132 (stereo)) Soundtrack to the James Bond film.

- You Only Live Twice (1967, United Artists UAL 4155 (mono), UAS 5155 (stereo)) Soundtrack to the James Bond film.

Basie, Count and His Orchestra

Count Basie was a giant in the world of jazz for decades, recording with Frank Sinatra and Ella Fitzgerald among others.

- Basie Meets Bond (1966, United Artists UAL 3480 (mono), UAS 6480 (stereo)) Basie covers various songs from the James Bond films released up to that time.

- Basie On The Beatles (1969, Happy Tiger HT-1007) Basie covers Beatles songs.

- Basie Swingin' Voices Singin' (1966, ABC-Paramount ABC 570 (mono), ABCS 570 (stereo); with **The Alan Copeland Singers**)

- Frankly Speaking (1966, Metro M/MS-592) This was a re-release of *More Hits of the '50's and '60's*.

- Half A Sixpence (1968, Dot DLP 25834) Songs from the British musical film.

- More Hits of the '50's and '60's (1963, Verve V-8563 (mono), V6-8563 (stereo) Re-released in 1966 as *Frankly Speaking*.

- Pop Goes the Basie (1965, Reprise R 6513 (mono), RS 6513 (stereo))

- This Time By Basie (1963, Reprise R-6070 (mono), RS-6070 (stereo))

Basile, Jo (aka **Jo Basile, Accordion and Orchestra)**

- Acapulco With Love (1967, Audio Fidelity AFSD 5947)

- Jazz Accordion (1968, Audio Fidelity AFSD 6210)

- Movie Theme Hits (1962, Audio Fidelity AFLP 1979)

- Rome With Love (1957, Audio Fidelity AFLP 1822 (mono); 1959, AFSD 5822 (stereo))

Bass, Sid (**and His Orchestra**; **Chorus**) (see also **Jackie Davis**)

- *From Another World* (1956, Vik LX-1053) A classic of the Space Age Pop genre.
- Sound and Fury (1957, Vik LX-1084)
- With Bells On (1958, Vik LX-1112; 1959, RCA Camden CAL-501 (mono), CAS-501 (stereo))

Baxter, Eddie

- Electronic Pipes (1958, Rendezvous RLP-1306)
- The Fantastic Sounds! (1962, Dot DLP 3551 (mono), DLP 25551 (stereo))
- Great Organ Themes from Movies and TV (1963, Dot DLP 3436 (mono), DLP 25436 (stereo))
- Holiday For Pipes (1958, Rendezvous RLP-1305)
- More Fantastic Sounds! (1963, Dot DLP 3607 (mono), DLP 25607 (stereo))
- Organ Blues 'N Boogie (1964, Hamilton HLP 136 (mono), HLP 12136 (stereo))
- Organ Festival (1960, Dot DLP 3277 (mono), DLP 25277 (stereo))
- Organ Melodies of Love (Dot DLP 3708 (mono), DLP 25708 (stereo))
- Organ Moods & Magic (1966, Hamilton HLP 175 (mono), HLP 12175 (stereo))
- Organ-Songs We Love (1963, Dot DLP 3435 (mono), DLP 25435 (stereo))
- Organ-Sounds Incredible (Dot DLP 3706 (mono), DLP 25706 (stereo))
- Speak Low (1957, Rendezvous RLP-1301)
- Super Organ (Concert Recording CR-E130)
- Temptation (1957, Rendezvous RLP-1302)
- This Love of Mine (1958, Rendezvous RLP-1303)
- Wedding Bells (Imperial LP-9111)

Baxter, Les (see also **Yma Sumac**)

Although Martin Denny might have been the father of Exotica, Les Baxter was assuredly its godfather, writing beautiful and groundbreaking music but also being an explorer in new realms of sound. Jungle climates, the mysterious Far East, sunken cities, even futuristic space colonies – these were the types of places that Baxter allowed listeners to experience, at least in their imaginations.

- The Academy Award Winners (1963, Reprise R-6079 (mono), R9-6079 (stereo))
- African Blue (1969, GNP Crescendo GNPS 2047; re-released in the UK as *Bugaloo in Brazil*, part of the KPM music library)
- African Jazz (1959, Capitol T-1117 (mono), ST-1117 (stereo))
- Alakazam the Great! (1960, Vee Jay LP-6000) *Alakazam the Great* was a Japanese animated feature that was released in American in 1961 by American International. Les Baxter was hired to provide new musical accompaniment.
- Barbarian (1960, American International LP-1001-M (mono), LP-1001-S (stereo); also called *Les Baxter's Barbarian*; re-released as *Goliath and the Barbarians* in 1979) Music from the motion picture *Goliath and the Barbarians.*
- Bora Bora (1970, American International ST-A-1029) Music from the film *Bora Bora.*
- Brazil Now (1967, GNP Crescendo GNP-2036 (mono), GNPS-2036 (stereo))
- Broadway '61 (1961, Capitol T-1480 (mono), ST-1480 (stereo))
- Caribbean Moonlight (1956, Capitol T-733)
- Confetti (1958, Capitol T-1029)
- The Dunwich Horror (1970, American International ST-A-1028) Music from the Lovecraftian horror film *The Dunwich Horror.*
- The Fabulous Sounds of Les Baxter: Strings, Guitars, Voices! (1965, Pickwick PC-3011 (mono), SPC-3011 (stereo); re-released by Sears in 1969 as *It's A Big, Wide Wonderful World of Les Baxter*)
- Hell's Belles (1969, Sidewalk ST-5919) Music from the film *Hell's Belles.*
- I Could Have Danced All Night (1966, Pickwick PC-3048 (mono), SPC-3048 (stereo))
- It's a Big, Wide, Wonderful World of Les Baxter (1969, Sears SP-409 (mono), SPS-409 (stereo); this was a re-release of *The Fabulous Sounds of Les Baxter* from 1965)
- *Jewels of the Sea* (1961, Capitol T-1537 (mono), ST-1537 (stereo) The absolute classic of the possible sub-genre (no pun intended) of Undersea Exotica.

- Jules Verne's Master of the World (1961, Vee Jay VJLP-4000 (mono), SR-4000 (stereo)) Music from the American International film *Jules Verne's Master of the World.*

- Jungle Jazz (1959, Capitol T-1184 (mono), ST-1184 (stereo))

- Kaleidoscope (1955, Capitol T-594)

- Love is a Fabulous Thing (1958, Capitol T-1088 (mono), ST-1088 (stereo))

- Love is Blue (1968, GNP Crescendo GNP 2042 (mono), GNPS 2042 (stereo))

- Midnight on the Cliffs (1957, Capitol T-843)

- Million Seller Hits Arranged and Conducted by Les Baxter (1970, Alshire S-5188; a re-release of *Les Baxter Conducts 101 Strings*, a UK-only release; released again in 1972 as *Exciting Sounds*, in quadraphonic; with **101 Strings**)

- Music Out of the Moon / Music for Peace of Mind (1953, Capitol P-390, T-390; this was a double-album re-release of two previous Capitol 10" discs; *Music For Peace of Mind* was by **Harry Revel**)

- Original Quiet Village (1964, Capitol T-1846 (mono), ST-1846 (stereo); re-released in 1969)

- Ports of Pleasure (1957, Capitol T-868 (mono), ST-868 (stereo))

- *The Primitive and the Passionate* (1962, Reprise R-6048 (mono), R9-6048 (stereo))

- *Que Mango!* (1970, Alshire S-5204; with **101 Strings**)

- *Ritual of the Savage (Le Sacre du Sauvage)* (1951, Capitol T-288; apparently released under its French title in 10" format)

- 'Round the World With Les Baxter (1957, Capitol T-780)

- The Sacred Idol (1960, Capitol T-1293 (mono), ST-1293 (stereo)) Music from the film *The Sacred Idol.*

- Sensational! (1961, Capitol T-1661 (mono), ST-1661 (stereo))

- Skins! (1957, Capitol T-774)

- The Soul of the Drums (1961, Reprise R-6100)

- South Pacific (1958, Capitol T-1012 (mono), ST-1012 (stereo)) Music from the stage production and film.

- *Space Escapade* (1958, Capitol T-968) One of the undisputed classics of Space Age Pop, this album sports one of the most easily-recognizable covers, too.

- Tamboo! (1955, Capitol T-655)

- Tangos (1951, Capitol T-279; re-released in 1960 as T-1372)

- Teen Drums (1960, Capitol T-1355 (mono), ST-1355 (stereo))

- Thinking Of You (1954, Capitol T-474)

- Voices in Rhythm (1961, Reprise R-6036)

- Wild Guitars (1959, Capitol T-1248 (mono), ST-1248 (stereo))
- Young Pops (1960, Capitol T-1399 (mono), ST-1399 (stereo))

Baxter, Terry and His Orchestra (and Chorus)

Grooved-up late-Now Sounds era song covers.

- The Best of '68 (1968, Columbia Music Treasuries P2S 5224) Two-disc set.
- The Best of '69 (1969, Columbia Music Treasuries P2S 5332) Two-disc set.
- The Best of '70 (1970, Columbia Music Treasuries P3S 5454) Three-disc set.
- The Best of '70 (1970, Columbia Music Treasuries DS 684) This is a single-disc album release of songs from the previous entry.
- The Best of '71 (1971, Columbia Music Treasuries P3S 5596) Three-disc set.
- The Best of '72 (1972, Columbia Music Treasuries P3S 5832) Three-disc set.
- The Burt Bacharach / Hal David Treasury (1971, Columbia Music Treasuries P4S 5578) Four-disc set.
- Feelin' Groovy (1970, Columbia Music Treasuries P2S 5503) Two-disc set.
- The Look of Love (1969, Columbia Music Treasuries P7S 5258) Seven-disc set.
- Song Sung Blue – The Very Best of 1972 (1972, Columbia House DS 1010)
- Today's Romantic Hits (1972, Columbia House DS 988)
- The Very Best of Burt Bacharach / Hal David (1971?, Columbia House DS 859)
- Yesterday – the Wonderful Music of The Beatles (1972, Columbia House P6S 5748) Six-disc set.

Bay, Francis aka The Bay Big Band

Francis Bay was born Frans Bayetz in Belgium in 1914. He also recorded under the pseudonyms **Don Catelli and the All Stars** and **John Evans and the Big Band**.

- The Bay Big Band's Latin Beat (1958, Omega OSL 20; also released as *Pradomania* on Mecca) The Big Bay Band do songs by Perez Prado.
- Pradomania (1958, Mecca OSL 20; also released as *The Bay Big Band's Latin Beat* on Omega)

Beirut, Ali (aka **Ali Beirut's Orientales**)

- Music of the Near East (1959, Promenade 2124; Pirouette FM 16) This is a song-for-song re-release of *The Music of Port Said* by

Mohammed El-Sulieman and His Oriental Ensemble, but with different titles for the songs.

Bell, Vincent 'Vinnie'

Vincent Bell was an accomplished seesion guitarist, but he is also remembered as the inventor of both the electric 12-string guitar and the electric sitar.

- Airport Love Theme (1970, Decca DL 75212)
- Good Morning Starshine (1969, Decca DL 75138)
- Pop Goes the Electric Sitar (1967, Decca DL 4938 (mono), DL 74938 (stereo))

Belmonte (and His Ochestra)

- Belmonte Plays Latin for Americans (1957, RCA Victor LPM-1571)
- Cha-Cha, Merengue, Bolero, and Mambo (1956, Columbia CL 802)
- Mambo at Midnight (Columbia CL 598; as 'Belmonte and His African-American Music')
- Rumba for Moderns (1958, RCA Victor LPM-1663 (mono), LSP-1663 (stereo))

Ben-Ahmed, Mohammed and The Bagdad Tribesmen

- East of Suez: Exotic Rhythms of the Middle East (Best B-508) This is a song-by-song reissue of *The Music of Port Said* by **Mohammed El-Sulieman and His Oriental Ensemble**, which was almost certainly another studio-cobbled group with a fakey name.

Bey, Chief and His Royal Household

Note that this apparently fictitious group is in no way related to the jazz artist known as Chief Bey.

- Congo Percussion (Pirouette RFM-11) This is another budget-label re-release (10 of the original 12 songs) of *Jungle Beat* by **Subri Moulin and His Equatorial Rhythm Group**.
- Taboo (1959, Pirouette FM-11) This seems to be a re-release of *Congo Percussion*, although it's difficult to say which came first. The same artwork and packaging would be reused for *Taboo* by **Cawanda's Group**; in fact, it appears to be the exact same album with very little difference.

Bianchi and The Jungle Sex-Tet

- Music to Play in the Dark (1959, Hi-Standard LP 101)

Bianco, Gene (aka **The Rainbow Sound of Bianco, His Harp, and Orchestra**)

- Hop, Skip, & Jump (1958, RCA Camden CAS 452; featuring **Mundell Lowe**)

- Music for a Summer Evening (1963, RCA Victor Record Club CPM 105 (mono), CSP 105 (stereo))
- Music to Make Your Heart Sing! (RCA Victor Record Club CSP 115)
- Stringin' the Standards (1957, RCA Camden CAL 366)
- Sweet Songs of Love (1964, RCA Victor CSP 107)
- Your All-Time Favorite Songs (1964, RCA Record Club CPM 110 (mono), CPM 110 (stereo))

Bilk, Acker (usually with **The Leon Young String Chorale**)

Mr. Acker Bilk was a British clarinet player whose primary claim to fame was the hit song "Stranger on the Shore."

- Above the Stars & Other Romantic Fancies (1962, Atco 33-144 (mono), SD 33-144 (stereo))
- Call Me Mister (1963, Atco 33-158 (mono), SD 33-158 (stereo))
- Great Themes From Foreign Films (1965, Atco 33-170 (mono), SD 33-170 (stereo))
- In Paris (1966, Atco 33-181 (mono), SD 33-181 (stereo))
- London is My Cup of Tea (1967, Atco 33-218 (mono), SD 33-218 (stereo))
- Mood For Love (1966, Atco 33-197 (mono), SD 33-197 (stereo))
- Only You (1962, Atco 33-150 (mono), SD 33-150 (stereo))
- Stranger on the Shore (1962, Atco 33-129 (mono), SD 33-129 (stereo))
- Together! (1965, Atco 33-175 (mono), SD 33-175 (stereo); as Acker Bilk and Bent Fabric)
- A Touch of Latin (1964, Atco 33-168 (mono), SD 33-168 (stereo))

Black, Stanley and His Orchestra

- Cuban Moonlight (1959, London PS 137)
- Exotic Percussion (1961, London SP 44004)
- Girls, Girls, Girls (1958, London LL 3012)
- Great Film Themes (1958, London PS 113)
- Melodies of Love (1958, Richmond B 20004)
- Moonlight Cocktail (London LL 1709)
- The Music of Lecuona (1959, London LL 1438)
- The Night Was Made For Love (1957, London LL 1307)
- Plays For Latin Lovers (1957, London LL 1681)
- Red Velvet (London LL 1592)
- Some Enchanted Evening (1955, London LL 1098)
- South of the Border (Richmond B 20003)
- Spain (1961, London SP 44016)

- Tropical Moonlight (1957, London LL 1615)

Bond, James and His Sextet

- The James Bond Songbook (1966, Mirwood MW 7001 (mono), MWS 7001 (stereo)) This is a collection of themes from James Bond films as well as, apparently, tunes inspired by the books – notice there is a song for "Moonraker" even though the film wouldn't come out for over a decade. The bandleader here really was named James Bond; Buddy Collette played flute and tenor sax. A fun album.

Borley, Clyde and His Percussions

- Music in 5 Dimensions (1965, Atco 33-195 (mono), SD 33-195 (stereo)) This album isn't for everyone, but its experimental nature, and the fact that it ranges between Exotica, Easy Listening, and other relevant genres, makes it eligible to be covered here.

Boston Pops – see **Arthur Fiedler**

Boutet, Phil and His Orchestra

- 100 Strings Play… (1959, Mercury Wing SRW 16143W)

Bowen, Hill and His Orchestra (see also the Compilations section)

- Instrumental Hits from Lerner and Loewe's 'Gigi' (1959, RCA Camden CAS 436)
- Kiss Me Kate (1958, RCA Camden CAS 482)
- Romantic Strings Play Dancing in the Dark (1963, RCA Custom/Readers Digest RD 28-M) Two-LP set.
- Selections from 'Redhead' (1959, RCA Camden CAL 521)
- South Pacific (1959, RCA Camden CAS 494)
- Standards in Stereo (1959, RCA Camden CAS 461)

Bradley, Harold

Bradley was a longtime session guitarist in Nashville.

- Guitar for Lovers Only (1966, Columbia CL 2456 (mono), CS 9256 (stereo))
- Guitar for Sentimental Lovers (1972, Heritage H 31324)
- Misty Guitar (1963, Columbia CL 2073 (mono), CS 8873 (stereo))

Brasil '66 – see **Sergio Mendes and Brasil '66**

Brass Breed, The

- Music to Watch Girls By (1967, Wyncote W-9191 (mono), SW-9191 (stereo))

Brass Impact Orchestra, The, Conducted by Warren Kime (aka **The Brass Choir**)

- 2 of a Kime (Replica 1008)
- Brass Impact (1967, Command RS 33 910 (mono), RS 910 SD (stereo))
- Dialog For Brass (1960, Columbia CL 1499 (stereo)), CS 8290 (stereo); the stereo version shows the title as *The Stereo Dialog for Brass* and the artist as The Stereo Brass Choir)
- Dynamic Brass Impact (1973, Command RSSD-961/2) Two-disc set.
- Explosive Brass Impact, Vol. 2 (1967, Command RS 33 919 (mono), RS 919 SD (stereo))
- Goin' Somplace! (1972, Command RS 935 SD)
- Jazz (Claremont C-778)

Brass Ring, The

- The Dis-Advantages of You (1967, Dunhill DS-50017) The title song for this album originally appeared in television commercials for Benson & Hedges cigarettes at the time. A single version was produced by a hastily-assembled studio group led by Mitch Leigh, the author of the tune; but the Brass Ring also released their own version, which outdid the original to peak at #36 on the Billboard charts.
- The Evolution of the Brass Ring (1969, Itco ILS-10002)
- Gazpacho (1968, Dunhill DS-50034)
- Lara's Theme/Guantanamera (1966, Dunhill DS-50012)
- Love Theme from The Flight of the Phoenix (1966, Dunhill DS-50008)
- The Now Sound of the Brass Ring (1967, Dunhill DS-50023)
- Only Love (1968, Dunhill DS-50044)
- Sunday Night at the Movies (1967, Dunhill DS 50015)

Brazilia '67

- Introducing Mas Que Nada and Guantanamera (1967, Wyncote W-9177 (mono), SW-9177 (stereo))

Brown, Brooke

- By Popular Demand (1967, Dino 28358)

Brown, Les (and His Band of Renown)

Most of Les Brown's music might be categorized as Big Band or Jazz, but some of it leaned enough toward Easy Listening or Exotica to be included in this volume.

- College Classics (1955, Capitol T-657)

- Dance to South Pacific (1958, Capitol T-1060 (mono), ST-1060 (stereo))
- Les Brown's In Town (1956, Capitol T-746)
- Plays for the World of the Young (1968, Decca DL-74965)
- Revolution in Sound (1962, Columbia CL 1818 (mono), CS 8618 (stereo))
- The Richard Rodgers Songbook (1962, CL 1914 (mono), CS 8714 (stereo))
- A Sign of the Times (1966, Decca DL-75768)
- The Swingin' Sound (1960, Signature SM 1019)
- That Sound of Renown (1956, Coral CRL 57030)
- The Young Beat (1963, Columbia CL 2119 (mono), CS 8919 (stereo))

Burger, Jack (aka **Jack 'Bongo' Burger**)
- ...The End on Bongos! (1957, HiFi R-804)
- Let's Play Bongos (1957, HiFi R-803) Bongo instructional record.
- Let's Play Congas (1958, HiFi R-809) Conga drum instructional record.
- Progressive Bongo Instruction (1966, Phonic JB-1001) More bongo instruction.

Burns, Ralph
- Illya Darling (1967, United Artists UAS 6606)
- New York's A Song (1959, Decca DL 79068)
- Swingin' Down the Lane (1962, Epic BN 26015)
- Where There's Burns There's Fire (1961, Warwick W 5001 ST)

Bushkin, Joe (see also **Eddie Heywood**)
- Blue Angels (1958, Capitol T-1094)
- Bushkin Spotlights Berlin (1958, Capitol T-911)
- A Fellow Needs a Girl (1956, Capitol T-832)
- I Get a Kick Out Of Porter (1958, Capitol T-1030 (mono), ST-1030 (stereo))
- In Concert, Town Hall (1964, Reprise R-6119 (mono), RS-6119 (stereo))
- Listen to the Quiet... (1959, Capitol ST-1165)
- Midnight Rhapsody (1956, Capitol T-711)
- Night Sounds – San Francisco (1966, Decca DL 4731 (mono), DL 74731 (stereo))
- Nightsounds (1958, Capitol T-983)
- Skylight Rhapsody (1957, Capitol T-759)

Buzon, John (aka **The John Buzon Trio**)

- Cha Cha on the Rocks (1959, Liberty LRP 3124 (mono), LST 7124 (stereo))
- Inferno! (1959, Liberty LRP 3108 (mono), LST 7108 (stereo))

Byrd, Jerry

Lap steel guitarist Jerry Byrd was primarily a country artist but did his share of Hawaiian/Polynesian style tunes also.

- Burning Sands, Pearly Shells, and Steel Guitars (1967, Monument MLP-8081 (mono), SLP-18081 (stereo))
- Byrd of Paradise (1961, Monument MLP-8009 (mono), SLP-18009 (stereo))
- Hawaiian Beach Party (1959, RCA Victor LPM-1687)
- Polynesian Suite (1968, Monument SLP-18107)

Caiola, Al

During his career Al Caiola was one of the foremost session guitarists, playing on dozens of albums and hit singles.

- 50 Fabulous Guitar Favorites (1964, United Artists UAL 3330 (mono), UAS 6330 (stereo))
- The Al Caiola Guitar (1966, Sears SPS 424) (re-issue of *Salute Italia!*)
- Ciao (1963, United Artists UAL 3276 (mono), UAS 6276 (stereo))
- Cleopatra and All That Jazz (1962, United Artists UAL 3299 (mono), UAS 6299 (stereo); as Al Caiola and the Nile River Boys)
- Deep in a Dream (1958, Savoy MG-12033)
- Give Me the Simple Life (1960, United Artists UAL 3280)
- Golden Guitar (1962, United Artists UAL 3240 (mono), UAS 6240 (stereo))
- Golden Hit Instrumentals (1960, United Artists UAL 3142 (mono), UAS 6142 (stereo))
- Greasy Kid Stuff (1963, United Artists UAL 3287 (mono), UAS 6287 (stereo))
- Guitar For Lovers (1964, United Artists UAL 3403 (mono), UAS 6403 (stereo))
- Guitar, Italian Style (1966, Pickwick SPC-3034) (re-issue of *Salute Italia!*)
- The Guitar Style of Al Caiola (1962, RCA Camden CAS-710)
- Guitars, Woodwinds, and Bongos (1960, United Artists WWS-8503)
- Have Guitar, Will Travel (1965, United Artists UAS 6405) Re-release of *Midnight in Moscow*. Probably retitled due to Cold War concerns.

- High Strung (1959, RCA Victor LSP-2031)
- Hit Instrumentals from Western TV Themes (1961, United Artists UAL 3161 (mono), UAS 6161 (stereo))
- Italian Guitars (1960, Time S/2023)
- King Guitar (1967, United Artists UAL 3586 (mono), UAS 6586 (stereo))
- Let the Sunshine In (1969, United Artists UAS 6712)
- The Magnificent Seven (1960, United Artists UAL 3133 (mono), UAS 6133 (stereo))
- Midnight Dance Party (1962, United Artists UAL 3228 (mono), UAS 6228 (stereo); as Al Caiola and His Magnificent Seven)
- Midnight in Moscow (1962, United Artists UAL 3200 (mono), UAS 6200 (stereo))
- Paradise Village (1963, United Artists UAL 3263 (mono), UAS 6263 (stereo); as Al Caiola and His Islanders)
- Percussion Espanol (1960, Time S/2006)
- The Return of the Seven and Other Themes (1967, United Artists UAL 3560 (mono), UAS 6560 (stereo))
- Roman Guitar (1968, Roulette SR 42008; re-issue of *Salute Italia!*)
- Romantico (1966, United Artists UAL 3527 (mono), UAS 6527 (stereo))
- Salute Italia! (1960, Roulette R 25108 (mono), SR 25108 (stereo))
- Solid Gold Guitar (1962, United Artists UAL 3180 (mono), UAS 6180 (stereo))
- Solid Gold Guitar Goes Hawaiian (1965, United Artists UAS 6418)
- Sounds for Spies and Private Eyes (1965, United Artists UAL 3435 (mono), UAS 6435 (stereo))
- Spanish Guitars (1962, Time S/2039)
- Tuff Guitar (1965, United Artists UAL 3389 (mono), UAS 6389 (stereo))
- Tuff Guitar English Style (1965, United Artists UAL 3453 (mono), UAS 6453 (stereo))
- Tuff Guitar Tijuana Style (1966, United Artists UAL 3473 (mono), UAS 6473 (stereo))

Caiola, Al and Ralph Marterie

- Acapulco 1922 & The Lonely Bull (1963, United Artists UAL 3256 (mono), UAS 6256 (stereo))

Calvert, Eddie

- Latin Carnival (1961, ABC-Paramount ABC-384 (mono), ABCS-384 (stereo))

- Lonely Night (1956, Capitol T-10007; with **Norrie Paramor and His Orchestra**)

- Presenting the Golden Trumpet of Eddie Calvert (1960, ABC-Paramount ABC-319 (mono), ABCS-319 (stereo))

Camarata (aka Tutti Camarata; see also **Tutti's Trumpets**)

Note: Tutti Camarata did numerous other works for Disney, most of which had vocals and/or narration, for the children's market.

- Autumn (1957, Disneyland WDL-3021 (mono), STER-3021 (stereo))
- Music for a Lazy Afternoon (Decca DL-8112)
- The Parent Trap! (1961, Buena Vista BV-3309 (mono), STER-3309 (stereo)) Music from the film and others.
- Songs from Brigadoon and Other Favorites (1966, Disneyland DQ-1299)
- Spring (1958, Disneyland WDL-3032 (mono), STER-3032 (stereo))
- Summer (1958, Disneyland WDL-3027 (mono), STER-3027 (stereo))
- Think Young (1965, Coliseum D 41001 (mono), DS 51001 (stereo))
- Winter (1957, Disneyland WDL-3026 (mono), STER-3026 (stereo))

Cano, Eddie (and His Orchestra; Quartet; Quintet; Sextet) (see also **Jack Costanzo and Eddie Cano**)

- 30 Latin American Favorites (Pickwick SPC-3017; also re-released as *Latin Discotheque*)
- Cano Plays Mancini (1961, Reprise R9-6068)
- Cha Cha con Cano (1959, United Artists UAL 3024)
- Cole Porter and Me (RCA Victor LPM-1340)
- Deep in a Drum (1958, RCA Victor LSP-1645)
- Eddie Cano at PJ's (1961, Reprise R-6030 (mono), R9-6030 (stereo))
- Here is the Fabulous Eddie Cano (1961, Reprise R-6055 (mono), R9-6055 (stereo))
- Right Now (Reprise RS-6124)
- The Sound of Music and The Sound of Cano (1965, Reprise R-6145 (mono), RS-6145 (stereo))
- Time For Cha Cha Cha (RCA Victor LPM-1672 (mono), LSP-1672 (stereo))

Cano, Eddie & Jack Costanzo with Tony Martinez and His Orchestra

- Dancing on the Sunset Strip (GNP Crescendo GNP-44)

Carle, Frankie (and His Orchestra)

Frankie Carle was a popular pianist and bandleader whose career spanned four decades.

- 37 Favorites for Dancing (1958, RCA Victor LPM 1868 (mono), LSP 1868 (stereo); as Frankie Carle and His Rhythm)
- April in Portugal (1966, RCA Camden CAL 963 (mono), CAS 963e (stereo))
- Around the World (1958, RCA Victor LPM 1499 (mono), LSP 1499 (stereo))
- A Carle-Load of Hits (1959, RCA Victor LPM 2148 (mono), LSP 2148 (stereo))
- Cocktail Time with Frankie Carle (1956, RCA Victor LPM 1221)
- Cocktail Time with Frankie Carle (1967, RCA Camden CAS 2118e) This is a completely different album from the previous entry.
- Easy to Love (1966, RCA Camden CAL 987 (mono), CAS 987e (stereo))
- The Fabulous Four Hands (1961, RCA Victor LPM 2288 (mono), LSP 2288 (stereo))
- Frankie Carle (1967, Dot DLP 25789)
- Frankie Carle and His Beautiful Dolls (1958, RCA Victor LPM 1559 (mono), LSP (stereo))
- Frankie Carle and His Girl Friends (1955, Columbia CL 642)
- A Frankie Carle Piano Bouquet (Harmony HL 7166)
- Frankie Carle's Piano Party (1953, Columbia CL 531)
- Frankie Carle Plays Cocktail Piano (1964, RCA CPM 112 (mono), CSP 112 (stereo))
- Frankie Carle Plays Cole Porter (1955, RCA Victor LPM 1064)
- Frankie Carle Plays the Big Imported Hits (1964, RCA Victor LPM 2920 (mono), LSP 2920 (stereo))
- Frankie Carle Plays the Great Piano Hits (1965, RCA Victor LPM 3425 (mono), LSP 3425 (stereo))
- Frankie Carle's Sweethearts (1956, RCA Victor LPM 1222)
- The Golden Touch (1959, RCA Victor LPM 2139 (mono), LSP 2139 (stereo))
- The Latin Syle of Frankie Carle (1966, RCA Victor LPM 3518 (mono), LSP 3518 (stereo))
- Let's Do It (1969, RCA Camden CAS 2370)
- Mediterranean Cruise (1956, RCA Victor LPM 1225)
- Music for the Cocktail Hour (1968, RCA Camden CAS 2277)
- The Piano Style of Frankie Carle (1959, RCA Camden CAL-478 (mono), CAS-478 (stereo))
- Play One For Me (RCA Camden CAL 585 (mono), CAS 585 (stereo))
- Roses in Rhythm (1956, Columbia CL 913)

- Short and Sweet (1965, RCA Victor LPM 3300 (mono), LSP 3300 (stereo))
- Show Stoppers in Dance Time (1959, RCA Victor LPM 1963 (mono), LSP 1963 (stereo))
- Somewhere My Love (1967, Dot DLP 25802)
- Top of the Mark (1960, RCA Victor LPM-2233 (mono), LSP-2233 (stereo))
- The Tropical Style of Frankie Carle (1966, RCA Victor LPM 3609 (mono), LSP 3609 (stereo))

Carlton, John, and the Craftsmen All-Star Orchestra
- All-Time Favorites (1957?, Craftsmen C8011)

Carroll, David and His Orchestra (see also **Dick Contino**)
- All the World Dances (1961, Mercury PPS 2022 (mono), PPS 6022 (stereo))
- Dance and Stay Young (1957, Mercury MG 20351 (mono), SR 60027 (stereo))
- Dance Date (Mercury Wing MGW 12106)
- Dancer's Delight (1955?, Mercury MG 20109)
- Dreams (1957, Mercury MG 20301)
- The Feathery Feeling (1958, Mercury MG 20286 (mono), SR 60026 (stereo))
- Happy Feet (1964, Mercury MG 20846 (mono), SR 60846 (stereo))
- House-Party Discotheque (1964, Mercury MG 20962 (mono), SR 60962 (stereo))
- Latin Percussion (1960, Mercury PPS 2000 (mono), PPS 600 (stereo))
- Let's Dance (1958, Mercury MG 20281 (mono), SR 60001 (stereo))
- Let's Dance Again! (1959, Mercury MG 20470 (mono), SR 60152 (stereo))
- Let's Dance Dance Dance (1961, Mercury MG 20649 (mono), SR 60649 (stereo))
- Mexico and 11 Other Great Hits (1961, Mercury MG 20660 (mono), SR 60660 (stereo))
- Music Makes Me Want to Dance (1964, Mercury MG 20926 (mono), SR 60926 (stereo))
- Percussion in Hi-Fi (1957, Mercury MG 20166 (mono); 1958, Mercury SR 60003 (stereo))
- Percussion Orientale (1960, PPS 2002 (mono), PPS 6002 (stereo))
- RePercussion (1959, Mercury MG 20389 (mono), SR 60029 (stereo))

- Serenade to a Princess (1956, Mercury MG 20156)
- Shimmering Strings (1962, Mercury MG 20154)
- Show Stoppers from the Fabulous Fifties (1959, Mercury MG 20411)
- Today's Top Hits! (1963, Mercury MG 20786 (mono), SR 60786 (stereo))

Castaway Strings, The

The Castaway Strings were actually Vee Jay's response to the success of **The Hollyridge Strings**, who interpreted the songs of the Beatles (and others) for an Easy Listening audience.

- The Castaway Strings Play Songs Made Famous by Andy Williams (1965, Vee Jay VJLP-1114 (mono), VJ-1114 (stereo))
- The Castaway Strings Play Songs Made Famous by Elvis Presley (1965, Vee Jay VJLP-1113 (mono), VJ-1113 (stereo))

Catelli, Don and the All Stars

'Don Catelli' was actually a pseudonum for Belgian bandleader Franz Bayetz, aka **Francis Bay**.

- Passionate Percussion (1960?, Directional Sound DS 5009)
- Potent Percussion (1960?, Directional Sound DS 5010)

Cates, George and His Chorus and Orchestra

- 1965's Great Hits (1965, Hamilton HLP 161 (mono), HLP 12161 (stereo))
- Exciting (1958, Coral CRL 57220)
- Hawaii (1968, Ranwood RLP 8039)
- Hit Songs, Hit Sounds (1964, Dot DLP 3564)
- Polynesian Percussion (1961, Dot DLP 3355 (mono), DLP 25355 (stereo))
- Third Man Theme (1962?, Dot DLP 25434)
- Twistin' Twelve Great Hits! (1962, Dot DLP 25422)
- Under European Skies (1957, Coral CRL 57126)

Cavallaro, Carmen

- 12 Easy Lessons in Love (1958, Decca DL 8747)
- Cavallaro With That Latin Beat (1959, Decca DL 8864 (mono), DL 78864 (stereo))
- The Carmen Cavallaro Camp Plays the 3 B's (1970, GWP ST 2011)
- Carmen Cavallaro Plays His Show Stoppers (1960, Decca DL 4018 (mono), DL 74018 (stereo))

- Carmen Cavallaro Plays the Hits (1968, Decca DL 4914 (mono), DL 74914 (stereo))

- Carmen Cavallaro Remembers Eddie Duchin (Decca DL 8661, DLM 8661)

- Cherry Blossom Time: Popular Melodies of Japan (1964, Decca DL 4545 (mono), DL 74545 (stereo))

- Cocktail Time (1962, Decca DL 4155 (mono), DL 74155 (stereo))

- Cocktails With Cavallaro (1960, Decca DL 8805 (mono), DL 78805 (stereo))

- Dancing in the Dark (Decca DL 8961 (mono), DL 78961 (stereo); also DL 8120, probably an earlier release)

- Easy Listening (1966, Decca DL 4743 (mono), DL 74743 (stereo))

- The Eddie Duchin Story (1959, Decca DL 8289 (mono), DL 78289 (stereo)) Film soundtrack.

- I Wish You Love: Fabulous French Songs (1964, Decca DL 4566 (mono), DL 74566 (stereo))

- Informally Yours (1960, Decca DL 4017 (mono), DL 74017 (stereo))

- Love Can Make You Happy (1960, Decca DL 75155)

- The Masters' Touch (1956, Decca DL 8288)

- More (1965, MCA MUPS 359)

- Rome At Night (1956, Decca DL 8359)

- Songs Everybody Knows (1964, Decca DL 4489 (mono), DL 74489 (stereo))

- Swingin' Easy (1962, Decca DL 4287 (mono), DL 74287 (stereo))

Cawanda's Group

- Taboo (1959, Promenade 2125) This is another budget-label re-release (10 of the original 12 songs) of *Jungle Beat* by **Subri Moulin and His Equatorial Rhythm Group**. The same artwork and packaging would be reused for *Taboo* by **Chief Bey and His Royal Household**. Oddly, six of the ten songs would be reused on a children's 7" 78-RPM record on the Peter Pan label also attributed to 'Cawanda's Group.'

Cesana, Otta and His Orchestra (aka **Cesana**) (see also **Bonnie Prudden**)

- Autumn Reverie (1967, Audio Fidelity AFLP 2170)

- Brief Interlude (1958, Capitol T-1032)

- Ecstasy (1955, Columbia CL-631) This was a compilation of two previous 10" releases by Cesana, *Ecstasy* and *Sugar and Spice*.

- Leaves in the Wind (1968, Audio Fidelity AFSD 6188)

- Lush & Lovely (1967, Audio Fidelity AFSD 6176)

- Night Magic (1967, Audio Fidelity AFSD 6179)

- Sheer Ecstasy (1960, Warner Brothers W 1390 (mono), WS 1390 (stereo))
- The Sound of Rome (1962, RCA Victor LSP-2600)
- Voices of Venus (1957, Columbia CL-971)

Cha-Cha Rhythm Boys, The (see also **Rene Touzet**)
- All Time Cha-Cha-Cha and Merengue Hit Parade (1959, Fiesta FLP 1210 (mono), FLPS 1210 (stereo))
- The Best of the Lot (1959, Fiesta FLP 1220)

Chacksfield, Frank and His Orchestra
Frank Chacksfield was a British composer and conductor, and became an important figure in the early history of 'Mood Music,' aka Easy Listening.
- Broadway Melody (1956, London LL-1509)
- Ebb Tide (1960, London-Richmond B 20078 (mono), S 20078 (stereo))
- Evening in Paris (1955, London LL-997)
- Evening in Rome... (1955, London LL-1205)
- First Hits of 1965 (1965, London LL-3416 (mono), PS-416 (stereo))
- Foreign Film Festival (1967, London SP-44112)
- The Great TV Themes (1966, London SP-44077)
- Hawaii (1967, London SP-44087)
- Hollywood Almanac (1957, London PSA-3201)
- Love Letters in the Sand... (1959, London LL-3027)
- The Million Sellers (1960, London-Richmond B 20045 (mono), S 20045 (stereo))
- The Music of George Gershwin (1956, London LL-1203)
- The New Ebb Tide (1964, London SP-44053)
- On the Beach (1959, London LL-3158) (music from the motion picture)
- Presenting Frank Chacksfield & His Orchestra (1954, London LL-1041)
- Romantic Europe (1961, London-Richmond B 20103)
- She Loves Me (1963, London LL-3316)
- Songs of Sunny Italy (1960, London-Richmond B 20080)
- South Sea Island Magic (1958, London LL-1538)
- Velvet (1956, London LL-1443)

Chaino (and His African Percussion Safari) Record company lore had it that percussionist Chaino was rescued by missionaries from deepest Africa and brought to civilization, but the truth was that he was a Chicago-raised veteran of the 'Chitlin' Circuit.'

- Africana (1959, Dot DLP 3240 (mono), DLP 25240 (stereo))
- Jungle Echoes (1959, Omega OSL 7)
- Jungle Mating Rhythms (1958, Verve MGV-2104)
- Jungle Rhythms (1958, Score SLP 4027)
- Night of the Spectre (1958, Tampa TP-4)
- Unbridled Passions of Love's Eerie Spectre (1957, Spectre SPECTRE-4)

Chango and the Polynesians

- Polynesian Percussion (1962, Directional Sound DM 5012 (mono), DS 5012 (stereo))

Charles, Ray (aka **The Ray Charles Singers/Choir**) (see also **Neal Hefti**, **Dick Van Dyke**)

Not *that* Ray Charles.

- Al-Di-La (1964, Command RS 33 870 (mono), RS 870 SD (stereo))
- At the Movies With the Ray Charles Singers (1967, Command RS 923)
- Autumn Nocturne (1954, MGM E-3145)
- Deep Night (1960, Decca DL 8988 (mono), DL 78988 (stereo))
- In the Evening By the Moonlight (1959, Decca DL 8874 (mono), DL 78874 (stereo))
- Love and Marriage (1958, Decca DL 8787 (mono), DL 78787 (stereo))
- MacArthur Park (1968, Command RS 936 SD)
- One of Those Songs (1966, Command RS 33 898 (mono), RS 898 SD (stereo))
- Paradise Islands (1962, Command RS 845 SD; re-released in 1972)
- Quiet Moments for Young Lovers (1964, Somerset P-21400 (mono), SF-21400 (stereo))
- Rome Revisited (1962, Command RS 839 SD; re-released in 1972)
- Something Special for Young Lovers (1964, Command SD 33 866 (mono), RS 866 SD (stereo); re-released in 1972)
- Something Wonderful (1961, Command RS 827 SD)
- Songs For Latin Lovers (1965, Command RS 33 886 (mono), RS 886 SD (stereo))
- Songs For Lonesome Lovers (1964, Command RS 33 874 (mono), RS 874 SD (stereo))

- A Special Something... (1967, Command RS 33 914 (mono), RS 914 SD (stereo))
- Summertime (1957, MGM E-3529)
- Take Me Along! (1968, Command RS 926 SD)
- We Love Paris (1963, MGM SE-4165)
- What the World Needs Now is Love! (1966, Command RS 903)
- Young Lovers in Far Away Places (1964, Somerset P-21500 (mono), SF-21500 (stereo))
- Young Lovers On-Broadway (1965, Command RS 33 890 (mono), RS 890 SD (stereo))

Cheltenham Orchestra and Chorus, The

- Great Themes from James Bond (1966, Wyncote W-9134 (mono), SW-9134 (stereo))
- Songs from Goldfinger and Other James Bond Favorites (1965, Wyncote W-9086 (mono), SW-9086 (stereo))

Chihuahua Marimba Band, The (see also **Guadalajara Brass and The Chihuahua Marimba Band**)

- Cry of the Wild Goose (Spin-O-Rama M-191 (mono), S-191 (stereo); Premier PS-9005)

Chillingworth, Sonny

Hawaiian slack-key guitarist.

- Los Hawaiianos (Makaha M-2019 (mono), MS-2019 (stereo))
- Sonny Chillingworth (1967, Makaha M-2014 (mono), MS-2014 (stereo); Lethua SL-2014)
- Waimea Cowboy (1972, Makaha M-2003; Lethua SL-2003)

Choco (aka **Choco and His Mafimba Drum Rhythms**)

- African Latin Voodoo Drums (1962, Audio Fidelity AFLP-2102 (mono) and AFSD-6102 (stereo)) This oddity from the Exotica era consists of basically nothing but drumming, with a bit of vocalization thrown in; no other instruments. For hardcore drumming or exotica fans only.

Christian, Bobby (and His Orchestra)

- Mr. Percussion (1958, Mercury MG 20335 (mono), SR 60015 (stereo))
- Percussion in Velvet (1959, Westminster WST 15046)
- Smooth Man (1959, Stepheny MF 4012)
- Strings for a Space Age (1962, Audio Fidelity AFSD 5959)

Clebanoff and His Orchestra (aka **The Clebanoff Strings**, etc.)

- Accent on Strings! (1960, Mercury MGD 16 (mono), SRD 16 (stereo))
- Clebanoff Plays More Songs from Great Films (1959, Mercury SR 60162)
- Clebanoff Plays Songs from Great Shows... (1959, MG 20416)
- Exciting Sounds of the Clebanoff Strings & Percussion (Mercury MG 20869 (mono), PPS 2012 (stereo); 1969, Mercury Wing SRW 16396 (re-release))
- A Film Concert by the Clebanoff Strings, Orchestra & Chorus (1964, Mercury MG 20887 (mono), SR 60887 (stereo))
- King of Kings and 11 Other Great Movie Themes (Mercury SR 60640)
- Love Themes from Great Films (Mercury MG 20578 (mono), SR 60238 (stereo))
- Lush, Latin, and Bossa Nova Too! (1963, Mercury MG 20824 (mono), SR 60824 (stereo))
- Moods in Music (1958, Mercury SR 60005)
- Music of Great Women of Films (Mercury Wing SRW 16399)
- Once Upon a Summertime (1968, Decca DL 74956)
- Songs from Great Films (1958, Mercury MG 20371)
- Strings Afire (1962, Mercury PPS-6019; SRW 16394 (later re-release))
- Teen Hits Played the Clebanoff Way (1964, Mercury MG 20929 (mono), SR 60929 (stereo))
- Today's Best Hits (1963, Mercury MG 20791 (mono), SR 60791 (stereo))
- Twelve Great Songs of All Time (Mercury MG 20720)

Coco, Johnny (see also **The Hawaiian Room Orchestra**)

- The Exotic Sounds of the Hawaii Kai (1965, Columbia CL 2329 (mono), CS 9129 (stereo))

Cole, Buddy

- Autumn Nocturne (Warner Brothers WS 1557)
- Backgrounds to Love (1960, Warner Brothers W 1384 (mono), WS 1384 (stereo))
- Buddy Cole Plays Cole Porter (1958, Warner Brothers W 1226 (mono), WS 1226 (stereo))
- Have Organ, Will Swing (1958, Warner Brothers W 1211 (mono), WS 1211 (stereo))
- Hot and Cole (1959, Warner Brothers W 1252)

- Ingenuity in Sound (1962, Warner Brothers B 1442 (mono), BS 1442 (stereo))
- Modern Pipe Organ (1963, Warner Brothers WS 1533)
- Organ Moods in Hi-Fi (1956, Columbia CL 874)
- Pipes, Pedals, and Fidelity (1957, Columbia CL 1003 (mono), CS 8065 (stereo))
- Powerhouse! (1959, Warner Brothers WS 1310)
- Sleepy Time Gal (1959, Warner Brothers W 1265)
- Sweet and Lovely (Tops L-1604; with **The Mellowaires**)
- Swing Fever (1960, Warner Brothers W 1373 (mono), WS 1373 (stereo))

Coleman, Cy

- The Art of Love (1965, Capitol T 2355 (mono), ST 2355 (stereo))
- Cool Coleman (1958, Westminster WST 15001)
- Cy Coleman (1958, Seeco CELP 402)
- Flower Drum Song (1958, Westminster WST 15038)
- Piano Witchcraft (1963, Capitol T 1952; re-released in 1979 with a slight change in song selection)
- Playboy's Penthouse (1960, Eve SDBR 1092)
- The Troublemaker (1964, Ava A 49 ST (mono), AS 49 ST (stereo))

Collette, Buddy (see also **Don Ralke and Buddy Collette**, and the Compilations section)

- The Girl from Ipanema... and Other Favorites (1964, Crown CLP-5460 (mno), CST-460 (stereo))
- The Polyhedric Buddy Collette (1961, Music LMP-2001) OK, this entry is a bit of a cheat since this album was apparently released only in Italy; but it's been re-issued a few times, including some recent vinyl and CD issues. But this is a very good example of Exotica/Space Age pop that *should* have been made available to American listeners.
- Polynesia (Music & Sound S-1001; as The Buddy Collette Septet)
- Porgy and Bess (1959, Interlude MO-505)

Colon, Augie

Colon was percussionist (and primary bird call vocalist) of **Martin Denny**'s group who took the time to put out these two solo albums with the blessing of his bandleader.

- Chant of the Jungle (1960, Liberty LRP-3148 (mono), LST-7148 (stereo))
- Sophisticated Savage (1959, Liberty LRP-3101) Apparently not released in stereo – why not?

Columbia Musical Treasuries Orchestra and Chorus

- Soundstage Spectacular (1968, Columbia Musical Treasuries P2S 5214)

- Soundstage Spectacular (1969, Columbia Musical Treasuries P2S 5284) This and the previous entry are two completely different albums, but share the same title and same basic cover design.

- Summer Wind (1967, Columbia Record Club DS 343)

- A Very Good Year (1967, Columbia Record Club D 285 (mono), DS 285 (stereo)

Columbia Salon Orchestra

- Quiet Music, Vol. 1: Easy Listening for Your Relaxation (1952, Columbia CL 510) Between 1952 and '53, Columbia released ten volumes of the Quiet Music: Easy Listening for Your Relaxation series. Each one features music by the Columbia Salon Orchestra and a few other artists. Each features instrumental music that might be perceived as a bridge between quieter selections from the 1940's, and what would come to be Easy Listening as we think of it today. Only this first one will be listed in this volume.

Comstock, Frank (aka **Project: Comstock**)

- *Music from Outer Space* (1962, Warner Brothers W 1463 (mono), WS 1463 (stereo)) One of the undisputed classics of what is known as 'Space Age Bachelor Pad Music.'

- Patterns (1958, Columbia CL 1156 (mono), CS 8003 (stereo))

- A Young Man's Fancy (1954, Columbia CL 1021)

Conniff, Ray (incl. **The Ray Conniff Singers**)

Although his records are now dragged out mostly at Christmas, at one time Ray Conniff and his Singers were the one of the most successful recording groups in the world; in the 1960's the Singers regularly dominated the charts, and by Conniff's death over 70 million albums had been sold worldwide.

- Bridge Over Troubled Water (1970, Columbia CS 1022)

- Broadway in Rhythm (1958, Columbia CL 1252 (mono), CS 8064 (stereo))

- Concert in Rhythm (1958, Columbia CL 1163 (mono), CS 8022 (stereo))

- Concert in Rhythm, Vol. 2 (1960, Columbia CL 1415 (mono), CS 8212 (stereo))

- Concert in Stereo / Live at the Sahara/Tahoe (1970, Columbia GA 30122)

- En Espanol! (1967, Columbia CL 2608 (mono), CS 9408 (stereo))

- Friendly Persuasion (1964, Columbia CL 2210 (mono), CS 9010 (stereo))

- The Happy Beat (1963, Columbia CL 1949 (mono), CS 8749 (stereo))
- Happiness Is (1966, Columbia CL 2461 (mono), CS 9261 (stereo))
- Hawaiian Album (1967, Columbia CL 2747 (mono), CS 9547 (stereo))
- Hollywood in Rhythm (1959, Columbia CL 1310 (mono), CS 8117 (stereo))
- Honey (1968, Columbia CS 9661)
- I Love How You Love Me (1969, Columbia CS 9777)
- I'd Like to Teach the World to Sing (1971, Columbia KC 31220)
- The Impossible Dream (1970, Harmony KH 30134)
- Invisible Tears (1964, Columbia CL 2264 (mono), CS 9064 (stereo))
- It Must Be Him (1967, Columbia CL 2795 (mono), CS 9595 (stereo))
- It's the Talk of the Town (1959, Columbia CL 1334 (mono), CS 8143 (stereo))
- Jean (1969, Columbia CS 9920)
- Love Affair (1965, Columbia CL 2352 (mono), CS 9152 (stereo))
- Love is a Many-Splendored Thing (1969, Harmony HS 11346)
- Love Story (1970, Columbia C 30498; also released in 1971 in quadraphonic)
- Memories Are Made of This (1960, Columbia CL 1574 (mono), CS 8374 (stereo))
- Music from Mary Poppins, The Sound of Music, My Fair Lady, & Other Great Movie Themes (1965, Columbia CL 2366 (mono), CS 9166 (stereo))
- Ray Conniff's World of Favorites (1967, Columbia Record Club D 267 (mono), DS 267 (stereo))
- Ray Conniff's World of Hits (1966, Columbia CL 2500 (mono), CS 9300 (stereo))
- Rhapsody in Rhythm (1962, Columbia CL 1878 (mono), CS 8678 (stereo))
- 'S Awful Nice (1958, Columbia CL 1137 (mono), CS 8001 (stereo))
- 'S Continental (1962, Columbia CL 1776 (mono), CS 8576 (stereo))
- 'S Marvelous (1957, Columbia CL 1074 (mono), CS 8037 (stereo))
- 'S Wonderful (1956, Columbia CL 925)
- Say it With Music – A Touch of Latin (1960, Columbia CL 1490 (mono), CS 8282 (stereo))

- So Much in Love (1962, Columbia CL 1720 (mono), CS 8520 (stereo); re-released in 1966)
- Somebody Loves Me (1961, Columbia CL 1642 (mono), CS 8442 (stereo))
- Somewhere My Love (1966, Columbia CL 2519 (mono), CS 9319 (stereo))
- Speak to Me of Love (1964, Columbia CL 2150 (mono), CS 8950 (stereo))
- Thanks For the Memory (1968, Columbia Record Club DS 357)
- This is My Song (1967, Columbia CL 2676 (mono), CS 9476 (stereo))
- Turn Around Look At Me (1968, Columbia CL 2912 (mono), CS 9712 (stereo))
- We've Only Just Begun (1970, Columbia C 30410)
- You Make Me Feel So Young (1964, Columbia CL 2118 (mono), CS 8918 (stereo))
- Young At Heart (1960, Columbia CL 1489 (mono), CS 8281 (stereo))

Conniff, Ray, and Billy Butterfield
- Conniff Meets Butterfield (1959, Columbia CL 1346 (mono), CS 8155 (stereo))
- Just Kiddin' Around (1963, Columbia CL 2022 (mono), CS 8822 (stereo))

Conrad, Paul
- Exotic Paradise (1960, Mahalo M-3010) One of the more sought-after exotica albums.

Contino, Dick (**and His Accordion; Orchestra**)
Gone are the days when an accordion player can become a major star, but Dick Contino managed to do so in the mid-1950's. In '58 he starred in a teen rebellion flick, *Daddy-O*.
- 12 Immortal Songs (Dot DLP 3609 (mono), DLP 25609 (stereo))
- Accordion Fiesta!! (Hamilton HLP 176 (mono), HLP 12176 (stereo))
- An Accordion in Paris (1956, Mercury MG 20142 (mono), Mercury Wing MGW 12147 (mono), 16147 (stereo); with **The David Carroll Orchestra**)
- Accordion Magic (1964, Hamilton HLP 135 (mono), HLP 12135 (stereo))
- Dick Contino and His Accordion (1956, Mercury MG 20141, Mercury Wing MGW 12122 (mono), SRW 16122 (stereo); with **The David Carroll Orchestra**)

- Dick Contino at the Fabulous Flamingo in Las Vegas (Mercury SR 60079)
- Hawaiian Holiday (1962, Mercury MG 20753 (mono), SR 60753 (stereo))
- It's Dance Time (1959, Mercury MG 20030 (mono), SR 60006 (stereo))
- Roman Holiday (1959, Mercury MG 20635 (mono), SR 60635 (stereo); with **The David Carroll Orchestra**)
- Something for the Girls (1959, Mercury MG 20141; with **The David Carroll Orchestra**)
- South American Holiday (1961, Mercury MG 20668 (mono), SR 60668 (stereo); with **The David Carroll Orchestra**)
- Squeeze Me! (Mercury MG 20414 (mono), SR 60090 (stereo))
- Twilight Time and Other Golden Hits (Dot DLP 3680 (mono), DLP 25680 (stereo))

Contino, Dick and Eddie Layton
- In the Mood (1959, Mercury MG 20471 (mono), SR 60153 (stereo))

Conway, Russ (and His Orchestra)
- All Time Movie Favorites (1962, MGM E 4021 (mono), SE 4021 (stereo); with **The Williams Singers** and **The Tony Osborne Orchestra**) Note: The bulk of Ross Conway's output was released in the UK and other countries, and thus is ineligible to be included in this volume.

Copeland, Alan (see also **Count Basie**)
- A Bubble Called You (1967, ABC ABC-617 (mono), ABCS-617 (stereo); as The Alan Copeland Conspiracy)
- If Loves Come With It (1969, A&M SP 4173; as The Alan Copeland Singers)
- No Sad Songs For Me (1957, Coral 57197)

Cordell, Frank and His Orchestra
- The Best of Everything (1967, United Artists UAL 3590 (mono), UAS 6590 (stereo)) Cordell is another artist whose work has largely appeared in the UK and elsewhere; he may have had a few more American releases than this one, though.

Costa, Don
- Days of Wine and Roses and Other Great Hits (Harmony HL 7347)
- The Don Costa Concept (1969, Mercury SR 61216)

- Don Costa's Instrumental Versions of Simon & Garfunkel (1968, Mercury SR 61177)

- Echoing Voices and Trombones (1960, United Artists WW-7501 (mono), WWS-8501 (stereo)

- The Golden Touch (1964, DCP International DCL 3802)

- Hits! Hits! Hits! (1963, Columbia CL 2041)

- Hollywood Premiere! (1962, Columbia CL 1880 (mono), CS 8680 (stereo))

- Modern Delights (1967, Verve V-8702 (mono), V6-8702 (stereo))

- Music to Break a Lease (1956, ABC-Paramount ABC-107)

- Music to Break a Sub-Lease (1958, ABC-Paramount ABC-212 (mono), ABCS-212 (stereo); as **Don Costa's Free-Loaders**) This and the preceding entry were composed of favorite sing-alongs recorded with multiple voices; but the humorous nature of the covers – with the theme of annoying one's neighbors by playing the records very loudly – have granted them a certain amount of notoriety. There was also a *More Music to Break a Lease*, although that one was by 'Sid Feller and His "Friends" (and Enemies)' – see separate entry.

- The Sound of the Million Sellers (1961, United Artists WW-3513 (mono), WS-8513 (stereo))

- The Theme from 'The Unforgiven' (1960, United Artists UAL-3119 (mono), UAS-6119 (stereo))

Costanzo, Jack (and His Orchestra; and His Afro Cuban Band) (see also the Compilations section)

Known as Mr. Bongo, Jack Costanzo started out as a dancer but switched to the percussive instrument after a handful of visits to Cuba. Eventually he would record with many singing stars of the 1950's as well as his own group.

- Afro Can-Can (1960, Liberty LRP 3137 (mono), LST 7137 (stereo))

- Bongo! Cha Cha Cha (1960, Golden Tone C-4061; also released as *Cha Cha Cha* on Clarity 804)

- Bongo Fever (1966, Sunset SUM-1134 (mono), SUS-5134 (stereo))

- Bongo Fever: Jack Costanzo at The Garden of Allah (1959, Liberty LRP 3109 (mono), LST 7109 (stereo))

- *Latin Fever* (1958, Liberty LRP 3093 (mono), LST 7020 (stereo))

- Learn – Play Bongos with 'Mr. Bongo' (1961, Liberty LRP 3177) As the title suggests, this is primarily an instructional record for learning to play the bongos.

- Mr. Bongo (1955, GNP GNP-19; later re-released as *Costanzo Cano & Bongos!*, see Jack Costanzo and Eddie Cano)

- Mr. Bongo (1964, Clarion 621 (mono), SD 621 (stereo)) His name is misspelled as 'Costanza' on the album cover and label as well. Note that this album is also completely different from the 1955 GNP release with the same title. Serenity now!

- Mr. Bongo Has Brass (1956, Zephyr ZP 12003 G)
- Mr. Bongo Plays Hi-Fi Cha Cha (1957, Tops L 1564)
- Naked City (1961, Liberty LRP 3195 (mono), LST 7195 (stereo))
- Spotlight on Dance Time (Tiara TMT 7529)

Costanzo, Jack and Eddie Cano

- Costanzo Cano & Bongos! (1963, GNP Crescendo GNP 90) This was a re-release of the 1955 *Mr. Bongo*.

Costanzo, Jack and Gerrie Woo

- Latin Percussion With Soul (1968, Tico LP 1177 (mono), SLP 1177 (stereo))
- Viva Tirado (1971, GNP Crescendo GNPS 2057)

Cottler, Irv

- Around the World in Percussion (1961, Somerset P-13900 (mono), SF-13900 (stereo))

Covington, Warren (and His Orchestra; and His Jazz Band; and the Commanders)

- Dancing Trombones (1962, Decca DL 4352 (mono), DL 74352 (stereo))
- Designed For Dancing (Decca DL 74448)
- Everybody Twist (1962, Decca DL 4271 (mono), DL 74271 (stereo))
- Golden Trombone Favorites (1966, Decca DL 4667 (mono), DL 74667 (stereo))
- Hits of the '60's, Vol. 1 (Re-Car RCS-2037)
- Hits of the '60's, Vol. 2 (Re-Car RCS-2038)
- Latin Dance Party (1967, Vocalion VL 3810 (mono), VL 73810 (stereo))
- Latin Si! (1961, Decca DL 4208 (mono), DL 74208 (stereo))
- Let's Dance Latin (1964, Decca DL 74491)
- Shall We Dance? (1956, Decca DL 8408; as Warren Covington and the Commanders)
- Teenage Hop (1957, Decca DL 8577; as Warren Covington and the Commanders)

Covington, Warren and The Tommy Dorsey Orchestra

- Dance and Romance (Decca DL 8904 (mono), DL 78904 (stereo))
- Dance to the Songs Everybody Knows (Decca DL 74120)

- The Fabulous Arrangements of Tommy Dorsey in Hi-Fi (1958, Decca DL 8802)

- It Takes Two... (Decca DL 8980 (mono), DL 78980 (stereo)) First song on this album is "Noche de Ferra (Cha Cha)."

- It Takes Two To... (1960, Decca DL 8996 (mono), DL 78996 (stereo)) First song on this album is "Bye Bye Blackbird." This is a completely different album from the previous entry.

- More Tea For Two Cha Chas (1960, Decca DL 8943 (mono), DL 78943 (stereo))

- Tea For Two Cha Chas (1959, Decca DL 8842 (mono), DL 78842 (stereo))

- Tricky Trombones (1960, Decca DL 4130 (mono), DL 74130 (stereo))

Craft, Morty and The Singing Strings (see also **The Singing Strings**)

- Percussion (1961, Warwick W 5004 ST)

- Percussion in Hollywood, Broadway, Television (Warwick W 5000 ST)

- World of Percussion (1961, Warwick W 5002 ST)

Crawford, Jesse

- Among My Souvenirs (1956, Decca DL 8276)

- Deep Purple (1957, Promenade 2074)

- Hits on the Hammond (1957, Decca DL 8470)

- A Lovely Way to Spend an Evening (1963, Decca DL 74477)

- Moon River (1967, Diplomat DS 2330)

- Moonlight Sonata (1957, Decca DL 8306)

- Organ Fantasies (Spin-O-Rama M-102)

- The Song is You (1959, Decca DL 8861 (mono), DL 78861 (stereo))

Crewe, Bob (aka **The Bob Crewe Generation**)

Crewe was a successful songwriter throughout the 1950's and 60's, and with his own group the Generation had a Top 20 hit with "Music to Watch Girls By."

- Barbarella (1968, Dynovoice DY-1908 (mono), DY-31908 (stereo)) Music from the film starring Jane Fonda.

- Let Me Touch You (1969, CGC Records CG-1000)

- Music to Watch Birds By (1967, Dynovoice DY 31902)

- Music to Watch Girls By (1967, Dynovoice LP 9003 (mono), SLP 9003 (stereo))

Crystal Studio Strings, The

- Strings in Stereo (1959, Waldorf Music Hall MHK 1409) 'Under the direction of Stuart Phillips.' Is this the **Stu Phillips** of **Hollyridge Strings** fame?

Cugat, Xavier and His Orchestra (see also the Compilations section)

For decades Xavier Cugat was one of the leading exponents of Latin music in the United States.

- Bang Bang (1966, Decca DL 4799 (mono), DL 74799 (stereo))
- Bread, Love, and Cha Cha Cha (1957, Columbia CL 1016)
- Cha Cha Cha (1955, Columbia CL 718)
- Chile Con Cugie (1959, RCA Victor LPM-1987 (mono), LSP-1987 (stereo))
- Cugat Caricatures (1964, Mercury MG 20888 (mono) SR 60888 (stereo))
- Cugat Cavalcade (1958, Columbia CL 1094 (mono), CS 8055 (stereo))
- Cugat in France, Spain, & Italy (1960, RCA Victor LPM-2173 (mono), LSP-2173 (stereo))
- Cugat in Spain (1959, RCA Victor LPM-1894 (mono), LSP-1894 (stereo))
- Cugat Plays Continental Hits (1962, Mercury PPS-2021 (mono), PPS-6021 (stereo))
- Cugat's Favorites (1955, Mercury MG 20065)
- Cugat's Golden Goodies (1963, Mercury MG 20798 (mono), SR 60798 (stereo))
- Cugi's Cockatils (1963, Mercury MG 20832 (mono), SR 60832 (stereo)) Each song on this album is named after an alcoholic mixed drink: "Cuba Libre," "Manhattan," etc.
- The Dance Beat of Xavier Cugat and His Orchestra (1967, Harmony HL 7242)
- Dance Party (1966, Decca DL 4740 (mono), DL 74740 (stereo))
- Feeling Good! (1965, Decca DL 4672 (mono), DL 74672 (stereo))
- Here's Cugat (1952, Mercury MG 25120)
- The King Plays Some Aces (1958, RCA Victor LPM-1882 (mono), LSP-1882 (stereo))
- Latin For Lovers (1959, RCA Camden CAL 516; previously released on 10" as *Rumbas*)
- Latin Reflections (1969, Musico MDS 1015)
- The Latin Rhythms of Xavier Cugat (1960, Harmony HL 7271)
- The Latin Soul of Xavier Cugat (1967, Pickwick SPC-3095)
- Mambo! (1957, Mercury MG 20108)
- Mambo at the Waldorf (1955, Columbia CL 732)

- Merengue! By Cugat! (1955, Columbia CL 733)
- Midnight Roses (1968, Decca DL 75046)
- Most Popular Movie Hits As Styled By Cugat (1962, Mercury MG 20745 (mono), SR 60745 (stereo))
- Ole! (1955, Columbia CL 618)
- Relaxing With Cugat: Quiet Music, Vol. 6 (1952, Columbia CL 515)
- Spanish Eyes (1970, Vocalion VL 73910; re-released by MCA Coral in 1973)
- That Latin Beat! (1959, RCA Camden CAL 323)
- Twist With Cugat (1962, Mercury MG 20705)
- Viva Cugat! (1961, Mercury PPS 2003 (mono), PPS 6003 (stereo))
- Xavier Cugat Plays the Music of Ernesto Lecuona (1964, Mercury MG 20936 (mono), SR 60936 (stereo))
- Xavier Cugat Today! (1967, Decca DL 74851)

Curbelo, Jose and His Orchestra
- Cha Cha Cha in Blue (1955, Fiesta FLP 1204)
- Cha Cha Cha, Mambo, Merengue (1955, Fiesta FLP 1207)
- Instrumental Cha Cha Cha, Mambo, Merengue (Fiesta FLP 1242 (mono), FLPS 1242 (stereo))
- Wine, Women, and Cha Cha (1955, Latin FLP 1219)

Dan & Dale (aka **The 'Sleepwalk' Guitars Of**; **The Sensational Guitars Of**)
- Batman and Robin (1966, Tifton 78002 (mono), S-78002 (stereo))
- Dear Heart (1964, Diplomat D-2340 (mono), DS-2340 (stereo))
- Dream Lovers (1964, Diplomat D-2362 (mono), DS-2362 (stereo))
- Falling In Love Again (1965, Diplomat D-2388 (mono), DS-2388 (stereo))
- Henry Mancini Favorites: Moon River (1964, Diplomat D-2366 (mono), DS-2366 (stereo))
- Love Is Blue – We Can Fly – Theme from Valley of the Dolls (1968, Diplomat DS-2441)
- Moonlight Memories (1965, Diplomat D-2391 (mono), DS-2391 (stereo))
- The Nearness of You (1965, Diplomat D-2390 (mono), DS-2390 (stereo))
- Somewhere My Love (1965, Diplomat D-2395 (mono), DS-2395 (stereo))
- Songs from The Great Race, Magnificent Men, Ship of Fools (1964, Diplomat D-2351 (mono), DS-2351 (stereo))

- The Theme from 'Hawaii' (1964, Diplomat D-2365 (mono), DS-2365 (stereo))
- Themes from Goldfinger and Zorba the Greek (1964, Diplomat D-2343 (mono), DS-2343 (stereo))
- Thunderball (1965, Diplomat D-2616 (mono), DS-2616 (stereo))
- Two Sleepy People (1965, Diplomat D-2389 (mono), DS-2389 (stereo))

Dant, Charles 'Bud', His Chorus and Orchestra
- The 50th State (1959, Coral CRL 57270)
- Isle of Enchantment (1959, Coral CRL 57249)

David, Russ
- Where There's Life... (1960, RCA Victor LPM-2191 (mono), LSP-2191 (stereo)) The cover for this one is interesting. It features a recursive photo – that is, one in which part of the photo repeats within the larger image – of a woman in a blue dress sitting at a portable record player; but her own image, in the same pose, can be seen on one of the album covers nearby. Also, a pair of male hands pours her a glass of beer from a Budweiser bottle where the brand label can be very clearly seen.

Davies, Lew and His Orchestra
- A Cheerful Earful (1963, Command RS 861 SD)
- Delicado (1963, Command RS 846 SD)
- Strange Interlude (1961, Command RS 33 829 (mono), RS 829 SD (stereo))
- Two Pianos & Twenty Voices (1960, Command RS 33-318 (mono), RS 813 SD (stereo))

Davis, Jackie
- Big Beat Hammond (1962, Capitol T-1686 (mono), ST-1686 (stereo))
- Chasing Shadows (1957, Capitol T-815)
- Easy Does It (1963, Warner Brothers W 1492 (mono), WS 1492 (stereo))
- Hammond Gone Cha-Cha (1959, Capitol T-1338 (mono), ST-1338 (stereo))
- The Hammond Organ of Jackie Davis Plus Voices! (1963, Warner Brothers W 1515 (mono), WS 1515 (stereo); with **The Sid Bass Chorus**)
- Hi-Fi Hammond (1956, Capitol T-686)
- Hi-Fi Hammond, Vol. 2 (1960, Capitol T-1517 (mono), ST-1517 (stereo))

- Jackie Davis Meets the Trombones (1959, Capitol T-1180 (mono), ST-1180 (stereo))
- Jumpin' Jackie (1958, Capitol T-974)
- Most Happy Hammond (1958, Capitol T-1046)
- Tiger on the Hammond (1960, Capitol T-1419 (mono), ST-1419 (stereo))

Davis, Maxwell

- Batman Theme! And Other Bat Songs (1966, Crown CLP-5509 (mono), CST-509 (stereo); 'Composed by **Neal Hefti**')

De Cara, Nick and Orchestra

- Happy Heart (1969, A&M SP 4176)

De Los Rios, Waldo

- Kiss of Fire (1957, Columbia CL 965)
- Waldo De Los Rios and His Symphony Pop Orchestra Play the International Hits (Vault SLP-126)

De Luca, Edmond

- Safari (1958, Somerset P 5500 (mono), SF 5500 (stereo))

Dee, Lenny

While Lenny Dee's long career at the organ had him playing many varieties of music, only a sample of his more Easy Listening-leaning material is included here.

- Dee-Latin: Hi-Fi Organ (1958, Decca DL 8718 (mono), DL 78718 (stereo))
- Gentle On My Mind (1968, Decca DL 74994)
- In the Mood (1966, Decca DL 4818 (mono), DL 74818 (stereo))
- Lenny Dee in Hollywood! (1962, Decca DL 4315 (mono), DL 74315 (stereo))
- Mellow-Dee (1958, Decca DL 8796 (mono), DL 78796 (stereo))
- My Favorite Things (1966, Decca DL 4706 (mono), DL 74706 (stereo))

Delugg, Milton

Among other accomplishments, accordionist and bandleader Delugg is remembered for writing the music for the kitsch classic film *Santa Claus Conquers the Martians.*

- Accordion My Way – Ole! (1967, RCA Victor LPM-3861 (mono), LSP-3861 (stereo))

- Gulliver's Travels Beyond the Moon (1966, Mainstream 54001 (mono), S/4001 (stereo); with Anne Delugg) Soundtrack to the animated film.

- Gypsy Girl (1966, Mainstream 56090 (mono), S/6090 (stereo); with Anne Delugg) Music from the Hayley Mills film.

- Presenting Milton Delugg and the Tonight Show Big Band (1967, RCA Victor LPM-3809 (mono), LSP-3809 (stereo))

Denny, Martin

Martin Denny single-handedly kicked a musical genre into being in 1959 when the stereo version of his group's album *Exotica* was released, and the single "Quiet Village" went to #2 in the *Billboard* charts. The music – with its foreign instruments and odd bird calls – made listeners dream of faraway places that they could never visit in reality. Denny went on to make a career out of such a musical style, although some of his later albums lean more toward Easy Listening than Exotica.

- 20 Golden Hawaiian Hits (1965, Liberty LRP 3415 (mono), LST 7415 (stereo))

- Afro-Desia (1959, Liberty LRP 3111 (mono), LST 7111 (stereo))

- Another Taste of Honey! (1963, Liberty LRP 3277 (mono), LST 7277 (stereo))

- The Enchanted Sea (1959, Liberty LRP 3141 (mono), LST 7141 (stereo))

- Exotic Love (1968, Liberty LST 7585)

- Exotic Moog (1969, Liberty LST 7621)

- Exotic Night (1968, Sunset SUS-5199)

- Exotic Percussion (1961, Liberty LRP 3168 (mono), LST 7168 (stereo))

- Exotic Sounds from the Silver Screen (1960, Liberty LRP 3158 (mono), LST 7158 (stereo))

- Exotic Sounds Visit Broadway (1960, Liberty LRP 3163 (mono), LST 7163 (stereo))

- *Exotica* (1957, Liberty LRP 3034; various re-releases, including stereo versions)

- Exotica, Vol. 2 (1957, Liberty LRP 3077; various re-releases, including stereo versions)

- Exotica, Vol. 3 (1959, Liberty LRP 3116 (mono), LST 7116 (stereo))

- Exotica Classica – For Those in Love (1967, Liberty LRP 3513 (mono), LST-7513 (stereo))

- Exotica Today (1966, Liberty LRP 3465 (mono), LST 7465 (stereo))

- Forbidden Island (1958, Liberty LRP 3081 (mono), LST 7001 (stereo))

- Golden Greats (1966, Liberty LRP 3467 (mono), LST 7467 (stereo))
- Hawaii (1967, Liberty LRP 3488 (mono), LST 7488 (stereo))
- Hawaii Tattoo (1964, Liberty LRP 3394 (mono), LST 7394 (stereo))
- Hawaii Goes A Go-Go! (1966, Liberty LRP 3445 (mono), LST 7445 (stereo))
- Hypnotique (1959, Liberty LRP 3102 (mono), LST 7102 (stereo))
- Latin Village (1964, Liberty LRP 3378 (mono), LST 7378 (stereo))
- Martin Denny! (1966, Liberty LRP 3438 (mono), LST 7438 (stereo))
- Martin Denny In Person (1962, Liberty LRP 3224 (mono), LST 7224 (stereo))
- Paradise Moods (1966, Sunset SUM-1102 (mono), SUS-5102 (stereo))
- Primitiva (1958, Liberty LRP 3087 (mono), LST 7023 (stereo))
- *Quiet Village* (1969, Liberty LRP 3122 (mono), LST 7122 (stereo); various re-releases)
- Romantica (1961, Liberty LRP 3207 (mono), LST 7207 (stereo))
- Sayonara (1967, Sunset SUM-1169 (mono), SUS-5169 (stereo))
- Spanish Village (1965, Liberty LRP 3409 (mono), LST 7409 (stereo))
- A Taste of Hits (1964, Liberty LRP 3328 (mono), LST 7328 (stereo))
- A Taste of Honey (1962, Liberty LRP 3237 (mono), LST 7237 (stereo))
- A Taste of India (1968, Liberty LRP 3550 (mono), LST 7550 (stereo))
- The Versatile Martin Denny (1963, Liberty LRP 3307 (mono), LST 7307 (stereo))

Denny, Martin and Si Zentner and His Orchestra
- Exotica Suite (1962, Liberty LMM 13020 (mono), LSS 14020 (stereo))

Dero, Pietro (see also **101 Strings**)
- Cocktails After Dark (1968, Somerset/Stereo Fidelity SF-30500)
- Continental Favorites at Cocktail Time (1968, Somersert/Stereo Fidelity SF-29800)

DeVol, Frank and His Orchestra

Frank De Vol was an arranger and conductor whose musical accomplishments included the theme songs for TV series such as *The Brady Bunch* and *My Three Sons*.

- The Columbia Album of Irving Berlin (Columbia C2L-12) Two-record set.
- The Columbia Album of Irving Berlin, Vol. 1 (1958, Columbia CL 1260 (mono), CS 8044 (stereo))
- Fabulous Hollywood! (1959, Columbia CL 1371 (mono), CS 8172 (stereo))
- Portraits (1958, Columbia CL 1108 (mono), CS 8010 (stereo))
- The Theme From Peyton Place and 11 Other Great Themes (1965, ABC-Paramount ABC-513)

Diamond Head Hula Boys, The

- Hawaiian Favorites (1957?, Craftsmen C8012)

Diamond, Leo (see also **Don Henry and Leo Diamond**)

Diamond was known as a master of the harmonica, and used experimental recording techniques and added sound effects to add to the versatility of his chosen instrument.

- Ebb Tide (Harmony HS-11328)
- Exciting Sounds From Exotic Places (1959, ABC-Paramount ABC-268 (mono), ABCS-268 (stereo))
- Exciting Sounds of the South Seas (1961, Reprise R-6002 (mono), R9-6002 (stereo))
- Harmonica Magic of Leo Diamond (1955, RCA Victor LPM-1042)
- Hi-Fi Harmonica (Roulette R-25019)
- Off Shore (Reprise R-6024 (mono), R9-6024 (stereo))
- Skin Diver Suite and Other Selections (1956, RCA Victor LMP-1165)
- Snuggled On Your Shoulder (1957, RCA Victor LMP-1442)
- Subliminal Sounds (1960, ABC-Paramount ABC-303 (mono), ABCS-303 (stereo))

Dorsey, Tommy Orchestra starring Warren Covington – see **Warren Covington and The Tommy Dorsey Orchestra**

Douglas, Johnny and His Orchestra

- Dance Party Discotheque (1965, RCA Camden CAL-883 (mono), CAS-883 (stereo))

Drasnin, Robert

- *Voodoo* (1959, Tops L1679; re-released in a handful of different formats between 1959 and 1960, sometimes under the title *Percussion Exotique* with a different cover) This album is one of the classics of the exotica genre. Drasnin was an employee at Tops Records when he was assigned the task of creating an exotica album to cash in on the then-surging musical trend. Drasnin wrote all twelve tracks.

Duffy, John

- Autumn Leaves (1966, Sunset SUM-1129 (mono), SUS-5129 (stereo))
- Born Free (1968, Sunset SUS-5178 (stereo))
- Carousel Music in Hi-Fi (1957, Liberty LRP 3053)
- An Excursion into Hi-Fi (1957, Liberty SL 9003)
- Giants! (1969, Sunset SUS-5256)
- John Duffy at the Mighty Columbia Square Wurlitzer (1955, Liberty LRP 3004)
- The Look of Love (1968, Sunset SUS-5223)
- Love Mood (1959, Edison International CL-5001 (mono), SDL-101 (stereo))

Edwards, Webley (with **Al Kealoha Perry**)

Webley Edwards was really taken with Hawaii and its musical heritage when he moved there in the late 1920's. He started a radio program devoted to Hawaiian music, *Hawaii Calls*, which lasted for 37 years.

- Hawaii Calls (1954, Capitol T-470)
- Hawaii Calls at Twilight (1956, Capitol T-582)
- Hawaii Calls: Best from the Beach at Waikiki (1966, Capitol T-2573 (mono), ST-2573 (stereo))
- Hawaii Calls: Blue Skies of Hawaii (1967, Capitol ST-2782)
- Hawaii Calls: Exotic Instrumentals – Favorites of the Islands, Vol. 4 (1961, Capitol T-1409 (mono), ST-1409 (stereo))
- Hawaii Calls: Favorite Instrumentals of the Islands (1957, Capitol T-715)
- Hawaii Calls: Fire Goddess (1958, Capitol T-1033 (mono), ST-1033 (stereo))
- Hawaii Calls: Hawaii Today (1966, Capitol T-2449 (mono), ST-2449 (stereo))
- Hawaii Calls: Hawaiian Shores – Favorite Instrumentals of the Islands, Vol. 2 (1957, Capitol T-904)
- Hawaii Calls: Hawaiian Strings (1959, Capitol T-1152 (mono), ST-1152 (stereo))
- Hawaii Calls: Holiday in Hawaii (1968, Tower DT-5102)

- Hawaii Calls: Romantic Instrumentals of the Islands (1964, Capitol T-1987 (mono), ST-1987 (stereo))
- Hawaii Calls: Waikiki (1957, Capitol T-772)
- Hawaii Calls: The Young Hawaiians (1969, Capitol ST-262)
- Hawaii: The Island of Dreams (Pickwick SPC-3062)
- Hula Island Favorites (1959, Capitol T-987)
- Island Paradise (1959, Capitol T-1229 (mono), ST-1229 (stereo))
- Let's Sing With Hawaii Calls (1961, Capitol KAO-1518 (mono), SKAO-1518 (stereo))
- Na Mele O Hawaii (1958, Capitol T-1092; with **The Kamehameha Alumni Glee Club**)
- Soft Hawaiian Guitars (1968, Capitol ST-2917)
- Sunkissed Hits of Hawaii (Pickwick SPC 3337)
- Webley Edwards Presents the Hawaii Calls Show (1962, Capitol TAO-1699 (mono), STAO-1699 (stereo))

El-Bakkar, Mohammed, and His Oriental Ensemble

- Dances of Port Said: Music of the Middle East, Vol. 5 (1960, Audio Fidelity AFLP 1922 (mono), AFSD 5922 (stereo))
- Exotic Music of the Belly Dancer (1966, Audio Fidelity AFLP 2154 (mono), AFSD 6154 (stereo))
- The Magic Carpet: Music of the Middle East, Vol. 4 (1958, Audio Fidelity AFLP 1895 (mono), AFSD 5895 (stereo))
- Music of the African Arab: Music of the Middle East, Vol. 3 (1958, Audio Fidelity AFLP 1858 (mono), AFSD 5858 (stereo)) The cover to this album shows a woman's bare breasts. I'm not complaining, just pointing it out.
- Port Said: Music of the Middle East (1957, Audio Fidelity AFLP 1833 (mono), AFSD 5833 (stereo))
- Sultan of Bagdad: Music of the Middle East, Vol. 2 (1957, Audio Fidelity AFLP 1384 (mono), AFSD 5834 (stereo))

El-Sulieman, Mohammed and His Oriental Ensemble

- The Music of Port Said (Coronet CX-55) Note that this album was reprinted song-for-song as *East of Suez* by **Mohammed Ben-Ahmed and the Bagdad Tribesmen**, as well as *East of Suez* (Broadway P 1027, in the Compilations section), and as *Music of the Near East* by **Ali Beirut's Orientales**, though the on the latter release, the songs were retitled. This disc, in turn, apparently reuses some of the songs from *Port of Suez: Exotic Music of the Middle East* (1958, Crown; see the Compilations section).

Electro-Sonic Orchestra, The

- Presenting a New Concept in Sound (1961, Coral CRL 757381)

Electronic Concept Orchestra, The

- Cinemoog (1970, Mercury SR 61279)
- Electric Love (1969, Limelight LS-86072)
- Moog Groove (1969, Limelight LS-86070)

Elliott, Dean and His Orchestra

- Zounds! What Sounds! (1962, Capitol T-1818 (mono), ST-1818 (stereo)) A classic of Space Age pop.

Elliott, Jack and His Orchestra

- Are You Lonesome Tonight? (1961, Kapp KL-1235)
- Forever (Kapp KL-1187)
- The Sound of Dynamic Woodwinds (1960, Medallion MS-7505)

Ellis, Ray and His Orchestra

- The Best of Peter Gunn (1960, MGM E 3813 (mono), SE 3813 (stereo))
- Big Hits for Swingers (1966, ATCO 33-187)
- Dancing With Gigi (1958, Columbia CL 1122 (mono), CS 8063 (stereo))
- Ellis in Wonderland (1957, Columbia CL 993)
- I'm in the Mood for Strings (1959, MGM E 3779 (mono), SE 3779 (stereo))
- I'm in the Mood to Swing (1960, MGM E 3820 (mono), SE 3820 (stereo))
- La Dolce Vita (1961, RCA Victor LPM-2410 (mono), LSP-2410 (stereo))
- Let's Get Away From It All (1958, Columbia CL 1097 (mono), CS 8051 (stereo))
- Our Man on Broadway (1963, RCA Victor LPM-2615 (mono), LSP-2615 (stereo))
- Ray Ellis Plays the Top 20 (1961, RCA Victor LPM-2400 (mono), LSP-2400 (stereo))

Epps, Preston

- Bongo Bongo Bongo (1960, Original Sound OSR-LPM-5002 (mono), OSR-LPS-8851 (stereo))
- Bongola (1961, Top Rank International RM 349 (mono), RS 649 (stereo))

- Surfin' Bongos (1963, Original Sound OSR-LPM-5009 (mono), OSR-LPS-8872 (stereo); with The Bongo Teens)

Esquivel, Juan Garcia (see also **Living Strings**)

Esquivel was a Mexican keyboardist and bandleader who came to the United States in 1958 to record an album of his unique, upbeat, somehow futuristic music, *Other Worlds, Other Sounds*.

- Exploring New Sounds in Hi-Fi (1959, RCA Victor LPM-1978 (mono), LSP-1978 (stereo))
- Four Corners of the World (1958, RCA Victor LPM-1749 (mono), LSP-1749 (stereo))
- The Genius of Esquivel (1967, RCA Victor LPM-3697 (mono), LSP-3697 (stereo))
- Infinity In Sound (1960, RCA Victor LPM-2225 (mono), LSP-2225 (stereo))
- Infinity In Sound, Vol. 2 (1961, RCA Victor LMP-2296 (mono), LSP-2296 (stereo))
- Latin-Esque (1962, RCA Victor LPM-2418 (mono), LSA-2418 (Stereo Action))
- More of Other Worlds, Other Sounds (1962, Reprise R-6046 (mono), R9-6046 (stereo))
- *Other Worlds, Other Sounds* (1958, RCA Victor LPM-1753 (mono), LSP-1753 (stereo)) One of the essentials of the Space Age Pop genre.
- Strings Aflame (1959, RCA Victor LMP-1988 (mono), LSP-1988 (stereo))
- To Love Again (1957, RCA Victor LPM-1345)

Etzel, Roy

- The Silence [Il Silencio] (1965, MGM E-4330 (mono), SE-4330 (stereo))
- Spanish Brass (1967, MGM SE-4349)

Evans, John and the Big Band

'John Evans' was actually a pseudonum for Belgian bandleader Franz Bayetz, aka **Francis Bay**.

- Cool Percussion (1962, Directional Sound DM 5011 (mono), DS 5011 (stereo))
- Exotic Percussion and Brilliant Brass (1961, Directional Sound DM 5003 (mono), DS 5003 (stereo))
- Latin Brass (1961, Directional Sound DM 5001 (mono), DS 5001 (stereo))
- Percussive Sound of the Big Band (1961, Directional Sound DM 5003 (mono), DS 5003 (stereo))

Evans, Lee

- Cinnamon & Clove (1967, MGM SE-4497)
- Lee Evans... In Concert (1963, Command RS 858 SD; as Lee Evans and His Orchestra)
- Lee Evans Plays Themes from Great Motion Pictures (1967, MGM E-4460 (mono), SE-4460 (stereo))
- The New and Exciting Piano Talent Plays the Best in 'Pops' (1964, Command RS 878 SD)
- Piano Plus (1962, Capitol T-1708)

Exotic Guitars, The

- All Time Guitar Hits (1971, Ranwood R-8090)
- Everybody's Talkin' (1969, Ranwood RLP-8061)
- The Exotic Guitars (1968, Ranwood RLP-8002)
- The Exotic Guitars (1972, Ranwood R-8104; this is a completely different collection of songs form the previous entry)
- Holly Holy (1970, Ranwood R-8073)
- I Can't Stop Loving You (1970, Ranwood R-8085)
- Indian Love Call (1969, Ranwood RLP-8051)
- Those Were the Days (1968, Ranwood RLP-8040)

Faith, Percy

His name was used as a punchline in the film *Good Morning Vietnam*, but Percy Faith was one of the grandmasters of Easy Listening music. For over a quarter of a century he recorded album after album for the Columbia label, each one showcasing his deft use of a string-heavy orchestra.

- Adventure in the Sun (1957, Columbia CL 1010)
- American Serenade (1963, Columbia CL 1957 (mono), CS 8757 (stereo))
- Amour, Amor, Amore (1956, Columbia CL 643)
- Bim! Bam!! Boom!!! (1966, Columbia CL 2529 (mono), CS 9329 (stereo))
- Bon Voyage! Continental Souvenirs (1960, Columbia CL 1417 (mono), CS 8214 (stereo))
- Delicado (1955, Columbia CL 681)
- Exotic Strings (1962, Columbia CL 1902 (mono), CS 8702 (stereo))
- For Those In Love (1968, Columbia CS 9610)
- Great Folk Themes (1964, Columbia CL 2108 (mono), CS 8908 (stereo))
- Held Over! Today's Great Movie Themes (1970, Columbia CS 1019)

- Hollywood's Great Themes (1962, Columbia CL 1783 (mono), CS 8583 (stereo))
- I Concentrate On You (1968, Columbia Musical Treasuries DS 390)
- I'll Take Romance (1969, Harmony HS 11292)
- Jealousy (1960, Columbia CL 1501 (mono), CS 8292 (stereo))
- Kismet (1954, Columbia CL 550 (mono), CS 8642 (stereo))
- Latin Themes for Young Lovers (1965, Columbia CL 2279 (mono), CS 9079 (stereo))
- Leaving on a Jet Plane (1970, Columbia CS 9983)
- Li'l Abner (1956, Columbia CL 955)
- Love Goddesses (1963, Columbia CL 2209 (mono), CS 9009 (stereo))
- Love Theme from "Romeo and Juliet" (1969, Columbia CS 9906)
- Malaguena: Music of Cuba (1958, Columbia CL 1267 (mono), CS 8081 (stereo))
- More Themes for Young Lovers (1964, Columbia CL 2167 (mono), CS 8967 (stereo))
- Movie Date (1967, Columbia Record Club D 318 (mono), DS 318 (stereo))
- Mucho Gusto! More Music of Mexico (1961, Columbia CL 1639 (mono), CS 8439 (stereo))
- Music For Her (1956, Columbia CL 705)
- Music From Hollywood (1954, Columbia CL 577)
- Music from Rodgers & Hammerstein's The Sound of Music (1960, Columbia CL 1418 (mono), CS 8215 (stereo))
- The Music of Brazil! (1962, Columbia CL 1822 (mono), CS 8622 (stereo))
- My Fair Lady (1956, Columbia CL 895)
- North and South of the Border (1958, Vocalion VL 3600)
- The Oscar (1966, Columbia Masterworks OL 6550 (mono), OS 2950 (stereo)). Soundtrack.
- Passport to Romance (1956, Columbia CL 880)
- Percy Faith Plays Continental Music (1953, Columbia CL 525)
- Percy Faith Plays Music from the Broadway Production of House of Flowers (1956, Columbia CL 640)
- Percy Faith Plays the Academy Award Winner Born Free and Other Great Movie Themes (1967, Columbia CS 9450)
- Percy Faith Plays Romantic Music (1953, Columbia CL 526)
- Porgy and Bess (1959, Columbia CL 1298 (mono), CS 8105 (stereo))

- Shangri-La! (1963, Columbia CL 2024 (mono), CS 8824 (stereo))
- Raindrops Keep Fallin' on My Head (1970, Harmony KH 30977)
- Soft Lights and Sweet Music (1954, RCA Victor LPM 1010)
- The Sounds of Music (1969, Harmony HS 11348; Columbia Special Projects P 13405)
- South Pacific (1958, Columbia CL 1105 (mono), CS 8005 (stereo); re-released as P 13559)
- Subways are For Sleeping (1961, Columbia CL 1733 (mono), CS 8533 (stereo))
- A Summer Place (1971, Harmony KH 30607)
- Tara's Theme from Gone With the Wind (1961, Columbia CL 1627 (mono), CS 8427 (stereo))
- Themes for the 'In' Crowd (1965, Columbia CL 2441 (mono), CS 9241 (stereo))
- Themes For Young Lovers (1963, Columbia CL 2023 (mono), CS 8823 (stereo))
- Viva! The Music of Mexico (1957, Columbia CL 1075 (mono), CS 8038 (stereo))
- Windmills of Your Mind (1970, Columbia CS 9835)
- Younger Than Springtime (1970, Harmony H 30020)

Faith, Percy and Russ Case

- Temptation (1963, Hurrah H-1059 (mono), HS-1059 (stereo))

Faith, Percy and Mitch Miller

- It's So Peaceful in the Country (1956, Columbia CL 779)
- Music Until Midnight (1954, Columbia CL 551)

Fantabulous Brass, The

Like Those Fantabulous Strings (next entry), this was a house band put together to capitalize on a trend; in this case it was to cash in on the sound of **Herb Alpert and the Tijuana Brass**.

- A Taste of Honey & Other Mariachi Hits (1967, MGM M-575 (mono), MS-575 (stereo))

Fantabulous Strings (aka **Those Fantabulous Strings**)

This was a house band for Metro/MGM designed to replicate the success of **The Hollyridge Strings** at playing pop hits using a string-heavy style for older listeners.

- Those Fantabulous Strings Play the Sonny & Cher Hits (1966, Metro M-557 (mono), MS-557 (stereo))
- Those Fantabulous Strings Play The Supremes Hits (1966, Metro M-554 (mono), MS-554 (stereo))

- Those Fantabulous Strings Play Thunderball and Other Big Movie Hits (1966, Metro M-551 (mono), MS-551 (stereo))

Farnon, Robert and His Orchestra

- Cocktails For Two (1958, Richmond/London B 20005)
- Light 'N Easy (1953, Richmond/London B 20033)
- Melody Fair (1956, London LL 1280)
- Robert Farnon and His Orchestra Play the Hits of Sinatra (1965, Phillips PHM 200-179)
- The Sensuous Strings of Robert Farnon (1962, Phillips PHS 600-038)

Farnon, Robert and Tony Coe

- Pop Makes Progress (1970, Chapter 1 CPS 39001)

Fascinating Strings, The

- The Heart & Soul of Spain (1968, Crown CLP-5559 (mono), CST-559 (stereo)
- Holiday Moods (1968, Crown CST-586)
- Love is a Many Splendored Thing (1968, Crown CST-587)
- Music from the Jet Set (1968, Custom CS-1091)
- On Cloud Nine (1970, Crown CST-617)
- Somewhere My Love (1968, Crown CLP-5567 (mono), CST-567 (stereo))
- Theme from Love Story (1971, Crown CST-628)

Felere, Pierre and His Orchestra

- Music for a French Dinner At Home (1959, RCA Victor LSP-1937)

Feller, Sid and His Orchestra

- Music for Expectant Mothers (1956, ABC-Paramount ABC-123)

Ferrante & Teicher (see also **Nelson Riddle**; **Roger Williams and Ferrante & Teicher**; Compilations section)

Ferrante and Teicher were a massively successful duo of piano players most closely associated with the Easy Listening music around which they built their careers, although in their early days they experimented with ways of making their instruments sound differently, so that their earlier records might be classified as Space Age Pop.

- Autumn Leaves (1966, ABC-Paramount ABC-558 (mono), ABCS-558 (stereo); this was a truncated re-release of *Postcards From Paris*, featuring 10 of the original 12 songs; there was also apparently a record club release by this title, ST-90693, which reproduced all 12 songs from *Postcards From Paris* in full)

- Autumn Leaves (1969, Harmony HS-11355; this is a completely separate release from the previous listing; only three songs overlap)
- Blast Off! (1958, ABC-Paramount ABC-285 (mono), ABCS-285 (stereo); re-released in 1966 as *We've Got Rhythm*)
- A Bouquet of Hits (1968, United Artists UAS-6659)
- Broadway to Hollywood (1961, Columbia CL 1607 (mono), CS 8407 (stereo))
- By Popular Demand (1965, United Artists UAL-3416 (mono), UAS-6416 (stereo))
- Concert For Lovers (1963, United Artists UAL-3315 (mono), UAS-6315 (stereo))
- Dream Concerto (1960, United Artists UAL-3087 (mono), UAS-6087 (stereo))
- Dynamic Twin Pianos (1960, United Artists Ultra Audio WW-7504 (mono), WWS-8504 (stereo); re-released in 1964 as *Keyboard Kapers*)
- The Enchanted World of Ferrante & Teicher (1964, United Artists UAL-3375 (mono), UAS-6375 (stereo))
- The Exciting Pianos of Ferrante & Teicher (1970, Pickwick PC-3003 (mono), SPC-3003 (stereo))
- The Ferrante & Teicher Concert (1965, United Artists UAL-3444 (mono), UAS-6444 (stereo))
- The Ferrante & Teicher Concert, Part 2 (1966, United Artists UAL-3475 (mono), UAS-6475 (stereo))
- Ferrante and Teicher Play Light Classics (1959, ABC-Paramount ABC-313 (mono), ABCS-313 (stereo))
- Ferrante and Teicher With Percussion (1958, ABC-Paramount ABC-248 (mono), ABCS-248 (stereo); re-released in 1966 as *Temptation*)
- Fireworks (1966, Columbia HS 11227; re-release of *Hi-Fireworks*)
- For Lovers of All Ages (1966, United Artists UAL-3483 (mono), UAS-6483 (stereo))
- Getting Together (1970, United Artists UAS-5501)
- Golden Piano Hits (1961, United Artists WWR-3505 (mono), WWS-8505 (stereo))
- Golden Themes from Motion Pictures (1962, United Artists UAL-3210 (mono), UAS-6210 (stereo))
- Heavenly Sounds in Hi-Fi (1957, ABC-Paramount ABC-221)
- The Heavenly Sounds of Ferrante & Teicher (1966, ABC-Paramount ABC-555 (mono), ABCS-555 (stereo))
- Hi-Fireworks (1955, Columbia CL 573; re-released in 1966 as *Fireworks*)

- Holiday For Pianos (1963, United Artists UAL-3298 (mono), UAS-6298 (stereo))
- In Love With Ferrante & Teicher (1967, Pickwick SPC-3077)
- In the Heat of the Night (1967, United Artists UAL-3624 (mono), UAS-6624 (stereo))
- The Incomparable Piano Stylings of Ferrante & Teicher (1968, Sunset SUS-5235)
- Keyboard Kapers (1964, United Artists UAS-6284; re-release of *Dynamic Twin Pianos*)
- The Keys to Her Apartment (1962, United Artists UAL-3247 (mono), UAS-6247 (stereo))
- Latin Pianos (1960, United Artists UAL-3135 (mono), UAS-6135 (stereo))
- Listen to the Movies With Ferrante & Teicher (1969, United Artists UAS-6701)
- Live For Life (1967, United Artists UAS-6632)
- Love in the Generation Gap (1968, United Artists UAS-6677)
- Love is a Soft Touch (1970, United Artists UAS-6771)
- Love Themes (1963, United Artists UAL-3282 (mono), UAS-6282 (stereo); re-released in 1966)
- A Man and a Woman and Other Motion Picture Themes (1967, United Artists UAL-3572 (mono), UAS-6572 (stereo))
- The Many Moods of Ferrante & Teicher (1962, United Artists UAL-3211 (mono), UAS-6211 (stereo))
- Memories (1966, ABC-Paramount ABC-554 (mono), ABCS-554 (stereo))
- Midnight Cowboy (1969, United Artists UAS-6725)
- Music from the Motion Picture West Side Story (1961, United Artists UAL-3166 (mono), UAS-6166 (stereo))
- My Fair Lady (1964, United Artists UAL-3361 (mono), UAS-6361 (stereo))
- Only the Best (1965, United Artists UAL-3434 (mono), UAS-6434 (stereo))
- Our Golden Favorites (1967, United Artists UAL-3556 (mono), UAS-6556 (stereo))
- The People's Choice (1964, United Artists UAL-3385 (mono), UAS-6385 (stereo))
- Pianos in Paradise (1962, United Artists UAL-3230 (mono), UAS-6230 (stereo))
- Postcards From Paris (1962, ABC-Paramount ABC-430 (mono), ABCS-430 (stereo); re-released as *Autumn Leaves*)
- Soundblast/Soundproof (1956, Westminster. The configuration of these two titles is a little confusing, but they basically represent three

different releases: A. *Soundblast*, mono, WP-6041; first song on Side 1 is "What is This Thing Called Love?" B. *Soundproof*, stereo, WP-6041; first song on Side 1 is "What is This Thing Called Love?" C. *Soundproof*, stereo, WST-15011; first song on Side 1 is "Peg-Leg Merengue.")

- Springtime (1964, United Artists UAL-3406 (mono), UAS-6406 (stereo))
- Temptation (1966, ABC-Paramount ABC-561 (mono), ABCS-561 (stereo); re-release of *Ferrante and Teicher With Percussion*)
- Themes From Broadway Shows (1960, ABC-Paramount ABC-336 (mono), ABCS-336 (stereo))
- Tonight (1962, United Artists UAL-3171 (mono), UAS-6171 (stereo))
- The Twin Piano Magic of Ferrante & Teicher (1964, Harmony HL-7325 (mono), HS-11125 (stereo))
- The Twin Piano Magic of Ferrante & Teicher, Vol. 1 (1966, ABC-Paramount ABC-557 (mono), ACBS-557 (stereo)) Note: This is a completely different album from the 1964 Harmony release, with completely different songs.
- Twin Pianos (1964, Guest Star G 1410 (mono), GS 1410 (stereo))
- We've Got Rhythm (1966, ABC-Paramount ABC-556 (mono), ABCS-556 (stereo); re-release of *Blast Off!*)
- The World's Greatest Themes (1960, United Artists UAL-3121 (mono), UAS-6121 (stereo)
- You Asked For It (1966, United Artists UAL-3526 (mono), UAS-6526 (stereo))

Fiedler, Arthur (**and The Boston Pops Orchestra**; **and His Orchestra**) (see also **Stan Getz and Arthur Fiedler**; **Peter Nero and Arthur Fiedler**)

- All the Things You Are (1966, RCA Victor Red Seal LM-2906 (mono), LSC-2906 (stereo))
- Arthur Fiedler and the Boston Pops Play the Beatles (1969 RCA Red Seal LSC-3117)
- Arthur Fiedler "Superstar" (1971, Polydor PD-5008)
- Boston Pops Picnic (1956, RCA Victor Red Seal LM-1985)
- Fabulous Broadway (1970, Polydor 24-5003)
- The Family All Together (1954, RCA Victor Red Seal LM-1879)
- Fiedler on Broadway (1958, RCA Victor Red Seal LM-2215)
- Have a Ball With Arthur (1970, RCA Red Seal LSC-3136)
- In the Latin Flavor (1956, RCA Victor Red Seal LM-2041)
- More Highlights From An Evening at the Pops (1966, RCA Victor Red Seal LM-2882 (mono), LSC-2882 (stereo))
- More Music from Million Dollar Movies (1965, RCA Victor Red Seal LM-2783 (mono), LSC-2782 (stereo))
- Motion Picture Classics (1970, RCA Red Seal VCS-7056)

- Music from Million Dollar Movies (1960, RCA Victor Red Seal LM-2380 (mono), LSC-2380 (stereo))
- Music from Million Dollar Shows (1967, RCA Victor LSC-2965)
- Our Man in Boston (1963, RCA Victor Red Seal LM-2599 (mono), LSC-2599 (stereo))
- Pops Roundup (1962, RCA Victor Red Seal LM-2595 (mono), LSC-2595 (stereo))
- Slaughter on Tenth Avenue (1964, RCA Victor Red Seal LM-2747 (mono), LSC-2747 (stereo))
- Salute to a Tower (1965, RCA Victor PRM 196) This was a promotional album produced for Allied Chemical Corp.
- Star Dust (1963, RCA Victor Red Seal LM-2670 (mono), LSC-2670 (stereo))
- Tenderly (1965, RCA Victor Red Seal LM-2798 (mono), LSC-2798 (stereo))
- Up Up and Away (1968, RCA Red Seal LSC-3041)

Fielding, Jerry and His Orchestra

- Near East Brass (1967, Command RS 922 SD)

Fields, Irving (aka **The Irving Fields Trio**)

- At the Emerald Room, Hotel Astor (1959, Decca DL 8901 (mono), DL 78901 (stereo))
- At the Latin Quarter (20th Century Fox FOX-1010)
- At the St. Moritz With the Irving Fields Trio: Cocktail Dance Time (1956, ABC-Paramount ABC-187)
- Bagels and Bongos (1959, Decca DL 8856 (mono), DL 78856 (stereo))
- Bikinis and Bongos (1962, Decca DL 4323 (mono), DL 74323 (stereo))
- Broadway Hits in Hi-Fi (ABC-Paramount ABC-154)
- Cha-Cha-Cha to America's Favorite Melodies (Oceanic OCP 519)
- Champagne and Bongos (1962, Decca DL 4238 (mono), DL 74238 (stereo))
- Classics Go Latin (1960, King 724 (mono), 724-S (stereo))
- Dance Date (1957, RCA Camden CAL-350)
- The Fabulous Fingers of Irving Fields (Fiesta FLP-1228)
- Irving Berlin Favorites (Craftsmen C8008)
- Irving Fields Plays Irving Berlin (1957, Tops L-1562)
- The Irving Fields Trio Featuring Herb Larson (Hi-Life SHLP-60)

- Live It Up! (1960, King, 709)
- Let's Have A Party (Dot DLP 25311)
- Lox, Latin, and Bongos (1960, King 742 (mono), 742-S (stereo))
- Melody Cruise to Havana (1957, Oceanic OCP 518)
- More Bagels and Bongos (1961, Decca DL 4114 (mono), DL 74114 (stereo))
- Pizzas and Bongos (1962, Decca DL 4175 (mono), DL 74175 (stereo))
- That Latin Beat for Dancing Feet (1959, Vox STVX-425.100)
- Twisting! (1961, Everest LPBR 5134; as The Irving Fields Orchestra)
- Year Round Party Fun (1953, Oceanic OCP 501)

Fields, Shep and His Orchestra

- Cocktails, Dinner, & Dancing (1957, Jubilee JGM-1056)

Fiesta Brass, The

- Viva Tijuana! (1966, Harmony HS 11183)

Finley, Greg and His Orchestra

- Come Dance With Us (1963, Golden Tone 14077; Al-Fi C 4077 with same cover artwork; also released as *Your Dancing Party*)
- Your Dancing Party (Westerfield S-14077; also released as *Come Dance With Us*)

Flanagan, Ralph and His Orchestra

- 1001 Nighters (1956, RCA Victor LPM 1274)
- Dance to the 'New Live' Sound of Ralph Flanagan and His Orchestra (1961, Coral CRL 757363)
- Dance to the Top Pops (1952, RCA Victor LPM 3084)
- Dancing Down Broadway (1956, RCA Camden CAL 322)
- Dancing in the Dark (1957, RCA Camden CAL 387)
- The Freshman-Sophomore Frolics (1954, RCA Victor 3190)
- Junior-Senior Prom (1954, RCA Victor LPM 3189)
- One Night Stand with Ralph Flanagan (1951, Joyce LP-1051)
- Ralph Flanagan in Hi-Fi (1958, LPM 1555 (mono), LSP 1555 (stereo))
- They're Playing Our Cha Cha! (1960, Imperial LP 12050)
- They're Playing Our Song (1958, Imperial LP 12006)

Florence, Bob (aka **The Bob Florence Big Band**)

- Bongos / Reeds / Brass (1960, HiFi L-1001, also the Life label; also called *Big Band Dance Party* on Stereo Sounds, SA-5)
- Pet Project (1967, World Pacific WP-1860 (mono), WPS-21860 (stereo))

Floyd, Chick and His Orchestra

This group played for a time at Don the Beachcomber's in Hawaii.

- Hula-La (1959, Liberty LRP 3106 (mono), LST 7106 (stereo))
- Little Grass Shack (1960, Liberty LRP 3129 (mono), LST 7129 (stereo))

Font, Ralph and His Orchestra

- Cha-Cha-Cha (1959, Westminster WP 6111 (mono), WST 15042 (stereo))
- Longhair Goes Cha Cha (1959, Westminster WP 6118 (mono), WST 15049 (stereo))
- Tabu (1959, Westminster WP 6077 (mono), WST 15012 (stereo))

Font, Ralph and His Orchestra and Bill Diablo and His Sextet

- The Best Cha Cha Cha of the Fabulous Fifties (1957, Kapp KL-1060)
- The Best Mambos of the Fabulous Fifties (1957, Kapp KL-1059)

Fontanna and His Orchestra (see also **Enoch Light and Fontanna Orchestras**)

- 12 For Two in Love (1957, Masterseal LS-33)
- Café Continental (1958, Masterseal MS-89 (mono), ST-9018)
- The Magic of Paris (Palace PST-632; as Fontanna and His 1001 Strings)
- Memories Are Made of These (1957, Masterseal MS-6 (mono), MS-33 (stereo); the Mono version says 'David Rose and His Orchestra' on the front but lists Fontanna as the artist on the back; a third version (Palace PST-614) says 'David Rose and Fontanna Orchestras' on the front. Also available on the Paris label)
- Music for Expectant Fathers (1957, Remington Musirama R-199-219)
- Rendezvous in Paris (1957, Masterseal MS-82; re-released 1964, Palace M-612 (mono), PST-612 (stereo))
- Vocal Highlights from Gigi (1958, Masterseal MS-71)

Fotine, Larry and His Orchestra

- Listening to Larry (1957, Bel Canto SR-1005)

Fountain, Pete

Pete Fountain was a clarinet player who became popular on *The Lawrence Welk Show*. Though much of his output could be described as New Orleans Jazz, some of it was more mainstream, and it is included here.

- Both Sides Now (1968, Coral CRL 757507)
- Golden Favorites (1970, Coral CRL 757511)
- I Love Paris (1961, Coral CRL 57378 (mono), CRL 757378 (stereo))
- I've Got You Under My Skin (1966, Coral CRL 57488 (mono), CRL 757488 (stereo))
- Make Your Own Kind of Music (1969, Coral 757510)
- Mood Indigo (1966, Coral CRL 57484 (mono), CRL 757484 (stereo))
- Music to Turn You On (1967, Coral CRL 57496 (mono), CRL 757496 (stereo))
- Pete Fountain Day (1959, Coral CRL 57313 (mono), CRL 757313 (stereo))
- Pete Fountain Plays Bert Kaempfert (1967, Coral CRL 57499 (mono), CRL 757499 (stereo))
- Something Misty (1970, Coral CRL 757516)
- A Taste of Honey (1966, Coral CRL 57486 (mono), CRL 757486 (stereo))
- Those Were the Days (1968, Coral CRL 757505)

Franconi, Dean (and His Sound Stage Orchestra)

- The Lush String Sounds of Dean Franconi and His Orchestra (1967, Design SDLP-261)
- Music from the Great Films (1962, Grand Prix KS-150)

Freedman, Bob and His Orchestra

- Music to Strip By (1962, Surprise SUR 100) This record came with a free lacey G-string which came draped across the main cover graphic, a cartoony (and non-anatomically correct) representation of a woman's midsection. Most modern copies, naturally, are missing this racy premium.

Frontiere, Dominic (and His Orchestra; Dom Frontiere and His Octet)

Frontiere is remembered today primarily for his film and television soundtracks.

- Billie (1965, United Artists UAL 4131 (mono), UAS 5131 (stereo). Soundtrack.
- Dom Frontiere and His El Dorado (1956, Liberty LRP 6002)
- Fabulous!! (1956, Liberty LRP 3015)

- Hang 'Em High (1968, United Artists UAS-5179) Music from the soundtrack.

- Love Eyes: The Moods of Romance (1960, Columbia CL 1427 (mono), CS 8224 (stereo))

- On Any Sunday (1971, Bell 1206) Music from the film.

- Pagan Festival: An Exotic Love Ritual for Orchestra (1959, Columbia CL 1273 (mono), CS 8084 (stereo))

- Popi (1969, United Artists UAS 5194) Soundtrack.

Galaxy Generation, The

Late-Now Sound era, generic-instrumental covers.

- Hair (1970, Design SDLP 302)

- Windmills of Your Mind (1970, Design SDLP 304)

Galladoro, Pete and The Surrey Latin Brass

This was almost certainly another Surrey label house band, a la The Surrey Brass and The Surrey Strings.

- Senor Swing (1966, Surrey S 1029 (mono), SS 1029 (stereo)) Generic Easy Listening with some exotica accents; a little too old-fashioned for its time. Were these songs previously released elsewhere?

Garcia, Russ and His Orchestra (see also **Walter Gross**; **Franklyn MacCormick and Russ Garcia**; **Si Zentner**)

Garcia was another composer/arranger who was known for his film and television score work, but it's a shame he didn't do more LP's because the man was clearly a genius.

- Carioca (1958, RCA Victor LPM 1691 (mono), LST 1691 (stereo))

- Enchantment (1957, Liberty LRP 3063)

- *Fantastica* (1958, Liberty LRP 3084 (mono), LST 7005 (stereo)) One of the classics of Space Age Pop.

- Four Horns and a Lush Life (1956, Bethlehem BCP-46)

- Hi-Fi Music for Children From 2 to 92 (1957, Liberty LRP 3065)

- The Johnny Evergreens (1956, ABC-Paramount ABC-147)

- Listen to the Music of Russell Garcia and His Orchestra (1957, Kapp KL-1050)

- *Sounds in the Night* (1957, Bethlehem BCP-5006; 1958, AAMCO ALP-309 (mono), ALPS-76 (stereo)) Although *Fantastica* is Garcia's best-known LP, this one is equally deserving of attention, and the musical styles it showcases are rather different.

- That Warm Feeling (1957, Verve MGV 2088; as Russell Garcia and Strings with Roy Eldridge)

Garson, Mort

Keyboardist Mort Garson did a wide variety of work in music, primarily in the 1960's, but it's his later, more experimental, output that more than qualifies him for this volume.

- The Connection (1968, Patch Cord Productions CF-2107) This odd little LP has music recorded only on side A; and that consists of TV ad jingles written by Garson. This was apparently a promotional item. Now sought after by collectors.
- Didn't You Hear? (1970, Custom Fidelity CFS-2379)
- Electronic Hair Pieces (1969, A&M SP-4209)
- Mother Earth's Plantasia (1976, Homewood H-101) Although it falls somewhat out of the time frame covered by this volume, *Plantasia* is a too good a disc to leave out of Garson's listing. The album originally came with a pamphlet, *Mother Earth's Indoor Plant Care Booklet.*
- Love Sounds (1968, Liberty LST-7559)

Geller, Harry (aka **The Harry Geller Orchestra**)

- Gypsy Mandolins (1962, Sunset SUS-5120)
- New York, New York (1955, RCA Victor LPM 1032)
- Play Gypsy Play! (1962, Liberty LMM-13023 (mono), LSS-14023 (stereo))
- Selections from The Eddie Duchin Story (1956, Capitol T-716)

Getz, Stan

Stan Getz was one of the heavy hitters of jazz during his career; but since this volume is concerned with other musical genres, only a small portion of his output will be included.

- Big Band Bossa Nova (1962, Verve V-8494 (mono), V6-8494 (stereo))
- Didn't We (1969, Verve V6-8780)
- Marrakesh Express (1970, MGM SE 4696)
- What the World Needs Now (1968, Verve V6-8752)

Getz, Stan and Laurindo Almeida

- Stan Getz with Guest Artist Laurindo Almeida (1963, Verve V-8665 (mono), V6-8665 (stereo))

Getz, Stan and Arthur Fiedler

- Stan Getz & Arthur Fiedler at Tanglewood (1967, RCA Victor Red Seal LSC-2925)

Getz, Stan and Astrud Gilberto

- Getz Au Go Go (1964, Verve V-8600 (mono), V6-8600 (stereo))

Getz, Stan and Joao Gilberto

- *Getz/Gilberto* (1964, Verve V-8545 (mono), V6-8545 (stereo)) Essential if only for the reason that it includes the original version of Astrud Gilberto singing "The Girl From Ipanema."

- Getz/Gilberto #2 (1965, Verve V-8623 (mono), V6-8623 (stereo))

Gil, Bobby and Members of the Perez Prado Orchestra

- Prado Mania / Mambo Jambo (1959, Crown CLP-5106 (mono), CST-137 (stereo); apparently pressed in red vinyl as well as black) This album can be found under either title, but both share the same catalog number, cover art, and song list; *Mambo Jambo* may be the title of the stereo version.

Gilberto, Astrud and Walter Wanderley

- *A Certain Smile, A Certain Sadness* (1966, Verve V-8673 (mono), V6-8673 (stereo)) Smooth as silk, this album stands as some of the best soft jazz/easy listening music of its era.

Gilberto, Joao

- The Boss of the Bossa Nova (1962, Atlantic 8070 (mono), SD-8070 (stereo))

- Brazil's Brilliant (1960, Capitol T-10280 (mono), ST-10280 (stereo); re-released as *Gilberto & Jobim*)

- The Warm World of Joao Gilberto (1963, Atlantic 8076)

Gilberto, Joao and Antonio Carlos Jobim

- Gilberto & Jobim (1964, Capitol T-10280 (mono), ST-10280 (stereo); this was a re-release of Gilberto's *Brazil's Brilliant*)

Glahe, Will

- Happy Days Are Here Again (1965, London LL 3397 (mono), PS 397 (stereo))

- More German Singalong (London TW 91419 (mono), SW 99419 (stereo))

Gleason, Jackie

He's remembered well as a comedic actor, but for several years starting in the early 1950's, Jackie Gleason was responsible for several best-selling albums of Easy Listening music. How much he personally contributed is disputed, but in any case he helped jump-start the nascent genre of romantic 'Mood Music,' as it was then known.

- Aphrodesia (1960, Capitol W-1250 (mono), SW-1250 (stereo))

- Come Saturday Morning (1970, Capitol ST-480)

- Doublin' in Brass (1968, Capitol W-2880 (mono), SW-2880 (stereo))

- The Gentle Touch (1961, Capitol W-1519 (mono), SW-1519 (stereo))
- How Sweet It Is For Lovers (1966, Capitol W-2582 (mono), SW-2582 (stereo))
- Irving Berlin's Music for Lovers (1968, Capitol SW-106)
- The Last Dance... for Lovers Only (1964, Capitol W-2144 (mono), SW-2144 (stereo))
- Lazy Lively Love (1960, Capitol W-1439 (mono), SW-1439 (stereo))
- Lonesome Echo (1955, Capitol W-627)
- Love Embers and Flame (1962, Capitol W-1689 (mono), SW-1689 (stereo))
- Lover's Portfolio (Capitol WBO-1619) This was a two-disc compilation of songs from previous albums, including the following two listings.
- Lover's Portfolio, Vol. 1 (1964, Capitol W-1979 (mono), SW-1979 (stereo))
- Lover's Portfolio, Vol. 2 (1964, Capitol W-1980 (mono), SW-1980 (stereo))
- The More I See You (1967, Pickwick/33 SPC-3150) Pickwick was able to re-release some of Capitol's back catalog starting in 1966. Songs which had originally been recorded in mono were rejiggered to accommodate modern stereo systems. These will usually say 'Digitally enhanced for stereo' on the album cover.
- The Most Beautiful Girl in the World (1967, Pickwick/33 SPC-3091)
- Movie Themes – For Lovers Only (1963, Capitol W-1877 (mono), SW-1877 (stereo))
- Music Around the World: For Lovers Only (1966, Capitol W-2471 (mono), SW-2471 (stereo))
- *Music For Lovers Only* (1953, Capitol W-352)
- Music For the Love Hours (1957, Capitol W-816 (mono), DW-816 (stereo))
- *Music, Martini, and Memories* (1954, Capitol W-509)
- Music to Change Her Mind (1956, Capitol W-632)
- Music to Make You Misty (1957, Capitol W-455; re-release of 10" disc from 1953)
- Music to Remember Her (1955, Capitol W-570)
- Night Winds (1956, Capitol W-717)
- The Now Sound... For Today's Lovers (1969, Capitol SW-2935)
- "Ooooh!" (1957, Capitol W-905 (mono), SW-905 (stereo))
- Opiate D'Amour (1960, Capitol W-1315 (mono), SW-1315 (stereo))

- Rebound (1958, Capitol W-1075 (mono), SW-1075 (stereo))
- Riff Jazz (1958, Capitol W-1020)
- Romantic Jazz (1955, Capitol W-568)
- Romeo and Juliet (1969, Capitol ST-398)
- Shangri-La (1966, Pickwick/33 SPC-3218)
- Silk 'N Brass (1965, Capitol W-2409 (mono), SW-2409 (stereo))
- Softly (1970, Capitol Creative Products SL-6664) 'Produced for Abbott Laboratories'.
- A Taste of Brass For Lovers Only (1967, Capitol W-2684 (mono), SW-2684 (stereo))
- That Moment (1959, Capitol W-1147 (mono), SW-1147 (stereo))
- Today's Romantic Hits: For Lovers Only (1963, Capitol W-1978 (mono), SW-1978 (stereo))
- Today's Romantic Hits: For Lovers Only, Vol. 2 (1964, Capitol W-2056 (mono), SW-2056 (stereo))
- The Torch With the Blue Flame (1961, Capitol W-961 (mono), SW-961 (stereo))
- Velvet Brass (1957, Capitol W-859 (mono), SW-859 (stereo))

Gold, Marty and His Orchestra (see also **Donald Hulme and Marty Gold Orchestra**)

- 24 Pieces of Gold (1962, RCA Victor VPM-6012 (mono), VPS-6012 (stereo))
- The Broadway Soundaroundus (1967, RCA Victor LSP-3689)
- By the Waters of the Minnetonka (1959, Kapp K-1125)
- Classic Bossa Nova (1965, RCA Victor LPM-3456 (mono), LSP-3456 (stereo))
- For Sound's Sake! (1964, RCA Victor LPM-2787 (mono), LSP-2787 (stereo))
- Hi Fi Fo Fum (1958, Vik LX-1133)
- Higher Than Fi (1957, Vik LX-1097)
- In A Young Mood (1964, RCA Victor LPM-2942 (mono), LSP-2942 (stereo))
- It's Magic (1961, RCA Victor LSA-2290) (Stereo Action)
- Lullabies for Sleepyheads (1960, RCA Camden CAL-1003)
- Moog Plays the Beatles (1969, Avco AVE 33003)
- Organized For Hi-Fi (1957, Vik LX-1069; as Marty Gold and His Organ Ensemble)
- Skin Tight (1960, RCA Victor LPM-2230 (mono), LSP-2230 (stereo))
- Something Special for Movie Lovers (1965, RCA Victor LSP-3342)

- The Soundaroundus (1966, RCA Victor LMP-3599 (mono), LSP-3599 (stereo))
- Soundpower! (1963, RCA Victor LPM-2620 (mono), LSP-2620 (stereo))
- Sounds Unlimited (1963, RCA Victor LPM-2714 (mono), LSP-2714 (stereo))
- Stereo Action Goes Hollywood (1961, RCA Victor LSA-2381) (Stereo Action)
- Sticks and Bones (1958, Vik LX-1126; 1959, RCA Victor LPM-2070 (mono), LSP-2070 (stereo))
- Sticks and Strings in Hi-Fi (1956, Vik LX-1082)
- Suddenly It's Springtime (1964, RCA Victor LPM-2882 (mono), LSP-2882 (stereo))
- Swingin' West (1960, RCA Victor LPM-2163 (mono), LSP-2163 (stereo))
- Wired For Sound (1956, Vik LX-1054)

Golden Gate Strings, The

This is apparently another **Stu Phillips** project, meant to replicate the success of **The Hollyridge Strings** for Epic.

- The Bob Dylan Song Book (1965, Epic LN 24158 (mono), BN 26158 (stereo))
- The Monkees Song Book (1967, Epic LN 26248 (mono), BN 26248 (stereo))
- A String of Hits (1965, Epic LN 24160 (mono), BN 24160 (stereo))

Golden Strings, The (aka **The Magnificent Golden Strings**)

- Around the World (Recar RCS 2070)
- Day Dreams (1961, Modern MST 810)
- Down Memory Lane (1962, Golden Tone C 4062)
- The Golden Strings (Recar RC 2010)
- The Golden Strings Play Golden Hits (1967, Recar RCS 2030)
- The Heart of Spain (1961, Modern MST 815)
- Holiday in Strings Around the World (1960, Golden Tone C4056)
- The Magnificent Golden Srings (Recar RC 2021)
- The Magnificent Golden Strings Play... (Recar RC 2017)
- Music For Dreaming (Riviera R0054)
- Music to Knit By (1956, Kapp KL-1037)

Gomez, Eddie and His Latin American Orchestra

- Caribbean Rendezvous (1957, Crown CLP-5043)

- Cuban Mist Cha Cha Cha (1957, Crown CLP-5032)

Gomez, Manuel and His Latin American Orchestra

Both Eddie and Manuel Gomez (and probably Tito Gomez in the next entry too) were almost certainly figments of the Crown Records management's imagination.

- Latin A-Go-Go (1968, Crown CLP-5568 (mono), CST-568 (stereo))

Gomez, Tito and His Orchestra

- Latin For Lovers (1970, Crown CST-621)

Goodman, Al and His Orchestra

- Cheek to Cheek (Pirouette FM 10)
- Curtain Time (Spin-O-Rama S-70)
- Music From Hollywood: Themes From Great Motion Pictures (1954, RCA Victor LPM-1007)
- Ringo's Theme (This Boy) and And I Love Her (1964, Diplomat D 2336 (mono), DS 2336 (stereo)) Music from the Beatles film *Hard Day's Night*.
- Sing Along With Al Goodman (1963, Spin-O-Rama M-3116 (mono), S-25 (stereo))
- South Pacific (1958, RCA Camden CAL-421; Spin-O-Rama S-3047)
- Speak Low (1957, RCA Camden CAL-317)
- Theme Music from Great Motion Pictures (RCA Victor LPT 1008)

Goodwin, Ron

- It Can't Be Wrong (1956 Capitol T-10078)
- Music For An Arabian Night (1959, Capitol T-10251 (mono), ST-10251 (stereo))
- Music in Orbit (1958, Capitol T-10188 (mono), ST-10188 (stereo))

Gordon, Jay (aka **The Jay Gordon Concert Orchestra**)

- Music from Another World (1957, Tops L 1552)
- Penthouse Serenade (1958, Tops L 1557)
- Silhouettes (1957, Tops L 1551)
- Strictly For Lovers (1958, Tops L 1558)

Gould, Morton and His Orchestra (see also **Larry Adler**)

The multi-talented Gould's music could range from jungle-themed Exotica to more classic Easy Listening.

- Beyond the Blue Horizon (1961, RCA Victor Red Seal LM-2552 (mono), LSC-2552 (stereo))

- Blues in the Night (1958, RCA Victor Red Seal LM-2104 (mono); 1960, RCA Victor Red Seal LSC-2104 (stereo))
- Coffee Time (1958, RCA Victor LPM-1656 (mono), LSP-1656 (stereo))
- Curtain Time (RCA Masterworks ML 4451)
- Good Night Sweetheart (1963, RCA Victor Red Seal LM-2682 (mono), LSC-2682 (stereo))
- Jungle Drums (1956, RCA Victor Red Seal LM-1994 (mono); 1960, RCA Victor Red Seal LSC-1994 (stereo))
- Kern/Porter Favorites (1960, RCA Victor Red Seal LM-2559 (mono), LSC-2559 (stereo))
- Latin, Lush and Lovely (1964, RCA Victor Red Seal LM-2752 (mono), LSC-2752 (strereo))
- Love Walked In (1962, RCA Victor Red Seal LM-2663 (mono), LSC-2663 (stereo))
- Moon, Wind, and Stars (1958, RCA Victor Red Seal LM-2232 (mono), LSC-2232 (stereo))
- Moonlight Sonata (1961, RCA Victor Red Seal LMP-2542 (mono), LSC-2542 (stereo))
- More Jungle Drums (1964, RCA Victor Red Seal LM-2768 (mono), LSC-2768 (stereo))
- Morton Gould Makes the Scene (1967, RCA Victor LPM-3771 (mono), LSP-3771 (stereo))
- Music of Lecuona/Springtime (1950, Columbia Masterworks ML 4361)
- Music for Summertime (1956, RCA Victor LM-2006)
- Starlight Serenade (1955, Columbia CL 664)
- Temptation (1957, RCA Victor Red Seal LM-2128)
- Windjammer (1958, Columbia CL 1158 (mono), CS 6851 (stereo)) Motion picture soundtrack.

Goupil, Augie (and His Royal Tahitians) and Thurston Knudson

- Tahitian Rhythms and Jungle Drums (Decca DL 8216) Goupil composed all of the songs on side A, Knudson the ones on side B.

Grand Award All Stars, The

Put together for Enoch Light's Grand Award record label, the All Stars consisted of top session musicians such as **Tony Mottola**, Doc Severinsen, and Phil Bodner.

- Brass, Bongos, Flutes, and Guitars (1961, Grand Award GA 33 427 (mono), GA 258 SD (stereo))
- Percussion and Brass (1960, Grand Award GA 33 423 (mono), GA 255 SD (stereo))

Grant, Earl

- Beyond the Reef and Other Instrumental Favorites (1962, Decca DL 4231 (mono), DL 74231 (stereo))
- Ebb Tide and Other Instrumental Favorites (1961, Decca DL 4165 (mono), DL 74165 (stereo))
- Just One More Time and Other Instrumental Favorites (1964, Decca DL 4576 (mono), DL 74576 (stereo))

Gray, Glen and the Casa Loma Orchestra

- Today's Best (1963, Capitol T-1938 (mono), ST-1938 (stereo))

Greeley, George

- The Best of the Popular Piano Concertos (1961, Warner Brothers X-1410 (mono), SX-1410 (stereo))
- Greeley Plays Gershwin (1969, Harmony HS-11309)
- The Most Beautiful Music of Hawaii (1960, Warner Brothers W-1366 (mono), WS-1366 (stereo); with **The Outriggers**)
- Piano Italiano (1961, Warner Brothers W-1402 (mono), WS-1402 (stereo))
- Piano Rhapsodies of Love (1961, Reprise R-6092 (mono), R6-6092 (stereo))
- Popular Piano Concertos from the Great Broadway Musicals (1961, Warner Brothers W-1415 (mono), WS-1415 (stereo))
- Popular Piano Concertos of Famous Film Themes (1961, Warner Brothers W-1427 (mono), WS-1427 (stereo))
- Popular Piano Concertos of the World's Great Love Themes (1960, Warner Brothers W-1387 (mono), WS-1387 (stereo))
- Themes from Mutiny on the Bounty and Other Great Films (1962, Warner Brothers W-1476 (mono), WS-1476 (stereo))

Green, Bernie and His Orchestra

- Futura (1961, RCA Victor LSA-2376) (Stereo Action)
- More Than You Can Stand in Hi-Fi (1957, San Francisco M33015; re-issued 1959, Barbary Coast BC 33015)
- Musically Mad (1959, RCA Victor LPM-1929 (mono), LSP-1929 (stereo); as Bernie Green with the Stereo Mad Men) True to its association with the irreverent *Mad* magazine, this album presents a number of well-known musical selections and medleys... well, as they would be if performed by the inmates of an insane asylum, anyway.

Green, Philip and His Orchestra

- Follow the Sun (Capitol T-10118)
- The Moods of London (1959, Capitol T-10059)

- Serenade in the Night (1954, MGM E3119)
- Wings of Song (1959, Jaro JAM 5002)

Green, Urbie and His Orchestra

- Green Power (1971, Project 3 Total Sound PR 5052 SD)
- His Trombone and Rhythm (1959, RCA Victor LPM-1969 (mono), LSP-1969 (stereo))
- The Persuasive Trombone of Urbie Green (1960, Command RS 33-815 (mono), RS 815 SD (stereo))
- The Persuasive Trombone of Urbie Green, Vol. 2 (1961, Command RS 33-838 (mono), RS 838 SD (stereo))
- Twenty-One Trombones (1967 Project 3 Total Sound PR 5014 SD; as Urbie Green and Twenty of the "World's Greatest")
- Twenty-One Trombones, Vol. 2 (1968 Project 3 Total Sound PR 5024 SD; as Urbie Green and Twenty of the "World's Greatest")

Gregory, Johnny and His [London] Orchestra

- Channel West! (1961, Columbia CL 1600)
- It's Bliss! (1956, Allegro 1744)
- Melodies of Japan (1963, Fontana MGF 27522)
- Show Music in Hi Fi (Rondo-lette A4)
- TV Thriller Themes (1961, Phillips PHS 600-027)

Gross, Walter

- Walter Gross Plays His Own Great Songs (1957, ABC-Paramount ABC-153; with **Russ Garcia and His Orchestra**)

Group I

- The Brothers Go to Mother's – and Others'! (1966, RCA Victor LPM 2524 (mono), LSP 3524 (stereo)) A nice interpretation of various Henry Mancini tunes.

Guadalajara Brass

This was one of the more obvious **Tijuana Brass** clone groups.

- Around the World (Coronet CXS-294; Premier PS-9000)
- The Guadalajara Brass (Premier PS-6015) Two-record set.
- Mame, The Work Song, and Other Hits (1967, Coronet CXS-285)
- Tijuana Taxi (1966, Spin-O-Rama M-164 (mono), S-164 (stereo))
- What Now My Love / Spanish Flea (1966, Spin-O-Rama S-174)
- Zorba the Greek, Whipped Cream, A Taste of Honey, and Others (1967, Coronet CXS-269)

Guadalajara Brass and The Chihuahua Marimba Band

- Guadalajara Brass and The Chihuahua Marimba Band (Premier K-44) Three-record set.

Guererra, Tito and His Latin American Orchestra

- Arriba (1960, Crown CLP-5164 (mono), CST-192 (stereo))

Guitar Underground

- 7 Great Guitars With the Now Sound (1966, Project 3 Total Sound PR 5015 SD)

Guitars Inc., The

- Invitation (1958, Warner Brothers B 1206 (mono), BS 1206 (stereo))
- Soft and Subtle (1958, Warner Brothers B 1246 (mono), BS 1246 (stereo))

Guitars Unlimited

- The Fantastic Sound of Guitars Unlimited (1970, London SP 44147)
- Quiet Nights & Brazilian Guitars (1966, Capitol T-2451 (mono), ST-2451 (stereo))
- Tender is the Night (1969, Capitol TST-173)

Guitars Unlimited Plus 7, The

- Crazy Rhythm (1961, RCA Victor LSA-2371) (Stereo Action)

Gunn, Johnny and Don Ralke

- Introspection IV (1960, Warner Brothers W 1372 (mono), WS 1372 (stereo)) This album consists of short stories/beatnik poems narrated by their author, Johnny Gunn, while Don Ralke and his orchestra play accompaniment. The stories are interesting, if a bit dated.

Hackett, Bobby

Jackie Gleason chose Bobby Hackett to translate his ideas into music for his series of best-selling albums, and Hackett stuck primarily to the Easy Listening style when he started producing his own LP's.

- Bobby Hackett Plays Henry Mancini (1964, Epic LN 24061 (mono), BN 26061 (stereo))
- Bobby Hackett Plays the Music of Bert Kaempfert (1964, Epic LN 24080 (mono), BN 26080 (stereo))
- Don't Take Your Love From Me (1958, Capitol T-1002)
- Dream Awhile (1961, Columbia CL 1602 (mono), CS 8402 (stereo))
- Hawaii Swings (1960, Capitol T-1316 (mono), ST-1316 (stereo))
- In a Mellow Mood (1955, Capitol T-575)

- The Most Beautiful Horn in the World (1962, Columbia CL 1729 (mono), CS 8529 (stereo); with '**Glenn Osser**'s Orchestral Pipe Organ Moods')

- Night Love (1962, Columbia CL 1895 (mono), CS 8695 (stereo); with **Glenn Osser** and **The Midnight Strings**)

- Rendezvous (1957, Capitol T-719)

- A Time For Love (Project 3 Total Sound PR 5066 SD)

- That Midnight Touch (1967, Project 3 Total Sound PR 5006 SD)

Hagan, Hans and His Orchestra

- South Pacific (1958, Crown CLP-5054 (mono), CST-111 (stereo))

- Symphony of the Sea (1958, Crown CLP-5076 (mono), CST-116 (stereo); as Hans Hagan and the Vienna World Pops Symphony Orchestra)

Hagen, Earle

- I Spy (1965, Warner Brothers W 1637 (mono), WS 1637 (stereo)) Music from the TV series starring Robert Culp and Bill Cosby.

- The New Interens (1964, Colpix CP 473 (mono), SCP 473 (stereo)) Music from the film.

Halletz, Erwin and His Orchestra

- The Girl From Budapest (1958, Decca DL 8797)

Harmonicats, The (aka **Jerry Murad's Harmonicats**)

The Harmonicats, led by Jerry Murad, were harmonica-based group whose early defining hit was "Peg O' My Heart." They performed for over twenty years, from the 1940's until at least the late 1960's.

- The Cats Meow (1956, Mercury MG 20136; re-released as *Harmonicats featuring Heartaches*)

- Cherry Pink and Apple Blossom White (1960, Columbia CL 1556 (mono), CS 8356 (stereo))

- Command Performance (1956, Mercury MG 20122)

- Dolls, Dolls, Dolls (1957, Mercury MG 20313; Mercury Wing MGW 12242 (mono), SRW 16242 (stereo))

- Fiesta! (1962, Columbia CL 1863 (mono), CS 8663 (stereo))

- Forgotten Dreams (1963, Columbia CL 1945 (mono), CS 8745 (stereo))

- Harmonica Cha-Cha (1958, Mercury MG 20391 (mono), SR 60061 (stereo); Mercury Wing MGW 12279 (mono), SRW 16279 (stereo))

- Harmonica Hits (1957, Mercury Wing MGW 12208 (mono), SRW 16208 (stereo))

- Harmonica Rhapsody (1965, Columbia CL 2341 (mono), CS 9141 (stereo))
- Harmonically Yours (1960, Mercury MG 20485; was there a stereo version?)
- Harmonicats (1958, RKO LP-131 (mono), SLP-1310 (stereo))
- The Harmonicats (1962, Design DLP-202; both mono and stereo versions seem to bear this number)
- Harmonicats featuring Heartaches (1967, Pickwick/33 SPC-3108; this was a re-release of *The Cats Meow* in stereo)
- In the Land of Hi-Fi (1959, Mercury MG 20362 (mono), SR 60028 (stereo))
- The Love Song of Tom Jones (1964, Columbia CL 2166 (mono), CS 8966 (stereo))
- Love Theme from El Cid and Other Motion Picture Songs and Themes (1962, Columbia CL 1753 (mono), CS 8553 (stereo))
- Peg O' My Heart (1961, Columbia CL 1637 (mono), CS 8437 (stereo))
- Selected Favorites (1955, Mercury MG 20074; Mercury Wing MGW 12133 (mono), SRW 16133 (stereo))
- Sentimental Serenade (1962, Columbia CL 1757 (mono), CS 8557 (stereo))
- The Soul of Italy: L'Anima d'Italia (1963, Columbia CL 1999 (mono), CS 8799 (stereo))
- South American Nights (1956, Mercury MG 20107; Mercury Wing MGW 12163 (mono), SRW 16163 (stereo))
- That New Gang of Mine! (1965, Columbia CL 2274 (mono), CS 9074 (stereo))
- Theme from The Avengers (1967, Columbia HL 7423 (mono), HS 11223 (stereo))
- Try A Little Tenderness (1963, Columbia CL 2090 (mono), CS 8890 (stereo))
- What's New Harmonicats? (1966, Columbia CL 2425 (mono), CS 9225 (stereo))

Harnell, Joe (and His Orchestra)

- Bossa Now! (1967, Columbia CL 2699 (mono), CS 9499 (stereo))
- Fly Me to the Moon and the Bossa Nova Pops (1963, Kapp KL-1318 (mono), KS-3318 (stereo))
- Golden Piano Hits (1966, Columbia CL 2466 (mono), CS 9266 (stereo))
- I Want to Be Happy (1960, Epic LN 3708 (mono), BN 573 (stereo))

- Joe Harnell & His Orchestra Play (1963, Kapp KL-1339 (mono), KS-3339 (stereo))
- Joe Harnell and His Trio (1963, Jubilee JGM 5020)
- More Bossa Nova Pops (1963, Kapp KL-1325 (mono), KS-3325 (stereo))
- Moving On!! (1969, Motown MS 698)
- The Piano Brilliance of Joe Harnell (1963, Epic LN 24048 (mono), BN 26048 (stereo))
- The Piano Inventions of Jo Harnell and His Trio (Jubilee LP 1015)
- The Rhythm and the Fire (1965, Kapp KL-1416 (mono), KS-3416 (stereo))
- The Sound of the Asphalt Jungle (1960, Kapp Medallion ML-7518 (mono), MS-7518 (stereo))

Harte, Roy and Milt Holland (aka **The 44 Instruments Of...**)

- Percussion Unabridged (Kimberly 11022; also released as *Perfect Percussion*)
- Perfect Percussion (1961, World Pacific WP-1405; also released as *Percussion Unabridged*)

Haskell, Jimmy and His Orchestra

- Count Down! (1959, Imperial LP-9068) This album is included because it fits in the 'Space Age Pop' category; it's basically rock and roll songs with 'futuristic' electronic sound effects mixed in. The cover puts one in mind of Les Baxter's Space Age Pop classic, *Space Escapade*, though the music is entirely different.

Hatch, Tony and His Orchestra (aka **The Tony Hatch Sound**)

- The Downtown Sound of Tony Hatch (1965, Warner Brothers W-1629 (mono), WS-1629 (stereo))
- A Latin Happening (1965, Warner Brothers W-1671 (mono), WS-1671 (stereo))

Hawaiian Hula Boys, The

- Hawaii in Stereo (1959, Capitol ST-10223)

Hawaiian Islanders, The

- 30 Hawaiian Favorites (1965, Wyncote W-9109 (mono), SW-9109 (stereo))
- Hawaii Tattoo and Other Hawaiian Favorites (1965, Wyncote W-9087 (mono), SW-9087 (stereo))
- Hawaiian Enchantment (1966, Wyncote W-9131 (mono), SW-9131 (stereo))

- Hawaiian Paradise (1964, Wyncote W-9034 (mono), SW-9034 (stereo))

Hawaiian Room Orchestra, The

'The Hawaiian Room Orchestra' consisted in part of George Hines and **Johnny Coco**. The Hawaiian Room was located in the Hotel Lexington, NYC.

- Hawaiian Room presents Melodies for Dancing from the Enchanted Islands (MGM E3498)

Hawaiian Strings, The

- Moonlight Time in Old Hawaii (1969, Vault SLP 127) Hawaii-themed tunes done in a string-heavy Easy Listening style. These versions almost certainly appeared on older releases before this.

Hawaiians, The

- Hawaii Tattoo (1964, Crown CLP-5454 (mono), CST-454 (stereo))
- Holiday in Hawaii (1958, Crown CLP-5080 (mono), CST-125 (stereo))
- Vacation in Hawaii (1961, Crown CLP-5214 (mono), CST-228 (stereo))

Hayman, Richard and His Orchestra

- Broadway Hits and Other Themes (Time S/328; as Richard Hayman and the Manhattan Pops Orchestra)
- Caramba! (1959, Mercury SR 60103)
- Cinemagic Sounds (1969, Command 941S)
- Come With Me to Far Away Places (1956, Mercury MG-20129; Mercury Wing SRW 16186)
- Genuine Electric Latin Love Machine (1969 Command COM 947S)
- Gypsy (Mercury PPS 6027 (mono), SR 60875 (stereo))
- Harmonica Holiday (1961, Mercury PPS 6005)
- Havana in Hi-Fi (1957, Mercury MG 20296 (mono), SR-60000 (stereo))
- Let's Get Together (Mercury Wing MGW 12100)
- Love is a Many Splendored Thing (1956, Mercury MG-20123)
- Melodies of Love (1967, Mainstream ST-91092)
- Music for a Quiet Evening (1954, Mercury MG-20048)
- Music for People Who Can't Sleep (1957, Mercury MG-20184)
- My Fair Lady (Mercury Wing SRW 16124)
- Only Memories (Mercury SR 60100)
- Reminiscing (1956, Mercury MG-20113)

- Richard Hayman Plays Great Motion Picture Themes of Victor Young (1958, Mercury MG-20369 (mono), SR-60012 (stereo))
- Serenade For Love (1956, Mercury MG 20115 (mono); Mercury Wing MGW 12239, SRW 16239 (stereo))
- Songs of Wonderful Girls (1962, Mercury MG 20733 (mono), SR 60733 (stereo); re-released 1964, Mercury Wing SRW 16285).
- Time For Listening (1956, Mercury MG-20103)
- Two Tickets to Paris (1957, Mercury 20220)
- Voodoo! (1959, Mercury MG-20465 (mono), SR-60147 (stereo))

Heath, Ted (usually as Ted Heath and His Music)
- All Time Top Twelve (1957, London LL 1716)
- The Big Ones (1970, London SP 44140)
- Gershwin for Moderns... (1955, London LL 1217)
- The Great Film Hits... (1959, London LL 3106 (mono), PS 159 (stereo))
- Hits I Missed (1958, London LL 3057)
- Pop Hits from the Classics (1959, London LL 3124 (mono), PS 171 (stereo))
- Pow! (1966, London SP 44079)
- Rodgers For Moderns (1956, London LL 1500)
- Satin, Strings, & Bouncing Brass (1963, London SP 44023)
- Shall We Dance? (1959, London LL 3062 (mono), PS 148 (stereo))
- Showcase (1957, London LL 1737)
- The Sound of Music (1965, London SP 44063)

Heath, Ted and Edmundo Ross and His Orchestra
- Heath Vs. Ros: Swing Vs. Latin (1964, London SP 44038)
- Heath Vs. Ros, Round 2 (1966, London SP 44089)

Heckscher, Ernie and His Fairmont Orchestra
- Dance Atop Knob Hill (1957, Verve MGV-4007)
- Dancing on Broadway (1960, Verve Verve MGV-4045)
- The Dancing Sounds of San Francisco (1964, Columbia CL 2256 (mono), CS 9056 (stereo))
- Hollywood Hits for Dancing (1960, Verve V-4047 (mono), V6-4047 (stereo))
- Listen and Dance to That San Francisco Beat! (1963, Columbia CL 2086 (mono), CS 8886 (stereo))
- Those Were the Days (1968, Earl EH 1600)

- The Whole World Dances (1965, Columbia CL 2332 (mono), CS 9132 (stereo))

Hefti, Neal and His Orchestra

He was known as Neal 'Batman theme' Hefti because he penned the popular tune, but he had wide range of musical experience including producing for Frank Sinatra's Reprise label.

- Barefoot in the Park (1967, Dot DLP 3803 (mono), DLP 25803 (stereo)) Motion picture soundtrack.
- Batman Theme and 11 Hefti Bat Songs (1966, RCA Victor LPM-3573 (mono), LSP-3573 (stereo)) Music 'inspired by' the *Batman* TV series, which premiered in January of that year. It's almost certain that Hefti had already written most or all of these songs, and they were simply retitled to take advantage of the show's sudden wild popularity.
- Boeing Boeing (1965, RCA Victor LOC-1121)
- Harlow (1965, Columbia Masterworks OL 6390 (mono), OS 2790 (stereo)) Motion picture soundtrack.
- Hefti in Gotham City (1966, RCA Victor LPM-3621 (mono), LSP-3621 (stereo). More music that was probably retitled to take advantage of Batmania in 1966. Although Hefti had a strong musical career by 1966, the public at large now knew him as Neal 'Batman theme' Hefti, and in fact that's how he was listed on the cover of this album.
- How to Murder Your Wife (1965, United Artists UAL 4119 (mono), UAS 5119 (stereo)) Motion picture soundtrack.
- The Leisurely Loveliness of Neal Hefti and His Orchestra (1965, Movietone MTM 1006 (mono), MTS 2006 (stereo))
- Li'l Darlin' (1964, 20th Century Fox TFM 4139 (mono), TFS 4139 (stereo))
- Light and Right! (1960, Columbia CL 1516 (mono), CS 8316 (stereo); as The Neal Hefti Quintet)
- Lord Love a Duck (1966, United Artists UAL 4137 (mono), UAS 5137 (stereo)) Motion picture soundtrack.
- Sex and the Single Girl (1960, Warner Brothers W 1572 (mono), WS 1572 (stereo)) Motion picture soundtrack.
- Synanon (1965, Liberty LRP-3143 (mono), LST-7413 (stereo)) Motion picture soundtrack.

Henke, Mel

- Dig (1955, Contemporary C5001)
- Dynamic Adventures in Sound (1962, Warner Brothers B 1447 (mono), BS 1447 (stereo))
- *La Dolce Henke* (1962, Warner Brothers W 1472 (mono), WS 1472 (stereo))
- Now Spin This! (1956, Contemporary C5003)

Henrique, Luiz

- Barra Limpa (1967, Verve V-8697 (mono), V6-8697 (stereo))
- Listen To Me (1967, Fontana SRF-67553)

Henrique, Luiz and Walter Wanderley

- Popcorn (1968, Verve V-8734 (mono), V6-8734 (stereo))

Henry, Don and Leo Diamond

- Hot Harmonica (1956, Regent MG 6025)

Herman, Woody

- Light My Fire (1969, Cadet LPS-819)

Herman, Woody and Tito Puente

- Herman's Heat & Puente's Beat! (1958, Everest LPBR-5010 (mono), SDBR-1010 (stereo))

Hernandez, Rene (aka **The Rene Hernandez Orchestra**) Is this artist the same as **Machito**?

- Percussive Cha Cha Latino (1962, Audio Fidelity AFSD 5973; this was a re-release of *Percussive Latino Cha Cha Cha*; with 'Pacheco')
- Percussive Latino Cha Cha Cha (1960, Audio Fidelity DFM 3003 (mono), DFS 7003 (stereo); re-released as *Percussive Cha Cha Latino*)

Heywood, Eddie (and His Orchestra) (see also **Hugo Winterhalter and Eddie Heywood**)

- An Affair to Remember (1966, Sunset SUS-5121)
- Breezin' Along With the Breeze (1959, Mercury MG 20445 (mono), SR 60115 (stereo); re-released in 1964)
- Canadian Sunset Bossa Nova (1963, Liberty LRP 3313 (mono), LST 7313 (stereo))
- Eddie Haywood Plays the Greatest! (1962, Liberty LRP 3210 (mono), LST 7210 (stereo))
- The Keys and I (1959, RCA Victor LMP-1900 (mono), LSP-1900 (stereo); with **Joe Reisman and His Orchestra**)
- Lightly and Politely (1956, Decca DL 8202)
- One For My Baby (1960, Mercury MG 20632)
- With Love and Strings (1967, Capitol ST 2833)

Hirt, Al

Al Hirt came out of the world of Dixieland jazz, but on many other recordings throughout the 1960's, he proved he could adapt easily to other musical styles.

- Al Hirt (1970, RCA Victor LSP-4247)
- Al Hirt Now! (1968, RCA Victor LSP-4101)
- Al Hirt Plays Bert Kaempfert (1968, RCA Victor LSP-3917)
- Gold (1970, GWP ST-2004; Romulus A-6054)
- The Happy Trumpet (1966, RCA Victor LPM-3579 (mono), LSP-3579 (stereo))
- Here in My Heart (1969, RCA Victor LSP-4161 (stereo))
- Honey in the Horn (1963, RCA Victor LPM-2733 (mono), LSP-2733 (stereo))
- The Horn Meets "The Hornet" (1966, RCA Victor LPM-3716 (mono), LSP-3716 (stereo))
- I'm In Love With You (1968, RCA Victor LSP-4020)
- Latin in the Horn (1966, RCA Victor LPM-3653 (mono), LSP-3653 (stereo))
- Music to Watch Girls By (1967, RCA Victor LPM-3773 (mono), LSP-3773 (stereo))
- Paint Your Wagon (1969, GWP ST-2002)
- Sugar Lips (1964, RCA Victor LPM-2965 (mono), LSP-2965 (stereo))
- That Honey Horn Sound (1965, RCA Victor LPM-3337 (mono), LSP-3337 (stereo))
- They're Playing Our Song (1966, RCA Victor LPM-3492 (mono), LSP-3492 (stereo))
- Trumpet and Strings (1962, RCA Victor LPM-2584 (mono), LSP-2584 (stereo))
- Unforgettable (1968, RCA Victor LPM-3979 (mono), LSP-3979 (stereo))

Hollyridge Strings, The (see also **Stu Phillips**)

Somebody at Capitol Records had the bright idea to take the unique songs of the then-white-hot Beatles, and adapt them for a more Easy Listening (i.e., older) audience. Meeting with success, producer **Stu Phillips** then went on to adapt the music of other popular artists. For copycat groups, see **The Castaway Strings**, **Those Fantabulous Strings, The Golden Gate Strings**, and **The Sunset Strings**.

- The Beach Boys Songbook: Romantic Instrumentals by The Hollyridge Strings (1964, Capitol T-2156 (mono), ST-2156 (stereo))
- The Beatles Song Book (1964, Capitol T-2116 (mono), ST-2116 (stereo))

- The Beatles Song Book, Vol. 2 (1964, Capitol T-2202 (mono), ST-2202 (stereo))
- The Beatles Songbook, Vol. 4 (1967, Capitol T-2656 (mono), ST-2656 (stereo))
- The Beatles Song Book, Vol. 5 (1968, Capitol ST-2876)
- Hits of the 70's (1972, Capitol ST-883)
- The Hollyridge Strings Play Hit Songs Made Famous by Elvis Presley (1964, Capitol T-2221 (mono), ST-2221 (stereo))
- The Hollyridge Strings Play Hits Made Famous by The Four Seasons (1964, Capitol T-2199 (mono), ST-2199 (stereo))
- The Hollyridge Strings Play the Hits of Simon & Garfunkel (1968, Capitol ST-2998)
- The Hollyridge Strings Play the Beach Boys Song Book, Vol. 2 (1967, Capitol T-2749 (mono), ST-2749 (stereo))
- The Nat King Cole Song Book (1965, Capitol T-2310 (mono), ST-2310 (stereo))
- The New Beatles Song Book (1966, Capitol T-2429 (mono), ST-2429 (stereo))
- Oldies But Goodies (1966, Capitol T-2564 (mono), ST-2564 (stereo))

Hollywood All Stars
- Moving Percussion in Pops (1960, Dyna-Disc SCH-810)

Hollywood Soundmakers, The
- Great Music from A Fistful of Dollars, For a Few Dollars More, The Good The Bad and The Ugly (1968, Unart S 21032; 1970, Sunset SUS-5286)

Hollywood Strings
- Hawaii and Other Songs of the Islands (1968, Crown CLP 5561 (mono), CST 561 (stereo))
- I Remember Nat King Cole (1966, Somerset SF-23800)

Hollywood Studio Orchestra, The
- Casino Royale (1967, Wyncote W-9202 (mono), SW-9202 (stereo))

Holmes, Leroy and His Orchestra
- 14 Big Hits (1963, United Artists UAL-3306 (mono), UAS-6306 (stereo); as The Leroy Holmes Singers)
- All Time Latin Favorites (1963, United Artists UAL-3272 (mono), UAS-6272 (stereo))

- Bossa Nova (1962, United Artists UAL-3242 (mono), UAS-6242 (stereo))
- Candlelight and Wine (1955, MGM E3288)
- College Prom (1959, MGM E3758 (mono), SE3758 (stereo))
- Everybody's Talkin' (1969, United Artists UAS-6731)
- For a Few Dollars More and Other Motion Picture Themes (1967, United Artists UAL-3608 (mono), UAS-6608 (stereo))
- The Good, The Bad, and The Ugly and Other Motion Picture Themes (1968, United Artists UAL-3633 (mono), UAS-6633 (stereo))
- Hawaii with a Bongo Beat (1960, MGM E3874 (mono), SE3874 (stereo))
- Lush Themes from Motion Pictures (1955, MGM E3172)
- Movie Themes for Teens (1962, MGM E3979 (mono), SE3979 (stereo))
- Music for Crazy Mixed-Up People (1957?, MGM E3608)
- Music from the Modern Screen (1959, MGM E3753 (mono), SE3753 (stereo))
- Snowflakes and Sweethears (1966, United Artists UAL-3481 (mono), UAS-6481 (stereo))
- A Song of Joy (1970, United Artists UAS-6769)
- Sophisticated Strings (1960, MGM E3833 (mono), SE3833 (stereo))
- Spectacular Guitars & Strings: A Fiesta in Sound (1961, MGM E3919 (mono), SE3919 (stereo))
- Take Me in Your Arms (1956?, MGM E3378)
- Themes from the New Provocative Films (1969, United Artists UAS-6742)

Honolulu Guitars, The

- Hawaii (1966, Power D 398 (mono), DS 398 (stereo))
- Songs of Hawaii (1966, Power D 397 (mono), DS 397 (stereo))

Horn, Paul (aka **The Paul Horn Quintet**)

The Paul Horn Quintet was a more conventional jazz combo throughout much of their career until about 1966; their last two albums are much farther into the category of Easy Listening.

- Here's That Rainy Day (1966, RCA Victor LPM-3519 (mono), LSP-3519 (stereo))
- Monday, Monday (1966, RCA Victor LPM-3613 (mono), LSP-3613 (stereo))

Hugo & Luigi Chorus, The

- Cascading Voices (Roulette R-25283 (mono), SR-25283 (stereo))
- The Cascading Voices of the Hugo & Luigi Chorus (1963, RCA Victor LPM-2641 (mono), LSP-2641 (stereo))
- The Cascading Voices of the Hugo & Luigi Chorus With Brass (1964, RCA Victor LPM-2789 (mono), LSP-2789 (stereo))
- The Cascading Voices of the Hugo & Luigi Chorus With Strings (1964, RCA Victor LPM-2863 (mono), LSP-2863 (stereo))
- Let's Fall in Love (1963, RCA Victor LPM-2717 (mono), LSP-2717 (stereo))

Hulme, Donald and The Marty Gold Orchestra

- Sounds Impossible (1972, Audio Fidelity AFSD 6248)

Hunter, Frank (aka **The Frank Hunter Orchestra**) (see also **Sam Makia and the Makapuu Beach Boys**)

- The Sound of Strings, Vol. 2 (1960, Kapp Medallion ML 7509 (mono), MS 7509 (stereo))
- Sounds of the Hunter (1955, Jubilee LP-1020)
- *White Goddess* (1959, Kapp KL 1136 (mono), KS 3019 (stereo))

Hyman, Dick (**and His Orchestra**)

Keyboard master Dick Hyman enjoyed a wide-ranging career playing in several different genres and styles.

- After Six (1960, MGM E 3827 (mono), SE 3827 (stereo); as Dick Hyman, His Piano and Trio)
- The Age of Electronicus (1969, Command COM 946-S)
- Beside a Shady Nook (1956, MGM E 3379; as The Dick Hyman Trio)
- Brasilian Impressions (1967, Command RS 911 SD)
- The Dick Hyman and His Trio (1961, Command RS 33 832 (mono), RS 832 SD (stereo))
- The Dick Hyman Trio Swings (1956, MGM E 3280)
- Electrodynamics (1963, Command RS 33 856 (mono), RS 856 SD (stereo))
- Fabulous (1963, Command RS 33 862 (mono), RS 862 SD (stereo))
- Fantomfingers (1971, Project 3 Total Sound PR 5057 SD)
- Gigi (1958, MGM E 3642; as The Dick Hyman Trio) Songs from the film.
- Happening! (1966, Command RS 899 SD; re-released as *Harpsichord Arrangements of Popular Tunes*)
- Harpsichord Arrangements of Popular Tunes (1970, Command 299 017; this was a re-release of *Happening!*)

- I'll Never Be the Same (1966, Sunset SUM-1140 (mono), SUS-1140 (stereo); as Dick Hyman and Strings)
- Keyboard Kaleidoscope (1964, Command RS 33 875 (mono), RS 875 SD (stereo))
- The Man From O.R.G.A.N. (1965, Command RS 33 891 (mono), RS 891 SD (stereo))
- Mirrors (1968, Command RS 924 SD; as Dick Hyman and 'The Group')
- Moog – The Electric Eclectics of Dick Hyman (1969, Command COM 938-S)
- Moon Gas (1963, MGM E 4119 (mono), SE 4119 (stereo); with Mary Maryo) A classic of Space Age Pop.
- Provocative Piano (1960, Command RS 33 811 (mono), RS 811 SD (stereo))
- Provocative Piano, Vol. 2 (1960, Command RS 33 824 (mono), RS 824 SD (stereo))
- Red Sails in the Sunset (1957, MGM E 3483)
- The Sensuous Piano of "D" (1971, Project 3 Total Sound PR 5054 SD) The title of this album was a play on a popular erotic novel of the time, *The Sensuous Woman*, whose author was listed as simply "J".
- September Song: Dick Hyman Plays the Music of Kurt Weill (1953, Proscenium CE 4001)
- Strictly Organic (1960, MGM E 3808 (mono), SE 3808 (stereo); as Dick Hyman and His Quintet)
- Sweet Sweet Soul (1968, Command RS 933 SD; as Dick Hyman and 'The Group')
- Swingin' Double Date (Lion L-70067; as The Dick Hyman Trio)
- The 'Unforgettable' Sound of the Dick Hyman Trio (1956, MGM E 3329)
- A Zillion Strings and Dick Hyman at the Piano (1960, Everest LPBR-5074 (mono), SDBR-1074 (stereo))

Ingmann, Jorgen

He didn't write it, but Dane Ingmann was known for having a huge hit in 1961 with the guitar song "Apache."
- Apache (1961, Atco 33-130)
- The Many Guitars of Jorgen Ingmann (1962, Atco 33-139)
- Swing Softly (1960, Mercury MG-20292) This album was called *Guitar in Hi-Fi* in its foreign releases.
- Swinging Guitar (1956, Mercury MG-20200)

International Pop Orchestra, The (often with '100 Men' or '100 Musicians')
- 110 Men (1963, Cameo C 2001 (mono), SC 2001 (stereo))

- 110 Musicians (1964, Wyncote W-9005 (mono), SW-9005 (stereo))
- Autumn Leaves (1967, Wyncote W-9174 (mono), SW-9174 (stereo))
- Cole Porter Favorites (1964, Wyncote W-9063 (mono), SW-9063 (stereo))
- An Exciting Evening At Home (1962, Cameo C 4001 (mono), SC 4001 (stereo))
- For Lovers Everywhere (1967, Wyncote W-9165 (mono), SW-9165 (stereo))
- The International Pop Orchestra Plays For Lovers Only (1964, Wyncote W-9021 (mono), SW-9021 (stereo))
- The International Pop Orchestra Plays Love Themes From The Classics (1964, Wyncote W-9040 (mono), SW-9040 (stereo))
- The International Pop Orchestra Visits the World's Fair (1964, Wyncote W-9014 (mono), SW-9014 (stereo))
- Let's Fall in Love (1967, Wyncote W-9193 (mono), SW-9193 (stereo))
- Musical Jewels (1960, Cameo C 1039 (mono), SC 1039 (stereo); re-released 1965, Wyncote W-9120 (mono), SW-9120 (stereo))
- Rhapsody in Blue (1964, Wyncote W-9084 (mono), SW-9084 (stereo))
- Songs That Will Live Forever (1960, Cameo C 1037 (mono), SC 1037 (stereo))
- The Sound of Music (1964, Wyncote W-9076 (mono), SW-9076; with The Cheltenham Chorus)
- Spanish Inferno (1962, Cameo C 4015 (mono), SC 4015 (stereo))
- Stardust (1964, Wyncote W-9059 (mono), SW-9059 (stereo))
- That's Life (1967, Wyncote W-9185 (mono), SW-9185 (stereo))
- When Lights Are Low (1966, Wyncote W-9124 (mono), SW-9124 (stereo))

Islanders, The (see also **Billy Mure and The Islanders**)
- The Enchanted Sound of The Islanders (1960, Mayflower M-633)

Jaffa, Max
- By Candlelight (1959, Capitol ST 10220)

Jaffee, Bill and His Islanders
- Hawaiian Paradise (1964, Strand SLS-1105)

Jankowski, Horst

- And We Got Love (1967, Mercury MG 21160 (mono), SR 61160 (stereo))
- Baby, But Grand! (1966, Mercury MG 21106 (mono), SR 61106 (stereo))
- Bravo Jankowski! (1964, Mercury MG 20993 (mono), SR 60993 (stereo); also released as *The Genius of Jankowski!*)
- The Genius of Jankowski! (1964, Mercury MG 20993 (mono), SR 60993 (stereo); also released as *Bravo Jankowski!*)
- More Genius of Horst Jankowski (1965, Mercury MG 21054 (mono), SR 61054 (stereo))
- Piano Affairs (1968, Mercury SR 61195)
- So What's New? (1966, Mercury MG 21093 (mono), SR 61093 (stereo))
- Still More Genius of Jankowski (1966, Mercury MG 21076 (mono), SR 61076 (stereo))
- A Walk in the Evergreens (1969, Mercury SR 61232)
- With Love (1967, Mercury MG 21125 (mono), SR 61125 (stereo))

Jarre, Maurice

- Doctor Zhivago (1965, MGM 1E-6ST (mono), S1E-6ST (stereo)) Soundtrack to the film starring Omar Sharif.
- Lawrence of Arabia (1962, Colpix CP 514 (mono), SCP 514 (stereo)) Soundtrack to the film starring Peter O'Toole.

Jazz All-Stars, The

Probably thrown together at the last minute, this collection of spy-movie theme music isn't very good.

- Thunderball & Other Secret Agent Themes (1966, Design DLP-206 (mono), SDLP-206 (stereo))

Jenkins, Gordon and His Orchestra and Chorus

- 26 Years of Academy Award Winning Songs (1960, CG Records CGM 1002 (mono), CGS 3002 (stereo))
- Blue Prelude (Sunset SUM-1149 (mono), SUS-5149 (stereo))
- Complete Manhattan Tower (1956, Capitol T-766)
- Dream Dust (1952, Capitol T-1023)
- Dreamer's Holiday (1958, Vocalion VL 3615)
- France (1962, Time 52061 (mono), S/2061 (stereo))
- Gordon Jenkins' Almanac (1955, Vik LXA-1026)
- Gordon Jenkins With His Orchestra Presents Marshall Royal (1960, Everest LPBR 5087 (mono), SDBR 1087 (stereo))

- Hawaiian Wedding Song (1962, Columbia CL 1764 (mono), CS 8564 (stereo); with The Ralph Brewster Singers)
- He Likes to Go Dancing (1957, Decca DL 8313; with The Commanders featuring Eddie Gray and Jerry Gray and His Orchestra)
- I Live Alone (1964, Kapp KL-1361 (mono), KS-3361 (stereo))
- In A Tender Mood (1963, Columbia CL 2009 (mono), CS 8809 (stereo))
- Let's Duet (1962, Warner Brothers W 1464 (mono), WS 1464 (stereo))
- The Magic World of Gordon Jenkins (1962, Columbia CL 1882; re-released CSRP 8682)
- My Heart Sings (1964, Decca DL 4714)
- Night Dreams (1957; Capitol T-781; with The Ralph Brewster Singers)
- Paris: I Wish You Love (Time 52130 (mono), S/2130 (stereo))
- P.S. I Love You (1952, Decca DL 8109)
- The Romantic Moods of Gordon Jenkins (Sears SPS-403)
- Seven Dreams (1953, Decca DL 9011 (mono), DL 79011 (stereo); did the stereo version come out later than '53?)
- Soft Soul (1966, Dot DLP 3752)
- Soul of a People (1962, Time 52050 (mono), S/52050 (stereo))
- Stolen Hours (1961, Capitol T-884 (mono), ST-884 (stereo))
- Tropicana Holiday (1958, Capitol T-1048)
- Yours (1967, Pickwick PC-3005 (mono), SPC-3005 (stereo))

Jerome, Henry and His Orchestra
- American Gold (1970, United Artists SQB 93113)
- Brazen Brass (1960, Decca DL 4056 (mono), DL 74056 (stereo))
- Brazen Brass Brings Back the Bands! (1961, Decca DL 4125 (mono), DL 74125 (stereo))
- Brazen Brass Features... Saxes (1961, Decca DL 4127 (mono), DL 74127 (stereo))
- Brazen Brass Goes Hollywood (1961, Decca DL 4085 (mono), DL 74085 (stereo))
- Brazen Brass Goes Latin (1962, Decca DL 4226 (mono), DL 74226 (stereo))
- Brazen Brass: New Sounds in Folk Music (1963, Decca DL 4344 (mono), DL 74344 (stereo))
- Brazen Brass Plays Songs Everybody Knows (Decca DL 41106 (mono), DL 741106 (stereo))
- Brazen Brass Zings the Strings (1961, Decca DL 4187 (mono), DL 74187 (stereo))

- Hello Nice People (1958, Roulette R-25056; re-issued Forum F 9015 (mono), SF 9015 (stereo))
- Henry's Trumpets (1967, United Artists UAL 3620 (mono), UAS 6620 (stereo))
- Memories of Hal Kemp (1957, Roulette R-25007)
- Vocal Velvet (1963, Decca DL 4440 (mono), DL 74440 (stereo))

Jones, J. J.

- Misty (1967, Wyncote W-9170 (mono), SW-9170 (stereo))

Jones, Quincy

The bulk of Quincy Jones's output isn't relevant for this volume, but these few might be.

- Big Band Bossa Nova (1962, Mercury MG 20751 (mono), SR 60751 (stereo))
- Quincy Jones Explores the Music of Henry Mancini (1964, Mercury MG 20863 (mono), SR 60863 (stereo))

Juarez, Ricardo and His Orchestra

- Ricardo Juarez and His Orchestra Play Happy Time Cha Chas (1960, Grand Award GA 33-422 (mono), GA 254 SD (stereo))

Jupp, Eric and His Orchestra

- Rockin' Violins (Capitol T 10240 (mono), ST 10240 (stereo))\

Kaapuni, Harry and His Royal Polynesians (see also **Billy Mure**)

- Aloha Hawaii (1960, Coronet CX-43 (mono), CXS-43 (stereo))

Note: The record label may give the title as either *Aloha Hawaii* or *Holiday in Hawaii*, but both give the same catalog number. This was also released as *Hawaiian Paradise* (Celebrity UT-135 (mono), UTS-135 (stereo)). This was apparently a re-release of *Hawaiian Holiday* by **Willie Alunuai and His Band**.

- Blue Hawaiian Waters (1960, Coronet CX-128 (mono), CXS-128 (stereo))

Kaempfert, Bert, and His Orchestra (see also the Compilations section)

Bert Kaempfert started out in his native Germany as a bandleader and arranger, but soon made his way to the U.S. where he became an A&R man for Polydor and signed a struggling young act calling themselves The Beatles. Kaempfert would go on to write and record his own creations, though his most famous songs became huge hits for others – including "Strangers in the Night" for Frank Sinatra and "Danke Schoen" for Wayne Newton.

- Afrikaan Beat and Other Favorites (1962, Decca DL 4273 (mono), DL 74273 (stereo))

- April in Portugal (1959, Decca DL 8881 (mono), DL 78881 (stereo))
- Bert Kaempfert Now! (1971, Decca DL 75305)
- Blue Midnight (1965, Decca DL 4569 (mono), DL 74569 (stereo))
- Bye Bye Blues (1966, Decca DL 4693 (mono), DL 74693 (stereo))
- Dancing in Wonderland (1960, Decca DL 4161 (mono), DL 74161 (stereo))
- Fabulous Fifties... And New Delights (1973, MCA MCA-314)
- Free and Easy (1970, Decca DL 75234)
- Gallery (1974, MCA MCA-447)
- The Happy Wonderland of Bert Kaempfert (1966, Polydor K2M 5051 (mono), K2S 5052 (stereo))
- Hold Me (1967, Decca DL 4860 (mono), DL 74860 (stereo))
- The Kaempfert Touch (1970, Decca DL 75175)
- Lights Out, Sweet Dreams (1963, Decca DL 4265 (mono), DL 74265 (stereo))
- Living It Up! (1963, Decca DL 4374 (mono), DL 74374 (stereo))
- Love That Bert Kaempfert (1967, Decca DL 4986 (mono), DL 74986 (stereo))
- The Magic Music of Far Away Places (1965, Decca DL 4616 (mono), DL 74616 (stereo))
- A Man Could Get Killed (1966, Decca DL 4750 (mono), DL 74750 (stereo)) Film soundtrack.
- The Most Beautiful Girl (1974, MCA MCA-402)
- My Way of Life (1968, Decca DL 75059)
- Orange Colored Sky (1970, Decca DL 75256)
- Strangers in the Night (1966, Decca DL 4795 (mono), DL 74795 (stereo))
- Sweet and Gentle (1963, Longines Symphonette Society LW 304 (mono), LWS 304 (stereo))
- That Happy Feeling (1962, Decca DL 4305 (mono), DL 74305 (stereo))
- That Latin Feeling... (1964, Decca DL 4490 (mono), DL 74490 (stereo))
- Three O'Clock in the Morning (1965, Decca DL 4670 (mono), DL 74670 (stereo))
- To the Good Life (1973, MCA MCA-368)
- Traces of Love (1969, Decca DL 75140)
- Warm and Wonderful (1969, Decca DL 75089)
- With a 'Sound' in My Heart (1962, Decca DL 4228 (mono), 74228 (stereo))

- Wonderland By Night (1960, Decca DL 4101 (mono), DL 74101 (stereo))
- The Wonderland of Bert Kaempfert (1961, Decca DL 4117 (mono), DL 74117 (stereo))
- The World We Knew (1967, Decca DL 4925 (mono), DL 74925 (stereo))

Kai, Lani and His Hawaiians
- Hawaiian Festival: 20 Golden Moments of Hawaiian Music (1967, Diplomat D-2424 (mono), DS-2424 (stereo))
- Hawaiian Magic (1964, Diplomat D-2326 (mono), DS-2326 (stereo))
- Hurrah Hawaii: 20 Golden Moments of Hawaiian Music (1967, Diplomat D-2425 (mono), DS-2425 (stereo))
- Island Love Songs (1963, Decca DL 4334 (mono), DL 74334 (stereo))

Kaiwaza
- Hawaiian Holiday (1964, Wyncote W-9006 (mono), SW-9006 (stereo))

Kamae, Eddie and The Sons of Hawaii (see also **Gabby Pahinui**)
- Eddie Kamae Presents the Sons of Hawaii (1975, Hawaii Sons HS-1001) Note: This and the next two entries are entirely different releases, each having a different selection of songs.
- Eddie Kamae Presents the Sons of Hawaii (1976, Hawaii Sons HS-2002)
- Eddie Kamae Presents the Sons of Hawaii (1977, Hawaii Sons HS-3003)
- The Folk Music of Hawaii (1971, Panini KN1001) This was a package that included the LP, a 7" 45 RPM record, and a booklet, 'On Hawaiian Folk Music'.
- Grassroots Music (1980, Hawaii Sons HS-6006)
- Ho'omau (1979, Hawaii Sons HS-5005)
- Music of Old Hawaii (1962, Hula H-506, HS-506; were there both mono and stereo versions?)
- This is Eddie Kamae and the Sons of Hawaii (1966, Hula H-512, HS-512)

Keack, Alex
- Surfers Paradise (1963, Crown CLP 5315 (mono), CST 315 (stereo))

Keating, Johnny (aka **The Johnny Keating Sound**) (see also **Sounds Galactic**)

- Here's Where It Is (1966, Warner Brothers W1666 (mono), WS 1666 (stereo); as The Johnny Keating Sound)
- Hotel (1966, Warner Brothers W 1682 (mono), WS 1682 (stereo) Film soundtrack.
- The Keating Sound (1966, London SP 44058; as Johnny Keating & 27 Men)
- Keating... Straight Ahead (1965, London SP 44072)
- Percussive Moods (1961, London SP 44005; as Johnny Keating's Kombo)
- Space Experience (1972, EMI TWO393; was this album only available in America in Quadrophonic?)
- Temptation (1963, London SP 44019)
- This Bird Has Flown (1966, Warner Brothers W 1638 (mono), WS 1638 (stereo); as The Johnny Keating Sound)

Keller and Constanze

- All Time Favorite Love Songs with Twin Pianos & Organ (1964, Wyncote W-9051 (mono), SW-9051 (stereo))

Kenton, Stan

A giant in the world of jazz, some of Kenton's later output can be classified as leaning toward softer Easy Listening material, so a representative sample is being included here.

- Artistry in Bossa Nova (1963, Capitol T-1931 (mono), ST-1931 (stereo))
- The Ballad Style of Kenton (1958, Capitol T-1068 (mono), ST-1068 (stereo))
- Hair (1969, Capitol ST-305)
- Lush Interlude (1959, Capitol T-1130 (mono), ST-1130 (stereo))
- Rendezvous With Kenton (1957, Capitol T-932 (mono), ST-932 (stereo))
- The Romantic Approach: In the Ballad Style of Stan Kenton (1961, Capitol T-1533 (mono), ST-1533 (stereo))
- Sophisticated Approach (1962, Capitol T-1674 (mono), ST-1674 (stereo))
- Stan Kenton Plays For Today (1966, Capitol T-2655 (mono), ST-2655 (stereo))
- Standards in Silhouette (1960, Capitol T-1394 (mono), ST-1394 (stereo))

Kerr, Anita (aka **The Anita Kerr Singers**; **The Anita Kerr Quartet**) (see also **The Mexicali Singers**)

Anita Kerr has been operating various versions of her vocal group, the Singers, since te late 1940's when she moved to Nashville from her native Memphis.

- All You Need is Love (1967, Warner Brothers WS 1724)
- And Now… The Anita Kerr Orchestra (1966, Warner Brothers W 1640 (mono), WS 1640 (stereo))
- The Anita Kerr Singers (1975, RCA Victor APL1-1166)
- The Anita Kerr Singers Reflect on the Hits of Burt Bacharach & Hal David (1969, Dot DLP 25906)
- Bert Kaempfert Turns Us On! (1967, Warner Brothers W 1707 (mono), WS 1707 (stereo))
- For You (1969, Vocalion VL 73899)
- For You, For Me, Forevermore (1960, Decca DL 4061 (mono), DL 74061 (stereo))
- From Nashville… The Hit Sound (1962, RCA Victor LPM-2480 (mono), LSP-2480 (stereo))
- 'The Genius' in Harmony (1962, RCA Victor LPM-2581 (mono), LSP-2581 (stereo))
- Georgia On My Mind (1968, RCA Camden CAS-2209)
- Grow to Know Me (1971, Ampex A-10136)
- Mellow Moods of Love (1965, RCA Victor LPM-3322 (mono), LSP-3322 (stereo))
- Slightly Baroque (1966, Warner Brothers W 1665 (mono), WS 1665 (stereo))
- Sounds (1968, Warner Brothers – Seven Arts W 1750 (mono), WS 1750 (stereo))
- A Sunday Serenade (1966, RCA Victor LPM-3485 (mono), LSP-3485 (stereo))
- Tender Words (1963, RCA Victor LPM 2679 (mono), LSP 2679 (stereo))
- Til the End of Time (1970, Decca DL 75159)
- Velvet Voices and Bold Brass (1969, Dot DLP 25951)
- Voices in Hi-Fi (1958, Decca DL 8647)
- We Dig Mancini (1965, RCA Victor LPM-3428 (mono), LSP-3428 (stereo))
- Yestergroovin': Anita Kerr Presents Les Tres Guitars (1969, Dot DLP 25916)

Kime, Warren – see **The Brass Impact Orchestra**

King, Pete (aka **The Pete King Orchestra and Chorale**)

- Funny Girl (Pickwick SPC 3131)
- Hits of the Fabulous Fifties (Kapp KL-1179 (mono), KS-3063 (stereo))
- Intermezzo (1967, Dot DLP 25810)
- The Last of the Secret Agents? (1966, Dot DLP 3714 (mono), DLP 25714 (stereo)) Music from the film.
- Mind If I Make Love To You (1959, Warner Brothers W 1294 (mono), WS 1294 (stereo))
- Moon River (1961, Kapp Medallion ML-7533 (mono), MS-7533 (stereo); 1962, Kapp KS-3288)
- More Hits (1962, Kapp KL-1291)
- Music for the Girl You Love (Liberty LRP 3942)
- Percussion Concert (1961, Kapp KL-1256 (mono), KS-3256 (stereo))
- A Pocketful of Hits (1960, Kapp KL-1295; 1962, Kapp Medallion ML-7535 (mono), MS-7535 (stereo))
- The Sound of Music (Kapp KL-1175 (mono), KS-3059 (stereo); ML-7533)
- Wildcat (1961, Kapp KL-1223 (mono), KS-3223 (stereo)) Music from the musical.

King, Vaughn (with 'His Golden Saxophone and Magic Violins')

- Waltzing in Paradise (1964, Musicor MM 2002 (mono), MS 3002 (stereo))

King, Wayne and His Orchestra

- Dance Date (1965, Decca DL 4702 (mono), DL 74702 (stereo))
- Dance to Music from Hollywood and Broadway (Decca DL 4232)
- Dance Time With Wayne King (1964, Decca DL 4551 (mono), DL 74551 (stereo))
- Dance to the Music of Wayne King His Saxophone and Orchestra (1966, Vocalion VL 73772)
- Dance to the Songs Everybody Knows (1961, Decca DL 4111 (mono), DL 74111 (stereo))
- Dream a Little Dream of Me (Decca DL 75070)
- Dream Time (1958, Decca DL 8663 (mono), 78663 (stereo))
- Enchanted Evening (Decca DL 8277)
- The Eyes of Love (1967, Decca DL 4916 (mono), DL 74916 (stereo))
- Golden Favorites (1962, Decca DL 4309 (mono), DL 74309 (stereo))

- Golden Favorites, Vol. 2 (Decca DLP 75134; MCA MCA-281)
- Gypsy Caravan (1961, Decca DL 4128 (mono), DL 74128 (stereo))
- Isle of Golden Dreams (1957 Decca DL 8496 (mono), DL 78496 (stereo))
- Lady Esther Serenade (1960, Decca DL 8951 (mono), DL 78951 (stereo)) This album took its title from a radio show that King hosted for nearly a decade; it was sponsored by Lady Esther cosmetics.
- Let's Dance (1955, RCA Camden CAL-277)
- Linger Awhile (1969, Vocalion VL 73898)
- Listening Time (1960, Decca DL 8972 (mono), DL 78972 (stereo))
- Marvelous Medleys (1968, Decca DL 74988; MCA MCA-270)
- Melodies of Love (Decca DL 8124)
- Melody of Love (1955, RCA Victor LPM-1117)
- Moonlight and Roses (1966, Decca DL 74805)
- The Night is Young (1956, RCA Camden CAL-358)
- Our Language of Love (Decca DL 4630 (mono), DL 74630 (stereo))
- Serenade to a Lady (1956, RCA Victor LPM-1216)
- Smoke Gets In Your Eyes (1968, Vocalion VL 73840)
- Smooth As Silk (Decca DL 8353)
- Songs of the Islands (1960, Decca DL 4023 (mono), DL 74023 (stereo))
- The Sound of Wayne King (1959, Decca DL 8823 (mono), DL 78823 (stereo))
- The Sweetest Sounds (1963, Decca DL 4368 (mono), DL 74368 (stereo))
- Under Italian Skies (Decca DL 4233 (mono), DL 74233 (stereo))
- Waltz Dreams (Decca DL 8145)
- Wayne King in Hi Fi (Decca DL 8751 (mono), DL 78751 (stereo))
- Wayne King's Dance Medleys (Decca DL 4848 (mono), DL 74848 (stereo))

Kinney, Ray and His Coral Islanders (see also the Compilations section)
- Hawaii (1966, Sunset SUS-5135)
- Hawaiian Favorites (1957, RCA Camden CAL-229)
- Remember Waikiki (1957, Liberty LRP 3054)
- Sweet Hawaiian Moonlight (Vocalion VL 3687; as Ray Kinney and His Hawaiians)
- The Voice of Aloha (1966, RCA Victor LPM-3446 (mono), LSP-3446 (stereo))

Klein, John

- Around the World on a Carillon (1959, Columbia WL 135)
- Bells in Toyland (1967, RCA Victor LSP-3832)

Klein, John and Sid Ramin

- The New Sound America Loves Best (1960, RCA Victor LPM-2237 (mono), LSP-2237 (stereo))

Knightsbridge Strings, The

- Latin Cameos (1960, Top Rank International RM 315 (mono); RS 615 (stereo))
- The Strings Sing (1959, Top Rank International RM 603; stereo exist also?)

Knudson, Thurston (see also **Augie Goupil and Thurston Knudson**)

- Primitive Percussion: African Jungle Drums (1961, Reprise R-6001 (mono), R9-6001 (stereo)) For hardcore fans of African drumming only.

Kokee Band

- Exotica 1970 (1967, Solid State SM 17004 (mono), SS 18004 (stereo))
- Hawaii and Other Exotic Movie Themes (1967, Solid State SM 17010 (mono), SS 18010 (stereo))

Kona, Rex and His Mandarins

- Wild Orchids (1964, Columbia CL 2174 (mono), CS 8974 (stereo))

Kostelanetz, Andre

Kostelanetz was one of the giants of Easy Listening, with a career spanning two decades.

- Andre Kostelanetz Plays Chicago (1971, Columbia C 31002)
- Andre Kostelanetz Plays Great Hits of Today (1973, Columbia KC 32415)
- Andre Kostelanetz Plays Hits from Funny Girl, Finian's Rainbow, & Star! (1968, Columbia CS 9724)
- Be My Love (1970, Harmony H 30014)
- Calendar Girl (1956, Columbia CL 811)
- The Columbia Album of Richard Rodgers (1957, Columbia C2L-3) This was a 2-record set; apparently the next year this was split up to become the next two entries listed below.
- The Columbia Album of Richard Rodgers, Vol. 1 (1958, Columbia CL 1140)

- The Columbia Album of Richard Rodgers, Vol. 2 (1958, Columbia CL 1181)
- Everything is Beautiful (1970, Columbia C 30037)
- Flower Drum Song (1959, Columbia CL 1280 (mono), CS 8095 (stereo))
- For All We Know (1971, Columbia C 30672)
- For the Young At Heart (1968, Columbia CS 9691)
- Gershwin Wonderland (1964, Columbia CL 2133 (mono), CS 8933 (stereo))
- Greatest Hits of the 60's (1970, Columbia CS 9973)
- Gypsy Passion (1960, Columbia CL 1431 (mono), CS 8228 (stereo))
- I Wish You Love (1964, Columbia CL 2185 (mono), CS 8985 (stereo))
- I'll Never Fall in Love Again (1970, Columbia CS 9998)
- The Kostelanetz Sound of Today (1967, Columbia CL 2609 (mono), CS 9409 (stereo))
- Last Tango in Paris (1973, Columbia C 32187)
- The Lure of France (1958, Columbia CL 1054 (mono), CS 8111 (stereo))
- Lure of Paradise (1959, Columbia CL 1335 (mono), CS 8144 (stereo))
- Lure of the Tropics (1955, Columbia CL 780 (mono); Columbia Masterworks ML 4822)
- The Magic of Music (1968, Harmony HS 11281)
- Music of George Gershwin (1955, Columbia CL 770)
- New York Wonderland (1964, Columbia CL 2138 (mono), CS 8938 (stereo))
- Richard Rodgers (1972, Harmony KH 31579)
- Scarborough Fair and Other Great Movie Hits (1968, Columbia CS 9623)
- Shadow of Your Smile (1966, Columbia CL 2467 (mono), CS 9267 (stereo))
- Showstoppers (1965, Columbia Masterworks ML 6129 (mono), MS 6729 (stereo))
- Stardust (1955, Columbia CL 781; Columbia Masterworks ML 4597)
- Today's Golden Hits (1966, Columbia CL 2534 (mono), CS 9334 (stereo))
- Today's Great Movie Hits (1967, Columbia CS 9556)
- Traces (1969, Columbia CS 9823)
- Wonderland of Golden Hits (1963, Columbia CL 2039 (mono), CS 8839 (stereo))

- Wonderland of Sound: Broadway's Greatest Hits (1962, Columbia CL 1827 (mono), CS 8627 (stereo))
- "Wonderland of Sound": Today's Great Hits (1961, Columbia CL 1657 (mono), CS 8457 (stereo))

Kothari, Chim
- Sound of Sitar (1966, Deram DE 16001 (mono), DES 18001 (stereo)) This is exactly what it appears to be: popular songs played with the sitar as the main instrument, often taking the place of the original vocals. Interesting, but grating after a while.

La Blanc, Pierre and His Orchestra
- Academy Award Hits (1959, Mercury Wing SRW-12504)

La Delle, Jack
- Hawaiian Holiday in Hi-Fi (1958, Design DLP 53 (mono), SDLP 53 (stereo))

Lamond, Don and His Orchestra
- Off Beat Percussion (1962, Command RS 33-842 (mono), RS 842 SD (stereo))

Latin All Stars, The
- Jazz Heat Bongo Beat (1960, Crown CLP-5159 (mono), CST-187 (stereo))

Lawrence, Elliot and His Orchestra
- Dream With the Elliot Lawrence Orchestra (1956, Fantasy 3-226; originally released in red vinyl)
- Hi Fi-ing Winds (1958, Vik LX-1124)
- Music for Trapping (Tender, That Is) (Top Rank International RM 304)
- Winds on Velvet (Surrey S 1019 (mono), SS 1019 (stereo))

Lawrence, Richard
- Romantic Moods (Waldorf Music Hall MHK 33-1228)

Layton, Eddie (see also **Dick Contino and Eddie Layton**)
- Better Layton Than Never (1960, Mercury MG 20377 (mono), SR 60031 (stereo))
- Caravan (1959, Mercury MG 20426 (mono), SR 60098 (stereo); re-released 1964, Mercury Wing MGW 12273 (mono), SRW 16273 (stereo))
- Eddie Layton at the Mighty Wurlitzer (1959, Mercury MG 20433 (mono), SR 60105 (stereo))

- Eddie Layton Plays Lawrence Welk's Greatest Hits (1966, Epic BN 26215)
- Great Organ Hits (1961, Mercury MG 20639 (mono), SR 60639 (stereo))
- In the Mood (1959, Mercury MG 20471 (mono), SR 60153 (stereo))
- No Blues on This Cruise (1957, Mercury MG 20308)
- Organ Moods (1955, Wing MGW 12004)
- Organ Moods in Hi-Fi (1957, Mercury MG 20208)
- Skatin' With Layton (1960, Mercury MG 20498 (mono), SR 60258 (stereo))

Layton, Eddie and Buddy Morrow

- Just We Two (1958, Mercury MG 20372 (mono), SR 60018 (stereo))

Leahy, Joe and His Orchestra

- Lovely Lady (1956, RKO-Unique ULP-106)

Leander, Mike (aka **The Mike Leander Orchestra**)

- The Folk Hits (1965, London LL 3453 (mono), PS 453 (stereo))
- Privilege (1967, UNI 3005 (mono), 73005 (stereo)) Soundtrack to the film.
- A Time for Young Love (1969, Decca DL 75144)

Legrand, Michel and His Orchestra

- At Shelly's Manne-Hole (1968, Verve V6-8760)
- Cinema Legrand (1967, MGM SE-4491; MGM ST-91296 (record club))
- The Happy Ending (1969, United Artists UAS 5203) Music from the motion picture.
- I Love Paris (1954, Columbia CL 555)
- Legrand Piano (1960, Columbia CL 1441 (mono), CS 8237 (stereo))
- Love is a Ball (1963, Phillips PHM 200-082 (mono), PHS 600-082 (stereo)) Music from the motion picture.
- A Matter of Innocence (1967, Decca DL 9160 (mono), DL 79160 (stereo)) Music from the motion picture.
- Michael Legrand Big Band Plays Richard Rodgers (1963, Phillips PHM 200-074 (mono), PHS 600-074 (stereo))
- Rendez-Vous a Paris (1962, Phillips PHM 200-045 (mono), PHS 600-045 (stereo))
- Scarlet Ribbons: Michael Legrand's Folksongs for Orchestra (1959, Columbia CL 1338 (mono), CS 8146 (stereo))

- The Umbrellas of Cherbourg (1964, Phillips PCC 216 (mono), PCC 616 (stereo)) Music from the motion picture.

Leighton, Michael and His Orchestra

- The Sound of Strings (1960, Medallion ML-7502 (mono), MS-7502 (stereo))

Leilani, Luke (see also **Billy Mure**)

- Hawaiian Delights (Spin-O-Rama M-188 (mono), S-188 (stereo); Premier 1010; as Luke Leilani and His Hawaiian Delights)
- Hawaiian Enchantment (Spin-O-Rama MK-3040 (mono), S-26 (stereo); there were other releases as well; first song is "Hawaiian Wedding Song")
- Hawaiian Holiday (Spin-O-Rame MK-3040; Parade SP 315; re-released as *Holiday in Hawaii*; first song is "Red Sails on the Sunset") This was apparently a re-release of **Willie Alunuai and His Band**'s *Hawaiian Holiday*... or was this the original?
- Hawaiian Moonbeams (Premier PS-6002) Two-record set.
- Hawaiian Paradise (Coronet CX-264 (mono), CXS-264 (stereo); re-release of *Heavenly Hawaii*)
- Heavenly Hawaii (Spin-O-Rama M-100 (mono), S-100 (stereo); as Luke Leilani and His Hawaiians; re-released as *Hawaiian Paradise*; first song is "Hawaiian Blues")
- Holiday in Hawaii (Omega, OSL-123; re-release of *Hawaiian Holiday*)
- Lure of Hawaii (Sutton SSU 220; re-release of *Hawaiian Holiday*)
- Passport to Romance (Spin-O-Rama MK-3015; re-release of *Hawaiian Holiday*; as Luke Leilani and His Hawaiian Rhythm, often sometimes leading to this album being called *Hawaiian Rhythm*)

Lester, Sonny and His Orchestra

- After Hours: Italy (1963, Time 52095 (mono), S/2095 (stereo))
- After Hours: Middle East (1963, Time 52096 (mono), S/2096 (stereo))
- After Hours: New York (1964, Time 52097 (mono), S/2097 (stereo))
- After Hours: Paris (1963, Time 52093 (mono), S/2093 (stereo))
- After Hours: Spain (1963, Time 52094 (mono), S/2094 (stereo))
- How to Belly Dance for Your Husband (1963, Roulette R-25202 (mono), SR-25202 (stereo); reissue Roulette SR-42041) This came with a small instructional booklet, ostensibly by Little Egypt herself, on how to accomplish the enticing dance.
- How to Strip for Your Husband (1963, Roulette R-25186 (mono), SR-25186 (stereo); aka 'Ann Corio Presents'...) Stripping

instructional record for housewives, or at least the music to accompany the act; also included a small instructional booklet. Ann Corio was then popular because she had created the stage show *This Was Burlesque*.

- More How to Belly Dance for Your Husband, Vol. 2 (1963, Roulette R-25225 (mono), SR-25225 (stereo); aka 'Little Egypt Presents'...) This also came with an instructional pamphlet.

- More How to Strip for Your Husband, Vol. 2 (1963, Roulette R-25224 (mono), SR-25224 (stereo)) This too included an instructional pamphlet.

Lewis and Bernard (aka **The Twin Pianos of Lewis and Bernard**) **and The Limelight Strings**

- My Cup Runneth Over (Power S 416)

Liberace

- New Sounds (1966, Dot DLP 3755 (mono), DLP 25755 (stereo)) At the risk of having to go back and include the rest of Liberace's voluminous output, the author is including this album from the master showman as proof of just how far the **Tijuana Brass** influence truly spread: here are included "Tijuana Taxi," "Spanish Flea," and "A Taste of Honey." When even Liberace latches onto a musical trend, you know it's finally hit the big time.

Liberace, George and His Orchestra

"I wish my brother George was here."

- Dine and Dance with George Liberace at the Beverly Hilton (1959, Crown CLP-5141 (mono), CST-174 (stereo))

- George Liberace Goes Latin (1960, Crown CLP-5151 (mono), CST-181 (stereo))

- Goes Teenage (1957, Imperial LP 9039) No jokes, please.

- Hawaiian Paradise (1961, Crown CLP-5198 (mono), CST-218 (stereo))

- Ooh La La Liberace (1960, Crown CLP-5178 (mono), CST-203 (stereo))

Light, Enoch (**and His Orchestra**; **and the Light Brigade**) (see also the Compilations section; **Vincent Lopez**)

Whatever talents Enoch Light had as a composer and arranger, it was his efforts on the other side of the recording console that will keep his name in notoriety. After creating and then selling the Grand Award record label, Light started another brand in 1959, Command, under which he would oversee the production of records that sought to take full advantage of the new stereo recording techniques. He would also later start a third label, Project 3 Total Sound.

- 12 Smash Hits (1968, Project 3 Total Sound PR 5021 SD; as The Enoch Light Singers)

- 1963 – The Year's Most Popular Themes (1963, Command RS 33 854 (mono), RS 854 SD (stereo))
- All the Things You Are (Grand Award GA 33-399)
- Around the World in 80 Days (Grand Award GA 214-SD)
- Beatles Classics (1974, Project 3 Total Sound PRS 5084)
- The Best of Hollywood: Movie Hits '68-'69 (1968, Project 3 Total Sound PR 5027 SD)
- The Best of the Movie Themes 1970 (1970, Project 3 Total Sound PR 5046 SD)
- Big Band Bossa Nova (1962, Command RS 33 844 (mono), RS 844 SD (stereo))
- Big Bold and Brassy (1960, Command RS 33 818 (mono), RS 818 SD (stereo))
- Big Brass & Percussion (Coronet CX-169 (mono), CXS-169 (stereo))
- Big Hits of the Seventies (1974, Project 3 Total Sound PR2 6003/4 SD) Two-record set.
- The Brass Menagerie 1973 (1972, Project 3 Total Sound PR 5060 SD)
- Command Performances (1964, Command RS 868 SD; was this available in mono?)
- Command Performances, Vol. 2 (1967, Command RS 915 SD)
- Dimension '3' (1964, Command RS 867 SD)
- Discotheque: The Discotheque Dance Album (1966, Command RS 33 892 (mono), RS 892 SD (stereo))
- Discotheque Dance... Dance... Dance (1964, Command RS 33-873 (mono), RS 873 SD (stereo))
- Discotheque Dance... Dance... Dance, Vol. 2 (1965, Command RS 882 SD)
- Enoch Light and the Brass Menagerie (1969, Project 3 Total Sound PR 5036 SD)
- Enoch Light and the Brass Menagerie, Vol. 2 (1969, Project 3 Total Sound PR 5042 SD)
- Enoch Light and the Glittering Guitars (1969, Project 3 Total Sound PR 5038 SD)
- Enoch Light and the Light Brigade Play Pops (Diplomat DS 2261 (mono), FM 98 (stereo))
- Familiar Songs From Foreign Lands (1973, Command RSSD 976-2)
- Far Away Places (1961, Command RS 33 822 (mono), RS 822 SD (stereo))
- Far Away Places, Vol. 2 (1963, Command RS 850 SD; no mono version?)

- Film Fame: Marvelous Movie Themes (1967, Project 3 Total Sound PR 5013 SD)
- Film on Film: Great Movie Themes (1966, Project 3 Total Sound PR 5005 SD)
- Future Sound Shock (1973, Project 3 Total Sound PR 5077 SD)
- Great Themes From Hit Films (1962, Command RS 33-835 (mono), RS 835 SD (stereo))
- Great Themes From Hit Films Recorded in Command's Dimension 3 Process (1964, Command RS 33-871 (mono), RS 871 SD (stereo))
- Happy Cha Cha's, Vol. 2 (1959?, Grand Award GA 33-391)
- I Want to Be Happy Cha Cha's (1959, Grand Award GA 33-388 (mono), GA 222 SD (stereo))
- Impelling Dances of Our Times (1973, Command RSSD 979-2) Two-record set.
- It's Happening... So Let's Dance! (1967, Project 3 Total Sound PR 5004 SD)
- Let's Dance the Bossa Nova (1963, Command RS 33 851 (mono), RS 851 SD (stereo))
- Magnificent Movie Themes (1965, Command RS 887 SD)
- The Million Dollar Sound of the World's Most Precious Violins (1959, Command RS 33 802 (mono), RS 802 SD (stereo))
- Movie Hits (1972, Project 3 Total Sound PR 5063 SD)
- Musical Explorations in Sound (1973, Command RSSD 970-2; as Enoch Light & The Command All-Stars)
- My Musical Coloring Book (1963, Command RS 33-848 (mono), RS 848 SD (stereo))
- A New Concept of Great Cole Porter Songs (1965, Command RS 879 SD)
- The Original Persuasive Percussion & Other Catalytic Sounds (1973, Command RSSD 960-2; as The Command All-Stars)
- Paperback Ballet (1963, Command RS 805 SD) This was a re-release of *The Private Life of a Private Eye*.
- The Paris I Love (1956, Grand Award GA 33-338)
- Permissive Polyphonics (1970, Project 3 Total Sound PR 5048 SD)
- Persuasive Percussion, Vol. 3 (Command RS 33 817 (mono), RS 817 SD (stereo); as The Command All-Stars)
- Persuasive Percussion, Vol. 4 (1962, Command ; as Enoch Light and the Command All Stars)
- Pertinent Percussion Cha-Cha's (1960, Command RS 33-814 (mono), RS 814 SD (stereo))

- Presenting Enoch Light (Tiara TMT 7540)
- The Private Life of a Private Eye (1959, Command RS 33-805 (mono), RS 805 SD (stereo); re-released as *Paperback Ballet*)
- Provocative Percussion (1959, Command RS 33 806 (mono), RS 806 SD (stereo); as The Command All-Stars)
- Provocative Percussion, Vol. 2 (1960, Command RS 33 810 (mono), RS 810 SD (stereo))
- Provocative Percussion, Vol. 3 (1961, Command RS 33 817 (mono), RS 817 SD (stereo))
- Provocative Percussion, Vol. 4 (1962, Command RS 33 834 (mono), RS 834 SD (stereo))
- Provocative Stereo Sounds of Our Time (1973, Command RSSD 981-2) Two-record set.
- Reeds and Percussion (1961, Command RS 33 820 (mono); RS 820 SD (stereo); as The Command All-Stars)
- Something To Remember You By (1959, Grand Award GA 33-410 (mono), GA 242 SD (stereo); as Enoch Light and His Vibrant Strings)
- The Sound of Strings (re-issue of The Million Dollar Sound of the World's Most Precious Violins, Vol. 2)
- Spaced Out (1968, Project 3 Total Sound PR 5043 SD)
- Spanish Strings (1966, Project 3 Total Sound PR 5000 SD)
- Stereo 35/MM (1961, Command RS 33 826 (mono), RS 826 SD (stereo))
- Stereo 35/MM, Vol. 2 (1961, Command RS 33 831 (mono), RS 831 SD (stereo))
- Tempestuous Latin Dance (1973, Command RSSD 974-2; as Enoch Light and The Command All-Stars with Bobby Byrne)
- Vibrations (1962, Command RS 33 833 (mono), RS 833 SD (stereo))
- Whoever You Are, I Love You (1968, Project 3 Total Sound PR 5030 SD; as The Enoch Light Singers)
- With My Eyes Wide Open I'm Dreaming (1960, Grand Award GA 238 SD)
- Young At Heart (Ambassador S/98050)

Light, Enoch Orchestra and The Fontanna Orchestra

- Sentimental... (Masterseal M-703)

Limelight Strings, The (see also **Lewis and Bernard and The Limelight Strings**)

- The Sound of Jerome Kern: All the Things You Are (Power S 421)

- The Sound of Music: Broadway's Best Loved Melodies (Power S 417)

Living Brass

The Living Brass, Living Strings, Living Guitars, etc., were all various groups of musicians gathered for recording sessions under the supervision of the bigwigs of RCA Camden, RCA's lower-end record label.

- A Henry Mancini Tribute (1967, RCA Camden CAS-2162)
- The Horse / Grazing in the Grass and Other Hits (1969, RCA Camden CAS-2297)
- In A Little Spanish Town (1967, RCA Camden CAS-2114)
- Knock Three Times and Other Hits (1971, RCA Camden CAS-2494)
- Living Brass Play Songs Made Famous by Aretha Franklin (1969, RCA Camden CAS-2396)
- Living Brass Play Songs Made Famous by Tom Jones (1969, RCA Camden CAS-2346)
- Mexican Shuffle (1965, RCA Camden CAL-907 (mono), CAS-907 (stereo))
- Mexico Lindo (1968, RCA Camden CAS-2197)
- Music from The Graduate and Other Simon and Garfunkel Hits (1969, RCA Camden CAS-2323)
- A Taste of Honey and Other Favorites (1966, RCA Camden CAL-949 (mono), CAS-949 (stereo))
- That's Life (1967, RCA Camden CAS-2143)
- What Now, My Love and Other Favorites (1966, RCA Camden CAL-996 (mono), CAS-996 (stereo))

Living Brass and Living Marimbas

- Living Brass & Living Marimbas Play Songs Made Famous by Herb Alpert (1969, RCA Camden CAS-2337)
- Mexico (1971, RCA Camden CAS-2485)

Living Guitars

- Am I That Easy to Forget (1973, RCA Camden ADL2-0305) Two-record set.
- The Big Guitar Sound (1963, RCA Camden CAL-766 (mono), CAS-766 (stereo))
- Dedicated to the One I Love (1967, RCA Camden CAS-2156)
- 'Flamingo' and Other Favorites (1967, RCA Camden CAS-2123)
- Guitar Man (1968, RCA Camden CAS-2245)

- The Heart and Soul of Italy (1970, RCA Camden CAS-2389)
- Let It Be and Other Hits (1970, RCA Camden CAS-2425)
- Living Guitars Play (1963, RCA Camden CAL-733 (mono), CAS-733 (stereo))
- Living Guitars Play Songs Made Famous by The Rolling Stones (1971, RCA Camden CAS-2521)
- Music from The Pink Panther and Other Hits (1964, RCA Camden CAL-827 (mono), CAS-827 (stereo))
- Ring Dang Doo (1966, RCA Camden CAL-940 (mono), CAS-940 (stereo))
- Rock 'n Roll with the Living Guitars (1970, RCA Camden CAS-2410)
- San Franciscan Nights (1968, RCA Camden CAS-2192)
- Shindig (1964, RCA Camden CAL-844 (mono), CAS-844 (stereo))
- Somewhere There's A Someone (1966, RCA Camden CAL-978 (mono), CAS-978 (stereo))
- Teen Beat Discotheque (1965, RCA Camden CAL-884 (mono), CAS-884 (stereo))

Living Jazz

- 'Dear Heart' and Other Favorites (1965, RCA Camden CAL-878 (mono), CAS-878 (stereo))
- The Fool on the Hill (1969, RCA Camden CAS-2298)
- The Girl from Ipanema and Other Hits (1964, RCA Camden CAL-848 (mono), CAS-848 (stereo))
- Hot Butter & Soul (1970, RCA Camden CAS-2436)
- A Lover's Concerto (1966, RCA Camden CAL-985 (mono), CAS-985 (stereo))
- Manha de Carnival (1973, RCA Camden ACL 1-0202)
- An Ode to Young Lovers (1968, RCA Camden CAS-2196)
- Quiet Nights (1965, RCA Camden CAL-914 (mono), CAS-914 (stereo))
- The Soul of Brazil (1967, RCA Camden CAS-2137)

Living Marimbas

- Georgy Girl and Other Music to Watch Girls By (1967, RCA Camden CAS-2149)
- Latin Soul (1966, RCA Camden CAL-2105 (mono), CAS-2105 (stereo))
- Love is Blue (1968, RCA Camden CAS-2253)
- Raindrops Keep Fallin' On My Head (1970, RCA Camden CAS-2400)

- Spanish Harlem and Other Hits (1971, RCA Camden CAS-2541)
- Sugar, Sugar (1970, RCA Camden CAS-2432)
- Tijuana Taxi (1966, RCA Camden CAL-961 (mono), CAS-961 (stereo))
- Tonight Carmen and Other Favorites (1967, RCA Camden CAL-2184 (mono), CAS-2184 (stereo))
- Zorba the Greek (1969, RCA Camden CAS-2308)

Living Percussion

- The Beat Goes On (1969, RCA Camden CAS-2255)

Living Series, The (aka **Living Brass**, **Living Strings**, **Living Voices**, **Living Marimbas**)

- From Hollywood With Love (1972, RCA Victor PRS-407)
- Great Hollywood Hits of the 60's (1967, RCA Camden CCM-0007 (mono), CCS-0007 (stereo))
- Happy Hits for Easy Listening (RCA Camden CCS-0671)
- Living Series Sampler (RCA DJL1-2417) This was a record used for demonstration only, and wasn't sold to the public.
- A Salute to the Tijuana Brass (1967, RCA Camden CCM-0008 (mono), CCS-0008 (stereo))
- Soft Lights and Sweet Music (1972, RCA Victor PRS-408)

Living Strings

- Airport Love Theme and Other Motion Picture Themes (1970, RCA Camden CAS-2420)
- At A Sidewalk Café (1963, RCA Camden CAL-762 (mono), CAS-762 (stereo))
- Bouquet of Roses (1967, RCA Camden CAS-2154)
- 'Charade' and Other Film Hits (1964, RCA Camden CAL-799 (mono), CAS-799 (stereo))
- Ebb Tide and Other Favorites (1969, RCA Camden CAS-2291)
- Everybody Loves Somebody (1965, RCA Camden CAL-864 (mono), CAS-864 (stereo))
- Finian's Rainbow (1968, RCA Camden CAS-2263)
- For Lovers Only (1973, RCA Camden CXS-9030) Two-record set.
- Hawaiian Memories (1970, RCA Camden CAS-2373)
- He Touched Me and Other Beautiful Songs (1966, RCA Camden CAL-951 (mono), CAS-951 (stereo))
- Holiday For Strings (1963, RCA Camden CAL-760 (mono), CAS-760 (stereo))

- Holiday For Two (1967, RCA Camden CCM-0010 (mono), CCS-0010 (stereo))
- I'm a Believer and Other Monkees' Hits (1966, RCA Camden CAL-2148 (mono), CAS-2148 (stereo))
- In a Mellow Mood (1962, RCA Camden CAL-709 (mono), CAS-709 (stereo)) The music on this album was actually arranged and conducted by **Juan Esquivel**.
- In the Still of the Night (1964, RCA Camden CAL-795 (mono), CAS-795 (stereo))
- Living Strings Play All the Music from Camelot (1961, RCA Camden CAL-657 (mono), CAS-657 (stereo))
- Living Strings Play All the Music from the Broadway Hit 'Carnival' (1961, RCA Camden CAL-678 (mono), CAS-678 (stereo))
- Living Strings Play Bert Kaempfert Hits (1969, RCA Camden CAS-2303)
- Living Strings Play Favorites Made Famous Again (1971, RCA Camden CAS-2453)
- Living Strings Play Henry Mancini (1963, RCA Camden CAL-736 (mono), CAS-736 (stereo))
- Living Strings Play Hit Motion Picture Themes (1962, RCA Camden CAL-673 (mono), CAS-673 (stereo))
- Living Strings Play Music For Romance (1960, RCA Camden CAL-637 (mono), CAS-637 (stereo))
- Living Strings Play Music from Gone With the Wind and Other Motion Pictures (1967, RCA Camden CAS-2161)
- Living Strings Play Music from Popi and Other Cinema Gems (1969, RCA Camden CAS-2364)
- Living Strings Play Music from the Motion Picture Camelot (1966, RCA Camden CAL-988 (mono), CAS-988 (stereo))
- Living Strings Play Music from West Side Story (1969, RCA Camden CAS-2313)
- Living Strings Play Music in the Night (1960, RCA Camden CAL-638 (mono), CAS-638 (stereo))
- Living Strings Play Music of Hawaii (1966, RCA Camden CAL-661 (mono), CAS-661 (stereo))
- Living Strings Play Music of the Sea (1960, RCA Camden CAL-639 (mono), CAS-639 (stereo))
- Living Strings Play South of the Border (1962, RCA Camden CAL-682 (mono), CAS-682 (stereo))
- Living Strings Plus Trumpet Play Music For Young Lovers (1963, RCA Camden CAL-739 (mono), CAS-739 (stereo))

- Living Strings Plus Two Pianos Play Songs That Will Live Forever (1962, RCA Camden CAL-721 (mono), CAS-721 (stereo))
- Living Strings Plus Two Pianos Play the Most Beautiful Music in the World (1962, RCA Camden CAL-687 (mono), CAS-687 (stereo))
- Marie (1966, RCA Camden CAL-962 (mono), CAS-962 (stereo))
- Melody of Love (1964, RCA Camden CAL-830 (mono), CAS-830 (stereo))
- Music from Doctor Zhivago and Other Motion Pictures (1967, RCA Camden CAS-2133)
- Music from Faraway Places (1967, RCA Camden CCS-0001)
- Music from Fiddler on the Roof (1968, RCA Camden CAS-2234)
- Music from 'The Sound of Music' (1965, RCA Camden CAL-869 (mono), CAS-869 (stereo))
- Music to Help You Stop Smoking (1964, RCA Camden CAL-821 (mono), CAS-821 (stereo)
- New From Broadway (1963, RCA Camden CAL-790 (mono), CAS-790 (stereo))
- Night Themes (1963, RCA Camden CAL-755 (mono), CAS-755 (stereo))
- Nostalgia (1971, RCA Camden CAS-2505)
- On A Sentimental Journey (1964, RCA Camden CAL-803 (mono), CAS-803 (stereo))
- The Shimmering Sounds of Living Strings (1963, RCA Camden CAL-761 (mono), CAS-761 (stereo))
- A Song of Joy and Other Favorites (1970, RCA Camden CAS-2441)
- Songs of the Swingin' Sixties (1970, RCA Camden CAS-2397)
- Songs to Remember (1965, RCA Camden CAL-857 (mono), CAS-857 (stereo))
- Souvenir D'Italie (1962, RCA Camden CAL-696 (mono), CAS-696 (stereo))
- Sunrise Serenade (1962, RCA Camden CAL-688 (mono), CAS-688 (stereo))
- The Sweetheart Tree and Other Film Favorites (1965, RCA Camden CAL-926 (mono), CAS-926 (stereo))
- Three O'Clock in the Morning (1965, RCA Camden CAL-915 (mono), CAS-915 (stereo))
- Too Beautiful for Words (1964, RCA Camden CAL-791 (mono), CAS-791 (stereo))
- Twilight Time (1966, RCA Camden CAL-930 (mono), CAS-930 (stereo); with **Bob Ralston**)

- When Irish Eyes Are Smiling (1965, RCA Camden CAL-859 (mono), CAS-859 (stereo))
- Where Did the Night Go (1963, RCA Camden CAL-738 (mono), CAS-738 (stereo))

Living Strings and Living Voices

- The Greatest Music Ever Sung (1963, RCA Camden CAL-730 (mono), CAS-730 (stereo))
- 'Mona Lisa' and Other Memorable Songs (1965, RCA Camden CAL-902 (mono), CAS-902 (stereo))
- What the World Needs Now is Love (1972, RCA Camden CAS-2542)
- The Windmills of Your Mind and Other Academy Award Winners (1969, RCA Camden CAS-2319)
- With a Happy Beat (1964, RCA Camden CAL-837 (mono), CAS-837 (stereo))

Living Trio

- Ballad of Easy Rider and Other Hits (1970, RCA Camden CAS-2401)
- Come Saturday Morning (1970, RCA Camden CAS-2437)
- Heart of My Heart (1967, RCA Camden CAL-2124 (mono), CAS-2124 (stereo))
- Honey and Other Hits (1968, RCA Camden CAS-2265)
- Love Theme from Romeo and Juliet (1969, RCA Camden CAS-2340)
- TV and Motion Picture Music (1968, RCA Camden CAS-2210)

Living Voices

- Angel of the Morning (1969, RCA Camden CAS-2307)
- Come to the Fair (1964, RCA Camden CAL-812 (mono), CAS-812 (stereo))
- Hootenanny Favorites (1963, RCA Camden CAL-786 (mono), CAS-786 (stereo))
- How Now, Dow Jones (1968, RCA Camden CAS-2189)
- Living Voices On Broadway (1962, RCA Camden CAL-692 (mono), CAS-692 (stereo))
- Living Voices Sing Indian Love Call (1962, RCA Camden CAL-697 (mono), CAS-697 (stereo))
- Living Voices Sing Irish Songs (1961, RCA Camden CAL-665 (mono), CAS-665 (stereo))
- Living Voices Sing Songs of Moonlight and Romance (1962, RCA Camden CAL-683 (mono), CAS-683 (stereo))

- Moonglow and Other Great Standards (1964, RCA Camden CAL-804 (mono), CAS-804 (stereo))
- Music from Mary Poppins (1965, RCA Camden CAL-881 (mono), CAS-881 (stereo))
- Music from The Happiest Millionaire (1967, RCA Camden CAS-2164)
- Music from the Motion Picture The Singing Nun (1966, RCA Camden CAL-974 (mono), CAS-974 (stereo))
- Nancy with the Laughing Face (1968, RCA Camden CAS-2240)
- Positively 4th Street and Other Message Folk Songs (1966, RCA Camden CAL-947 (mono), CAS-947 (stereo))
- Ramblin' Rose and Other Hits (1963, RCA Camden CAL-748 (mono), CAS-748 (stereo))
- Sing Along with the Living Voices (1962, RCA Camden CAL-712 (mono), CAS-712 (stereo))
- Smoke Gets In Your Eyes (1963, RCA Camden CAL-764 (mono), CAS-764 (stereo))
- Song Fest: Fun at Home (1962, RCA Camden CAL-714 (mono), CAS-714 (stereo))
- Wish Me a Rainbow (1967, RCA Camden CAL-2147 (mono), CAS-2147 (stereo))

Lockyer, Malcolm and His Orchestra

Most of this English pianist and bandleader's output was released in his native country.

- The Seasons of Love (1957, Mercury MG 20205)

Loco, Joe (**and His Band**; **Orchestra**; **Quintet**)

- Calypso Dance (1957, Mercury MG 20302)
- Cha Cha Cha (1959, Fantasy 3277 (mono), 8022 (stereo); apparently released in both red and black vinyl)
- Dance! (1966, Sunset SUM-1133 (mono), SUS-5133 (stereo); as Joe Loco and His Pachanga Band)
- Goin' Loco (1955, Tico LP 1006; also released as *Mambo Moods*, with different cover artwork)
- Happy-Go-Loco (1959, Imperial LP 9073 (mono), LP 12019 (stereo))
- Joe Loco – His Piano and Rhythm (1957, Ansonia ALP 1221)
- Latin Jewels (1960, Fantasy 3294 (mono), 8041 (stereo); released in red and black vinyl)
- Let's Go Loco (1959, Imperial LP 9070 (mono), LP 12014 (stereo))
- Loco Motion (1955, Columbia CL 760)
- Make Mine Mambo (1955, Tico LP 1008)

- Mambo Fantasy (1956, Tico LP 1012)
- Mambo Moods (1955, Tico LP 1006; also released as *Goin' Loco*, with different cover artwork)
- Ole! Ole! Ole! Ole! (1959, Fantasy 3285 (mono), 8028 (stereo))
- Pachanga Twist (1962, Imperial LP 9166 (mono), LP 12079 (stereo))
- Puerto Rico '68 (1968, Sunset SUS-5219)
- Rockin' Cha (1958, Mercury MG 20373)
- Vaya! (1956, Columbia CL 827)
- Viva Mambo (1956, Tico LP 1013)

Londonderry Strings, The

- The Londonderry Strings Play the Liverpool Songbook (1964, Warner Brothers W 1580 (mono), WS 1580 (stereo))

Lopez, Miguel and His Orchestra

- Latin Favorites (1957?, Craftsmen C8015) Mary Tyler Moore is the model for the cover of this budget gem.

Lopez, Vincent

- Come Saturday Morning (Ambassador S 98096)
- Lopez Playing (1960, CL 1433 (mono), CS 8229 (stereo))
- Music Out Of Century 21 (1962, World's Fair Records XTV 82023) 'An official souvenir of the Seattle World's Fair.'
- The Theme From Love Story (Ambassador S 98100)

Lopez, Vincent and Enoch Light and Their Orchestras

- Moments to Remember (1958, Waldorf Music Hall MHK 33-1214) Jayne Mansfield is featured on the cover of this album.

Lorber, Alan (aka **The Alan Lorber Orchestra**)

- The Lotus Palace (1967, Verve V6-8711)

Los Admiradores

Similar to the **Command All Stars**, this studio group was sort of a heavy-hitter collection of musicians brought together just for these recordings.

- Bongos (aka Bongos Bongos Bongos) (1959, Command RS 33 809 (mono), RS 809 SD (stereo))
- Bongos Flutes Guitars (1960, Command RS 33 812 (mono), RS 812 SD (stereo))

Los Bandidos

- Tijuana Beat: That Happy Tijuana Sound (Oscar OS-110) Given that this includes the word 'Tijuana' in the title and features the songs "A Taste of Honey" and "Whipped Cream," it's safe to say that this was another attempt to cash in on the popularity of Herb Alpert's **Tijuana Brass**.

- Tijuana Beat, Vol. 2 (Oscar OS-132)

Los Cinco Caballeros

- Latin Hurricane (1960, Crown CLP-5184 (mono), CST-209 (stereo))

Los Indios Tabajaras

This was actually two guitarist brothers from Brazil, who (at least early on in their career) dressed in 'traditonal' costumes to perform.

- Always in My Heart (1964, RCA Victor LPM-2912 (mono), LSP-2912 (stereo))

- The Fascinating Rhythms of Their Brazil (1968, RCA Victor LSP-3905)

- The Many-Splendored Guitars of Los Indios Tabajaras (1965, RCA Victor LPM-3413 (mono), LSP-3413 (stereo))

- Maria Elena (1964, RCA Victor LPM-2822 (mono), LSP-2822 (stereo))

- The Mellow Guitar Moods of Los Indios Tabajaras (1964, RCA Victor LPM-2959 (mono), LSP-2959 (stereo))

- Popular and Folk Songs of Latin America (1957, Vox STPL 515-080)

- Softly, As in a Morning Sunrise (1972, RCA Victor FSP-310)

- Sweet and Savage (1958, RCA Victor LPM-1788 (mono), LSP-1788 (stereo))

- Their Very Special Touch (1967, RCA Victor LPM-3723 (mono), LSP-3723 (stereo))

- Twin Guitars – In a Mood for Lovers (1966, RCA Victor LPM-3611 (mono), LSP-3611 (stereo))

- The Very Thought of You (1971, RCA Victor LSP-4496)

- What the World Needs Now (1971, RCA Victor LSP-4615)

Los Norte Americanos

This was a house band for Somerset (and later Alshire) created specifically to cash in on the popularity of the **Tijuana Brass**'s sound.

- The Band I Heard in Tijuana (1966, Somerset S-246 (mono), SF-24600 (stereo)) Also cheekily titled *The Brass I Heard in Tijuana*; this might have been the original title and changed due to threat of legal action by A&M.

- The Band I Heard in Tijuana, Vol. 2 (1967, Somerset S-257 (mono), SF-25700 (stereo))
- The Band I Heard in Tijuana, Vol. 3 (1968, Somerset S-284 (mono), SF-28400 (stereo))
- More Happy Tijuana Sounds (Alshire S-5178)
- The Tijuana Sound: Los Norte Americanos Go British (Alshire S-5165)

Lowe, Mundell (and His All Stars) (see also **Gene Bianco**)
- Guitar Moods (1956, Riverside RLP 12-208)
- Porgy & Bess (1959, RCA Camden CAL-490 (mono), CAS-490 (stereo))
- TV Action Jazz! (1959, RCA Camden CAL-522 (mono), CAS-522 (stereo))
Themes from Mr. Lucky, The Untouchables, and Other TV Action Jazz (1960, RCA Camden CAL-627 (mono), CAS-627 (stereo))

Luboff, Norman (aka **The Norman Luboff Choir**)
- Aloha from Norman Luboff (1963, RCA Victor LPM-2602 (mono), LSP-2602 (stereo))
- Apasionada (1961, RCA Victor LPM-2341 (mono), LSP-2341 (stereo))
- Blues – Right Now! (1965, RCA Victor LPM-3312 (mono), LSP-3312 (stereo))
- Broadway! (1958, Columbia CL 1110 (mono), CS 8052 (stereo))
- But Beautiful (1959, Columbia CL 1296 (mono), CS 8114 (stereo))
- Calypso Holiday (1957, Columbia CL 1000)
- A Choral Spectacular (1962, RCA Victor LPM-2522 (mono), LSP-2522 (stereo))
- Easy to Remember (1955, Columbia CL 545)
- Grand Tour (1963, RCA Victor LPM-2521 (mono), LSP-2521 (stereo))
- Great Movie Themes (1964, RCA Victor LPM-2895 (mono), LSP-2895 (stereo))
- Greensleeves (1965, Harmony HL 7343 (mono), HS 11143 (stereo))
- Just a Song… (1956, Columbia CL 890)
- The Latin Luboff (1966, RCA Victor LPM-3637 (mono), LSP-3637 (stereo))
- Moments to Remember (1960, Columbia CL 1423 (mono), CS 8220 (stereo))
- Moonglow (Harmony H 30935)

- Remember (1965, RCA Victor LPM-3400 (mono), LSP-3400 (stereo))
- Reverie (1959, Columbia CL 1256 (mono), CS 8074 (stereo))
- Serenade (1967, Harmony HL-7406 (mono), HS-11206 (stereo))
- Side By Side (1967, RCA Camden CAL-2129 (mono), CAS-2129 (stereo))
- Sing! It's Good For You (1962, RCA Victor LPM-2475 (mono), LSP-2475 (stereo))
- Sleepy Time Songs / Wide Awake Songs (1958, Columbia CL 1179) This album had two 'front' covers, with one of the titles on each.
- Songs of the British Isles (1959, Columbia CL 1348 (mono), CS 8157 (stereo))
- Songs of the Caribbean (1959, Columbia CL 1357; did this come out only in mono?)
- Songs of the World (1958, Columbia C2L 13) Two-disc set.
- Songs of the World, Vol. 1 (1958, Columbia CS 8140) This was a release of the first album from the previous entry, sold separately...
- Songs of the World, Vol. 2 (1958, Columbia CS 8141) ...and this was the second album from that set.
- This is Norman Luboff! (1961, RCA Victor LPM-2342 (mono), LSP-2342 (stereo))
- Windows of the World (1969, Columbia Musical Treasuries P2S 5310) Two-disc set.
- You're My Girl (1961, RCA Victor LPM-2368 (mono), LSP-2368 (stereo))

Luboff, Norman Choir and The Melachrino Strings

- Sentimental Memories (1970, Longines Symphonette Society SYS 5229)

Lush Strings

- Autumn Leaves (1960, Custom CM-2009 (mono), CS-1009 (stereo))
- Ebb Tide (1960, Custom C-2013 (mono), CS-1013 (stereo))
- Fascination (1960, Custom CM-2012 (mono), CS-1012 (stereo))
- The Heart of Spain (1960, Custom CM-2020 (mono), CS-1020 (stereo))
- Holiday For Strings (Custom CM-2063 (mono), CS-1063 (stereo))
- Imagination (1960, Custom CM-2008 (mono), CS-1008 (stereo))
- Lush Strings Play for Listening (1967, Custom CM-2064 (mono), CS-1064 (stereo))

- Moon of Manakoora (Custom CS-1006) Note: This album has the same basic cover and catalog number as *Sweet Leilani and Other Hawaiian Favorites* below, but a completely different song list.

- More Lush Strings For Lovers (1967, Custom CS-1067)

- Old Favorites (1967, Custom CS-1066)

- Spellbound (Custom CM-2007 (mono), CS-1007 (stereo))

- Stormy Weather (1960, Custom CM-2014 (mono), CS-1014 (stereo))

- Sweet Leilani and Other Hawaiian Favorites (Custom CM-2006 (mono), CS-1006 (stereo)) Note: This album has the same basic cover and catalog number as *Moon of Manakoora* above, but a completely different song list.

- Theme From Goldfinger (Custom CM-2032 (mono), CS-1032 (stereo))

Lyman, Arthur

One of the giants of exotica, Arthur Lyman was practically destined for success in the genre. His family moved to Hawaii when he was a boy, and he took up the vibraphone as his chosen instrument. As a young man he played on Martin Denny's seminal *Exotica* album, and would soon go on to a solo career during which he and Denny would compete for record sales – but the two men remained friends until Lyman's death in 2002.

- Aloha, Amigo (1966, HiFi L-1034 (mono), SL-1034 (stereo))

- Aphrodesia (1968, HiFi SL-1038)

- Arthur Lyman at the Port of Los Angeles (1967, HiFi SL-1036)

- Arthur Lyman on Broadway (1959, HiFi R-818 (mono), SR-818 (stereo))

- Bahia (1959, HiFi R-815 (mono), SR-815 (stereo))

- Blowin' in the Wind (1964, HiFi L-1014 (mono), SL-1014 (stereo))

- Bwana A (1959, HiFi R-808 (mono), SR-808 (stereo))

- Call of the Midnight Sun (1965, HiFi L-1024 (mono), SL-1024 (stereo))

- Cast Your Fate To The Wind (1965, GNP Crescendo GNP-607 (mono), GNPS-607 (stereo))

- The Colorful Percussions of Arthur Lyman (1962, HiFi L-1005 (mono), SL-1005 (stereo))

- Cotton Fields (1963, HiFi L-1010 (mono), SL-1010 (stereo))

- The Exotic Sounds of Arthur Lyman at the Crescendo (1963, GNP Crescendo GNP-605 (mono), GNP-605S (stereo))

- Hawaiian Sunset (1959, HiFi R-807 (mono), SR-807 (stereo))

- Hawaiian Sunset, Vol. 2 (1965, HiFi L-1025 (mono), SL-1025 (stereo))

- I Wish You Love (1963, HiFi L-1009 (mono), SL-1009 (stereo); also released as *Love For Sale!* with the same catalog number)
- Ilikai (1967, HiFi L-1035 (mono), SL-1035 (stereo))
- Isle of Enchantment (1964, HiFi L-1023 (mono), SL-1023 (stereo))
- Latitude 20 (1967, HiFi SL-1027)
- The Legend of Pele (1959, HiFi R-813 (mono), SR-813 (stereo))
- Leis of Jazz (1959, HiFi R-607 (mono), SR-607 (stereo))
- Love For Sale! (1963, HiFi L-1009 (mono), SL-1009 (stereo); also released as *I Wish You Love* with the same catalog number)
- Lyman '66 (1966, HiFi L-1031 (mono), SL-1031 (stereo))
- The Many Moods of Arthur Lyman (1962, HiFi L-1007 (mono), SL-1007 (stereo))
- Paradise (1964, GNP Crescendo GNP-606 (mono), GNPS-606 (stereo); also W-90038; also released as *Pearly Shells* with the same GNP(S)-606 catalog number)
- Pearly Shells (1964, GNP Crescendo GNP-606 (mono), GNPS-606 (stereo); also released as *Paradise* with (sometimes, apparently) the same catalog number)
- *Percussion Spectacular* (1961, HiFi L-1004 (mono), SL-1004 (stereo); a retitling of *Yellow Bird* with the same catalog number)
- Polynesia (1965, HiFi L-1027 (mono), SL-1027 (stereo))
- Puka Shells (1975, GNP Crescendo GNPS-901) 'Introducing Kapiolani' – apparently Arthur brought his lovely daughter into the band as a singer and musician during this time.
- The Shadow of Your Smile (1966, HiFi L-1033 (mono), SL-1033 (stereo))
- Taboo (1958, HiFi R-806 (mono), SR-806 (stereo))
- Taboo, Vol, 2 (1960, HiFi R-822 (mono), SR-822 (stereo))
- Today's Greatest Hits (1969, HiFi SL-1040)
- The Winner's Circle (1969, HiFi SL-1039)
- *Yellow Bird* (1961, HiFi L-1004 (mono), SL-1004 (stereo); also released as *Percussion Spectacular* with the same catalog number, as well as several other re-releases)

MacCormick, Franklyn and The Russ Garcia Orchestra

- The Torch is Burning (1958, Liberty LRP 3086 (mono), LST 7086 (stereo)) The vocalist is credited as 'The poetic voice of…' because he doesn't actually *sing* the lyrics, he recites them in a heartfelt and passionate manner. Which is fine, but for an entire album? Russ Garcia and his boys are impeccable as usual.

Machito and His Orchestra

- Asia Minor Cha Cha Cha (1964, Forum F 9043 (mono), SF 9043 (stereo))
- Kenya Afro Cuban Jazz (1958, Roulette R-52006 (mono), SR-52006 (stereo))
- Mi Amigo, Machito (1958, Tico LP 1053 (mono), SLP 1053 (stereo))
- The New Sound of Machito (1963, Tico LP 1084 (mono), TRSLP 1084 (stereo))
- A Night Out (1960, Tico LP 1074 (mono), SLP 1074 (stereo))
- Si-Si, No-No (1958, Tico LP 1033 (mono), SLP 1033 (stereo))
- Soul of Machito (1968, Cotique C/CS-1019)
- The World's Greatest Latin Band (1962, GNP Crescendo GNP 72 (mono), GNPS 72 (stereo))

Magnante, Charles, His Accordion and Orchestra

- Accordion Bellicosity (1973, Command RSSD 971-2) Two-record set.
- Accordiana (1957, Harmony HL 7014)
- Carnival in Far Away Places (1957, Command RS 33 907 (mono), RS 907 SD (stereo))
- Fiesta! (1964, Command RS 33 869 (mono), RS 869 SD (stereo))
- Holiday in Paris (1962, Waldorf Music Hall MHK 33-1218)
- Moods For Moderns (1959, Grand Award GA 33 413 (mono), GA 245 SD (stereo))
- Percussion Italiano (1961, Grand Award GA 33 426 (mono), GA 257 SD (stereo))
- Roman Accordion (1963, Command RS 33 852 (mono), RS 852 SD (stereo))
- Roman Carnival (1962, Grand Award GA 33 429 (mono), GA 260 SD (stereo))
- Roman Spectacular (1956?, Grand Award GA 33 205 (mono), GA 205 SD (stereo); first song is "Oh Marie"; re-released in 1966 – or was "Oh Marie" only the first song on the re-release?)
- Roman Spectacular (1957, Grand Award GA 33 361; first song is "Tarantella Calabrese"; different selection of songs from previous version)
- Roman Spectacular (ABC-Paramount ABC-489 (mono), ABCS-489 (stereo); first song is "Nel blu dipinto di blu"; the cover back says it is a re-release of the Grand Award GA 205 SD version; this version contains the same song selection, but in a different order)
- Roman Spectacular, Vol. 2 (Grand Award GA 33 374 (mono), GA 233 SD (stereo))

- Romantic Accordion (1965, Command RS 33 888 (mono), RS 888 SD (stereo))
- Spanish Spectacular (Command RS 33 379 (mono), GA 212 SD (stereo))

Magne, Michel and His Orchestra
- Tropical Fantasy (1962, Columbia CL 1693 (mono), CS 8493 (stereo))

Makamia and His Moana Islanders
- Holiday in Hawaii (1957, Remington R-199-244)

Makia, Sam
- Hawaii: The Fabulous Fiftieth State (1959, Kapp KL-1144 (mono), KS-3027 (stereo); 'Hawaii in Stereo' for the stereo version; 'With Orchestra Directed by **Frank Hunter**'; as Sam Makia and the Makapuu Beach Boys)
- Hawaiian Favorites (Springboard 4064)
- Hawaiian Island Magic (1965, Forum Circle FC-9087 (mono), FCS-9087 (stereo); as Sam Makia and His Surf Riders) The stereo version of this was apparently retitled to *The Magic of Hawaii.*
- How to Hula at Home: 15 Hawaiian Favorites (Musicor MM 2013 (mono), MS 3013 (stereo); as Sam Makia and His Royal Islanders)
- Live Hawaiian Party (Tifton TS 83; as Sam Makia and His Hawaiian Islanders)
- The Lure of Hawaii (1961, Riverside RLP 7503 (mono), RLP 97503 (stereo); as Sam Makia and His Islanders)
- The Magic of Hawaii (Forum Circle FCS-9087; as Sam Makia and His Surf Riders) This is apparently the stereo version of *Hawaiian Island Magic.*
- Music of the Islands: Hawaiian Holiday (Mercury MG 20158; as Sam Makia and His Waikikians)
- Songs of the Islands (Surrey S-1035 (mono), SS-1035 (stereo); as Sam Makia and His Islanders)

Mancini, Henry

Henry Mancini's big breakthrough came when Blake Edwards asked him to provide music for Edwards's new TV series, *Peter Gunn*. The music was an instant hit with viewers, so an album of music from the soundtrack was quickly put out and proved instantly successful. Another big success came with Edwards's film *Breakfast At Tiffany's*, for which Mancini wrote the tune "Moon River." Mancini went on to become one of the most successful film music composers of all time, and was also a dominating force on the record charts throughout the 1960's.

- Academy Award Songs, Vol. 2 (RCA Victor PRS-175; created as a premium for B.F. Goodrich)
- Arabesque (1966, RCA Victor LPM-3623 (mono), LSP-3623 (stereo))
- The Big Latin Band of Henry Mancini (1968, RCA Victor LSP-4049)
- The Blues and the Beat (1960, RCA Victor LPM-2147 (mono), LSP-2147 (stereo))
- Breakfast at Tiffany's (1961, RCA Victor LPM-2362 (mono), LSP-2362 (stereo)) Music from the film.
- Charade (1963, RCA Victor LPM-2755 (mono), LSP-2755 (stereo)) Music from the film.
- Combo! (1961, RCA Victor LPM-2258 (mono), LSP-2258 (stereo))
- The Concert Sound of Henry Mancini (1964, RCA Victor LPM-2897 (mono), LSP-2897 (stereo))
- Days of Wine and Roses & Others (1973, RCA Camden ACL 7035; re-released on Pickwick ACL-7035)
- Dear Heart and Other Songs About Love (1965, RCA Victor LPM-2990 (mono), LSP-2990 (stereo))
- Debut! (1969, RCA Red Seal LSC-3106; with The Philadelphia Orchestra Pops)
- Dream Of You (1971, RCA Camden CAS-2510)
- Driftwood and Dreams (Liberty LRP-3049; re-release of *The Versatile Henry Mancini and His Orchestra*)
- Encore! More of the Concert Sound of Henry Mancini (1967, RCA Victor LPM-3887 (mono), LSP-3887 (stereo))
- Experiment in Terror (1962, RCA Victor LPM-2442 (mono), LSP-2442 (stereo))
- Gaily, Gaily (1969, United Artists UAS-5202) Music from the film.
- The Great Race (1965, RCA Victor LPM-3402 (mono), LSP-3402 (stereo)) Music from the film.
- Gunn... Number One! (1967, RCA Victor LPM-3840 (mono), LSP-3840 (stereo)) Music from the film *Gunn*.
- Hangin' Out (1974, RCA Victor CPL-1-0672)

- Hatari! (1962, RCA Victor LPM-2559 (mono), LSP-2559 (stereo)) Music from the film.

- The Hawaiians (1970, United Artists UAS-5210) Music from the film.

- Henry Mancini Presents the Academy Award Songs (1966, RCA Victor LPM-6013 (mono), LSP-6013 (stereo))

- Henry Mancini Favorites (1964, Crown CLP 5459 (mono), CST 459 (stereo))

- His Sound is His Signature (1969, RCA SPS-33-557) This was a promotional album given to radio stations, consisting mostly of interviews with Mancini; side 2 also interspersed a couple of his more famous songs into the mix.

- The Latin Sound of Henry Mancini (1965, RCA Victor LPM-3356 (mono), LSP-3356 (stereo))

- Mancini '67 (1967, RCA Victor LSP-3694)

- Mancini Concert (1971, RCA Victor LSP-4542)

- Mancini Plays Mancini and Other Composers (1967, RCA Camden CAL-2158 (mono), CAS-2158 (stereo))

- Mancini Plays the Great Academy Award Songs (1964, RCA Victor PRM-151 (mono), PRS-151 (stereo))

- Mancini Plays the Theme from Love Story (1970, RCA Victor LSP-4466)

- The Mancini Sound (1968, RCA Victor LPM-3943 (mono), LSP-3943 (stereo)) 'Special Club Edition' on cover. Was this distributed differently?

- The Mancini Touch (1960, RCA Victor LPM-2101 (mono), LSP-2101 (stereo))

- Me, Natalie (1969, Columbia OS 3350; with Rod McKuen) Music from the film.

- The Molly Maguires (1970, Paramount PAS-6000) Music from the film.

- More Music from Peter Gunn (1959, RCA Victor LPM-2040 (mono), LSP-2040 (stereo)) Music from the TV series.

- Mr. Lucky Goes Latin (1961, RCA Victor LPM-2360 (mono), LSP-2360 (stereo))

- Music from Mr. Lucky (1960, RCA Victor LPM-2198 (mono), LSP-2198 (stereo)) Music from the TV series.

- *The Music from Peter Gunn* (1959, RCA Victor LPM-1956 (mono), LSP-1956 (stereo)) Music from the TV series. An absolute classic of the Crime Jazz genre.

- Music from the Motion Picture Score 'High Time' (1960, RCA Victor LPM-2314 (mono), LSP-2314 (stereo) Music from the film.

- Music of Hawaii (1966, RCA Victor LPM-3713 (mono), LSP-3713 (stereo))

- Our Man in Hollywood (1963, RCA Victor LPM-2604 (mono), LSP-2604 (stereo))
- The Party (1968, RCA Victor LPM-3997 (mono), LSP-3997 (stereo)) Music from the film.
- The Pink Panther (1963, RCA Victor LPM-2795 (mono), LSP-2795 (stereo)) Music from the film.
- The Second Time Around and Others (1966, RCA Camden CAL-928 (mono), CAS-928 (stereo))
- Six Hours Past Sunset (1969, RCA Victor LSP-4239)
- The Sounds & Voices of Henry Mancini (1966, Sunset SUM-1105 (mono), SUS-5105 (stereo))
- Sunflower (1970, Avco Embassy AVE-0-11001) Music from the film.
- Symphonic Soul (1975, RCA Victor APL1-1025)
- Theme From "Z" and Other Film Music (1970, RCA Victor LSP-4350)
- Touch of Evil (1958, Challenge LP-602) Music from the film.
- Two for the Road (1967, RCA Victor LPM-3802 (mono), LSP-3802 (stereo)) Music from the film.
- Uniquely Mancini (1963, RCA Victor LPM-2692 (mono), LSP-2692 (stereo))
- The Versatile Henry Mancini and His Orchestra (1959, Liberty LRP-3121 (mono), LST-7121 (stereo); re-released as *Driftwood and Dreams*)
- A Warm Shade of Ivory (1969, RCA Victor LSP-4140)
- What Did You Do in the War, Daddy? (1966, RCA Victor LPM-3648 (mono), LSP-3648 (stereo)) Music from the film.
- The Wild Side of Henry Mancini (1962, Challenge CH 615)

Mancini, Henry and Doc Severinsen

- Brass On Ivory (1972, RCA Victor LSP-4629)

Mann, George (aka **The George Mann Orchestra featuring The Golden Trumpet**)

- Music to Watch Girls By (1968, CST-573)

Mann, Johnny Singers (see also **Si Zentner and The Johnny Mann Singers**)

- At Our Best (1969, Sunset SUS-5288)
- Ballads of the King (1961, Liberty LRP-3198 (mono), LST-7198 (stereo)) The Singers interpret songs originally done by Elvis Presley...
- Ballads of the King: The Songs of Sinatra (1961, Liberty LRP-3217 (mono), LST-7217 (stereo)) ...and Frank Sinatra.
- Beatle Ballads (1964, Liberty LRP-3391 (mono), LST-7391 (stereo))

- Daydream (1966, Liberty LRP-3447 (mono), LST-7447 (stereo))
- Don't Look Back (1967, Liberty LRP-3535 (mono), LST-7535 (stereo))
- Flowing Voices of the Johnny Mann Singers (1966, Sunset SUM-1115 (mono), SUS-5115 (stereo))
- Golden Folk Song Hits (1962, Liberty LRP-3253 (mono), LST-7253 (stereo))
- Golden Folk Song Hits, Vol. 2 (1963, Liberty LRP-3296 (mono), LST-7296 (stereo))
- Golden Folk Song Hits, Vol. 3 (1964, Liberty LRP-3355 (mono), LST-7355 (stereo))
- Golden Mann (1969, Liberty LST-7629)
- Goodnight My Love (1969, Liberty LST-7620)
- Heart Full of Song (1968, Sunset SUS-5196)
- If I Loved You, and Other Hits of the Day (1965, Liberty LRP-3411 (mono), LST-7411 (stereo))
- I'll Remember You (1966, Liberty LRP-3436 (mono), LST-7436 (stereo))
- Invisible Tears (1964, Liberty LRP-3387 (mono), LST-7387 (stereo))
- Love is Blue (1968, Liberty LST-7553)
- A Man and a Woman (1966, Liberty LRP-3490 (mono), LST-7490 (stereo))
- Midnight Special (Liberty L2S 5204) 'Exclusive release for Columbia Record Club.'
- Night (1956, Liberty LRP-3021) Two enticing album covers exist for this release; one features a woman sitting in a sheer neglgee, the other shows a nude woman smoking, partially in shadow.
- Roses and Rainbows (1965, Liberty LRP-3422 (mono), LST-7422 (stereo))
- Stand Up and Sing (1973, Longines Symphonette Society LS-306-A) Five-disc set.
- Stand Up and Cheer (1973, Columbia KE-31954) This album took its title from a syndicated musical variety show of the time which was hosted by Johnny Mann and featured his Singers; it lasted for three seasons between 1971 and 1974.
- This Guy's In Love With You, The Look of Love (1968, Liberty LST-7587)
- We Can Fly! Up-Up and Away (1967, Liberty LRP-3523 (mono), LST-7523 (stereo))

Mann, Sy and Nick Tagg

- 2 Organs & Percussion (1961, Grand Award GA 33-425 (mono), GA 256 SD (stereo))

Mantovani

Mantovani was a giant of the Easy Listening genre, whose music never strayed far from the lush but unadventurous 'Mantovani Sound' that the artist perfected early in his recording career.

- All-American Showcase (1959, London LL 3122/3133 (mono), PS 165/166 (stereo)) Two-disc set.
- Bravo! Mantovani (London SS-11)
- Candlelight (1956, London LL 1502)
- Continental Encores (1959, London LL 3004 (mono), PS 147 (stereo))
- Film Encores (1957, London LL 1700 (mono), 1959, London PS 124 (stereo))
- Film Encores, Vol. 2 (1959, London LL 3117 (mono), PS 164 (stereo))
- From Monty, With Love (1971, London XPS 585/586) Two-disc set.
- Gems Forever (1958, London 3032 (mono), PS 106 (stereo))
- Hollywood (1967, London LL 3516 (mono), PS 516 (stereo))
- The Incomparable Mantovani (1964, London LL 3392 (mono), PS 392 (stereo))
- Italia Mia (1961, London LL 3239 (mono), PS 232 (stereo))
- Latin Rendezvous (1963, London LL 3295 (mono), PS 295 (stereo))
- Manhattan (1963, London LL 3328 (mono), PS 328 (stereo))
- Mantovani Magic (1966, London LL 3448 (mono), PS 448 (stereo))
- Mantovani Ole (1965, London LL 3422 (mono), PS 422 (stereo))
- Mantovani Plays Music from Exodus and Other Great Themes (1960, London LL 3231 (mono), PS 224 (stereo))
- The Mantovani Scene (1969, London PS 548)
- The Mantovani Sound – Big Hits from Broadway and Hollywood (1965, London LL 3419 (mono), PS 419 (stereo))
- Mantovani Today (1970, London PS 572)
- The Mantovani Touch (1968, LL 3526 (mono), PS 526 (stereo))
- Memories (1969, PS 542)
- Moon River and Other Great Film Themes (1962, London LL 3261 (mono), PS 249 (stereo))
- The Most Beautiful Mood Music in the World (1965, London *nn*) Four-album set. This collected four previous Mantovani albums in

stereo: *Gems Forever*, *Continental Encores*, *American Waltzes*, and *Latin Rendezvous*.

- Mr. Music... (1966, London LL 3474 (mono), PS 474 (stereo))
- The Music of Victor Herbert (1953, London LL 746)
- Romantic Melodies (1954, London LL 979)
- Showcase (1959, London MS 5 (mono), SS 1 (stereo))
- Song Hits From Theatreland (1955, London LL 1219 (mono); 1959, London PS 125 (stereo))
- Songs to Remember (1960, London LL 3149 (mono), PS 193 (stereo))
- Stop the World – I Want to Get Off / Oliver! (1962, London LL 3270 (mono), PS 270 (stereo))
- Theme from Carnival and Other Great Broadway Hits (1961, London LL 3250 (mono), PS 242 (stereo))
- To Lovers Everywhere (1971, London XPS 598)
- The Wonderful World of Melody (London SS-10)
- The World of Mantovani (1969, London PS 565)
- The World's Favorite Love Songs (1957, London LL 1748)

Manzanilla Sound, The

This trumpet-heavy instrumental music was what supermarkets throughout America sounded like from the late 60's to the mid-70's.

- Make Mine Manzanilla (1972, GNP Crescendo GNPS 2062)
- The Manzanilla Sound (1968, GNP Crescendo GNPS 2058)

Mariachi Brass, The ('featuring Chet Baker')

This was a hastily-assembled group put together to mimic the sound (and success) of the **Tijuana Brass**; the difference here was the inclusion of jazz great Chet Baker in the band, which the record label was careful to highlight.

- Double Shot (1966, World Pacific WP-1852 (mono), WPS-21852 (stereo))
- Hats Off (1966, World Pacific WP-1842 (mono), WPS-21842 (stereo))
- In the Mood (1966, World Pacific WP-1859 (mono), WPS-21859 (stereo))
- A Taste of Tequila (1966, World Pacific WP-1839 (mono), WPS-21839 (stereo))

Marimba Chiapas

- Marimbas Mexicanas (1957, Capitol T-10043)
- Marimbas South of the Border (1964, Capitol T-10358 (mono), ST-10358 (stereo))

- Mexican Marimba Music (1959, Capitol T-10183)

Marino, Richard

- The Magic Beat! The Unique Rhythms of Richard Marino (1961, Liberty LMM 13003 (mono), LSS 14003 (stereo))
- *Out of This World* (1961, Liberty LMM 13007 (mono), LSS 14007 (stereo)) The epitome of Space Age pop, this album incorporates retro-futuristic sound effects with lush orchestration.

Mark, Paul and His Orchestra

- 12-1/2 Geishas Must Be Right (1963, Sounds of Hawaii SHS 5010; as Paul Mark and His Orchestra and the Geishas)
- East to West (1961, Imperial LP 9120 (mono), LP 12057 (stereo))

Markko Polo Adventurers, The

An effort by the record company to cater to the then-current craze for exotica, *Orienta* offers a dizzying storybook of songs and sounds meant to evoke faraway ports and foreign shores. Put together by industry professionals, the album mixes the familiar and the exotic, in both music and sound effects, into a dazzling tour de force.

- *Orienta* (1959, RCA Victor LPM-1919 (mono), LSP-1919 (stereo))

Marowitz, Sam

- Sounds in the Night (1958, Roulette R 25099 (mono), SR 25099 (stereo))

Marshall, Jack

- Soundsville! (1959, Capitol T-1194 (mono), ST-1194 (stereo))

Marshall, Jack and Shelly Manne

- Sounds! (1966, Capitol T-2610 (mono), ST-2610 (stereo))
- Sounds Unheard Of! (1962, Contemporary M5006 (mono), S9006 (stereo))

Marterie, Ralph (**and His Orchestra/His Marlboro Men**) (see also **Al Caiola and Ralph Marterie**)

- Alone Together (1954, Mercury MG 20054; this was apparently re-released the next year as *Music for Smoochin'*)
- Music for a Private Eye (1959, Mercury MG 20437 (mono), SR 60109 (stereo); Mercury Wing MGW 12238 (mono), SRW 16238 (stereo))
- Music for Smoochin' (1955, Mercury MG 20054; this was a re-release of 1954's *Alone Together*)

Martin, Freddy and His Orchestra

- As Time Goes By (1964, Capitol T-2347 (mono), ST-2347 (stereo))
- Best of the New Favorites (1965, Capitol T-2098 (mono), ST-2098 (stereo))
- C'Mon Let's Dance! (1961, Capitol T-1269 (mono), ST-1269 (stereo))
- Dancing Party (1956, RCA Camden CAL-264)
- Dancing Tonight (1963, Kapp KL-1286 (mono), KS-3286 (stereo))
- Freddy Martin at the Cocoanut Grove (1957, RCA Victor LPM-1414)
- Freddy Martin in Hi-Fi (Capitol W-900)
- Freddy Martin Plays the Hits, Vol. 2 (1964, Capitol T-2163 (mono), ST-2163 (stereo); this was a re-release of *Salute to the Smooth Bands*)
- In a Sentimental Mood (1962, Capitol T-1889 (mono), ST-1889 (stereo))
- Lush and Latin (1958, Capitol T-998)
- Make Believe (1957, RCA Camden CAL-315)
- Midnight Music (1957, RCA Victor LPM-1360)
- The Most Beautiful Girl... (1966, Kapp KL-1490 (mono), KS-3490 (stereo))
- Most Requested (1967, Decca DL 4839 (mono), DL 74839 (stereo))
- Salute to the Smooth Bands (1959, Capitol T-1116 (mono), ST-1116 (stereo); re-released as *Freddy Martin Plays the Hits, Vol. 2*)
- Seems Like Old Times (1961, Capitol T-1486 (mono), ST-1486 (stereo))
- Shall We Dance? (1956, RCA Victor LPM-1160)
- Tonight We Love (1963, Capitol T-2018 (mono), ST-2018 (stereo))

Martin, Ray and His Orchestra (aka **Ray Martin and His Picadilly Strings**)

- Comic Strip Favorites (1966, RCA Camden CAL-2102 (mono), CAS-2102 (stereo))
- Dancing After Dark (1962, Strand SL 1037 (mono), SLS 1037 (stereo))
- Dynamica (1961, RCA Victor LSA-2287) (Stereo Action)
- Excitement, Incorporated (1962, RCA Victor LSA-2422) (Stereo Action)
- Global Hop (1957, Capitol T-10101)
- Goldfinger and Other Music from James Bond Thrillers (1965, RCA Camden CAL-913 (mono), CAS-913 (stereo))
- International Vibrations (1957, Capitol T-10066)

- Love of My Life (1959, Imperial LP 9083 (mono), LP 12018 (stereo))
- Martin Goes Latin (1959, Imperial LP 9087 (mono), LP 12022 (stereo))
- Michelle Going for Baroque (1966, RCA Camden CAL-976 (mono), CAS-976 (stereo))
- Rainy Night in London (1956, Capitol T-10017)
- The Rockin' Strings of Ray Martin (1959, RCA Victor LPM-2130 (mono), LSP-2130 (stereo))
- The Sound of Sight (1964, London SP 44040) The album cover artwork was done by Jack Davis.
- Thunderball and Other Thriller Music (1965, RCA Camden CAL-927 (mono), CAS-927 (stereo))
- Up-Up and Away (1967, RCA Camden CAS-2181)
- Witchcraft...! (1958, Jubilee JGM 1055)

Martin, Skip (and **The Video All-Stars**) (see also **The Video All-Stars**)
- 8 Brass 5 Sax 4 Rhythm (1959, MGM E3743 (mono), SE3743 (stereo))
- Dance to Swingin' Things from Can-Can (1961, Somerset P-12400 (mono), SF-12400 (stereo))
- The Music from Mickey Spillane's Mike Hammer (1959, RCA Victor LPM-2140 (mono), LSP-2140 (stereo))
- Perspectives in Percussion, Vol. 1 (1961, Somerset P-13200 (mono), SF-13200 (stereo))
- Perspectives in Percussion, Vol. 2 (1961, Somerset P-13300 (mono), SF-13300 (stereo))
- Scheherajazz (1959, Somerset P-9700 (mono), SF-9700 (stereo)) This album was an odd attempt to combine modern jazz notions with a full symphony orchestra to do a unique interpretation of a classical work. The result doesn't quite work for some listeners, while others find it very satisfying. Either way, it's interesting.
- Songs and Sounds from the Era of The Untouchables (1958, Somerset P-12900 (mono), SF-12900 (stereo); as Skip Martin and His Prohibitionists)
- Swingin' With Prince Igor (1962, Somerset P-16000 (mono), SF-16000 (stereo)) More melding of jazz and classical music.

Martinelli, Louis and the Continentals
- Arrivaderci Roma (1964, Crown CLP-5441 (mono), CST-441 (stereo))
- Cocktails for Two (1959, Crown CLP-5096 (mono), CST-126 (stereo))

- L'amore D'Italia (1960, Crown CLP-5165 (mono), CST-193 (stereo); stereo version pressed on both black and red vinyl)
- Latin Twist (1960, Crown CLP-5171 (mono), CST-197 (stereo))

Martinez, Willie and His Orchestra
- I Could Have Cha Cha'd All Night (1958, Decca DL 8694)

Marx, Harpo
- Harpo at Work! (1958, Mercury MG 20263 (mono), SR 60016 (stereo); each has a different cover) Yes, this is Harpo of the Marx brothers, who really could play the harp and does so on these releases of standards.
- Harpo in Hi-Fi (1957, Mercury MG 20232)

Mathews, Mat
- Come Travel With Me (1959, ABC-Paramount ABC 269)
- Mat Mathews With the Surrey Strings (Surrey S 1020 (mono), SS 1020 (stereo))

Mauriat, Paul and His Orchestra (see also **Baden Powell**)
This French orchestra leader produced smooth Easy Listening music for years; his big breakthrough was a cover of "Love is Blue" in 1968.
- Blooming Hits (1967, Phillips PHM 200-248 (mono), PHS 600-248 (stereo))
- Doing My Thing (1969, Phillips PHS 600-292)
- El Condor Pasa (1971, Phillips PHS 600-352)
- From Paris With Love (1967, Mercury Wing SRW 16403)
- Gone is Love (1970, Phillips PHS 600-345)
- Listen Too! (1965, Phillips PHM 200-197 (mono), PHS 600-197 (stereo))
- L.O.V.E. (1969, Phillips PHS 600-320)
- Love Theme from The Godfather (1972, MGM SE4838)
- Mauriat Magic (1968, Phillips PHS 600-270)
- Midnight Cowboy / Let the Sunshine In (1970, Phillips PHS 600-337)
- More Mauriat (1967, Phillips PHM 200-226 (mono), PHS 600-226 (stereo))
- Of Vodka and Caviar (1966, Phillips PHM 200-215 (mono), PHS 600-215 (stereo))
- Paris By Night (Fantasy Fant 8380)
- Prevailing Airs (1969, Phillips PHS 600-280)
- The Soul of Paul Mauriat (1969, Phillips 600-299)

- Theme from A Summer Place (1972, MGM/Verve MV 5087)
Actress Angela Cartwright is featured on this album's cover.

Mauu, Charles and The Royal Polynesians

- Polynesia! Native Songs and Dances from the South Seas (1954, Capitol T-483)

Maxin, Ernest and His Orchestra

- F#... Where There is Music (1959, Top Rank International RM 307 (mono), RS 607 (stereo))
- The Nearness of You (1969?, Altair 35783)
- With My Love (1960?, Top Rank International RM 321 (mono), RS 621 (stereo))

Maxwell, Robert and His Orchestra

- Harpistry in Rhythm (1972, Command RS 932-S)
- Let's Get Away From It All (1966, Decca DL 4723 (mono), DL 74723 (stereo))
- Music to Make You Starry-Eyed (1957, MGM E-3571)
- Peg O' My Heart (1964, Decca DL 4563 (mono), DL 74563 (stereo))
- Shangri-La (1963, Decca DL 4421 (mono), DL 74421 (stereo); re-released as *Bewitched* with the same catalog number)
- A Song For All Seasons (1965, Decca DL 4609 (mono), DL 74609 (stereo))

May, Billy and His Orchestra (see also **Verlye Mills and Billy May**; **Jack Webb**)

A naturally talented arranger as well as a composer, Billy May enjoyed a wide-ranging career, including being part of Glenn Miller's orchestra, to backing Sinatra on his classic *Come Fly With Me* album, to producing records for children. May also started the earlier 'Brass Movement' (not the later Tijuana-themed one) with his album *Billy May's Big Fat Brass* in 1958. Creative, dynamic, and seemingly everywhere one cares to look, May is one of the most important figures mentioned in this book.

- Arthur Murray: Cha Cha Mambos (1955, Capitol T-578; as Billy May's Rico Mambo Orchestra)
- Arthur Murray Favorites: Mambos (Capitol T-261; as The Rico Mambo Orchestra)
- Bill's Bag (1964, Capitol T-1888 (mono), ST-1888 (stereo))
- Billy May Plays for Fancy Dancin' (1956, Capitol T-771)
- Billy May Today! (1966, Capitol T-2560 (mono), ST-2560 (stereo))
- Billy May's Bacchanalia! (1955, Capitol T-374)

- Billy May's Big Fat Brass (1958, Capitol T-1043 (mono), ST-1043 (stereo))
- Cha Cha! (1960, Capitol T-1329 (mono), ST-1329 (stereo))
- The Fuzzy Pink Nightgown (1957, Imperial LP-9042) Music from the film.
- The Girls and Boys on Broadway (1960, Capitol T-1418 (mono), ST-1418 (stereo))
- The Green Hornet (1966, 20th Century Fox 3186) Music from the TV series.
- Hey, It's May (1962, Pickwick/33 PC-3010 (mono), SPC-3010 (stereo); as Billy May & His Big Band)
- Johnny Cool (1963, United Artists UAL 4111 (mono), UAS 5111 (stereo)) Music from the film.
- Music For Uptight Guys (1967, Stereo Sounds SA-12)
- No Strings (1962, Capitol T-1709 (mono), ST-1709 (stereo))
- Pow! (1960, Capitol T-1377 (mono), ST-1377 (stereo))
- Process 70 (1962, Time 52064 (mono), S/2064 (stereo))
- Sorta-May (1955, Capitol T-562)

McEachern, Murray

- Caress (1957, Capitol T-899)
- Music for Sleepwalkers Only (1956, Key LP-711)

McFarland, John

- Provocatif (1959, United Artists UAL 4053)

McIntire, Lonnie

- Hawaiian Moonlight (Pickwick/33 SPC-3038)

Medallion Strings, The

- The Sound of Hollywood (1960, Kapp Medallion ML-7513 (mono), MS-7513 (stereo))
- The Sound of Musical Pictures (1960, Kapp Medallion ML-7501 (mono), MS-7501 (stereo))

Melachrino, George and His Orchestra (aka **The Melachrino Strings**) (see also **The Norman Luboff Choir and The Melachrino Strings**)

Robert Melachrino was one of the most important creators within the Easy Listening genre.

- All the Hits from Oliver! (1963, RCA Victor LPM-2660 (mono), LSP-2660 (stereo); music from the stage musical)
- The Ballads of Irving Berlin (1962, RCA Victor LPM-2817 (mono), LSP-2817 (stereo))

- Bells Are Ringing (1960, RCA Victor LPM-2279 (mono), LSP-2279 (stereo))
- Lisbon at Twilight (1958, RCA Victor LPM-1762 (mono), LSP-1762 (stereo))
- Love Story (1970, Pickwick SPC-3263)
- Love Walked In (1970, Pickwick SPC-3234; as The Now Melachrino Strings)
- The Magic of the Melachrino Strings (1952, Vocalion VL 73808)
- Masquerade (1956, RCA Victor LPM-1184)
- Melachrino on Broadway (1963, RCA Victor LPM-1307)
- More Music for Dining (1962, RCA Victor LPM-2412 (mono), LSP-2412 (stereo))
- More Music for Relaxation (1961, RCA Victor LPM-2278 (mono), LPS-2278 (stereo))
- Music for Courage and Confidence (1953, RCA Victor LPM-1005)
- Music for Daydreaming (1954, RCA Victor LPM-1028)
- Music for Dining (1952, RCA Victor LPM-1000; later re-released in stereo also)
- Music for Reading (1958, RCA Victor LPM-1002 (mono), LSP-1002 (stereo))
- Music for Relaxation (1958, RCA Victor LPM-1001 (mono), LSP-1001 (stereo))
- Music for Romance (1964, RCA Victor LPM-2979 (mono), LSP-2979 (stereo))
- Music for the Nostalgic Traveler (1955, RCA Victor LPM-1053)
- Music for Two People Alone (1954, RCA Victor LPM-1027)
- The Music of Jerome Kern (1961, RCA Victor LPM-2283 (mono), LSP-2283 (stereo))
- The Music of Rodgers and Hammerstein (1962, RCA Victor LPM-2513 (mono), LSP-2513 (stereo))
- Music from Lionel Bart's Oliver! (1968, RCA Camden CAS-2282)
- Music to Help You Sleep (1958, RCA Victor LPM-1006 (mono), LSP-1006 (stereo))
- Music to Work or Study By (1954, RCA Victor LPM-1029)
- The New Sound of Broadway (1965, RCA Victor LPM-3323 (mono), LSP-3323 (stereo))
- Our Man in London (1963, RCA Victor LPM-2608 (mono), LSP-2608 (stereo))
- Something to Remember You By (1965, RCA Victor LPM-3398 (mono), LSP-3398 (stereo))

- You and the Night and the Music (1964, RCA Victor LPM-2866 (mono), LSP-2866 (stereo))

Melavano and His Orchestra

- My Memories (1957, Argo LP 619)

Melis, Jose

- At Midnight (1959, Seeco CELP-414 (mono), CELP-4140 (stereo))
- Bon Amigo (Seeco B-23764)
- The Exciting Jose Melis (1958, Harmony HL 7150)
- Jose Melis and the Metropolitan Strings (Diplomat 2260)
- Jose Melis in Movieland (1961, Mercury MG 20648 (mono), SR 60648 (stereo))
- Jose Melis on Broadway (1961, Mercury MG 20610 (mono), SR 60610 (stereo))
- Jose Melis Plays His TV Favorties (1961, Mercury MG 20683 (mono), SR 60683 (stereo))
- Jose Melis Plays the Latin Way (1959, Seeco CELP-445 (mono), CELP-4450 (stereo))
- Latin American Stylings (1957, Mercury MG 20127)
- The Many Moods of Jose Melis (1959, Seeco CELP-436 (mono), CELP-4360 (stereo))
- Tonight (1959, Seeco CELP-411 (mono), CELP-4110 (stereo))
- Tonight It's Music (1958, Mercury MG 20275)

Melvoin, Mike

- Keys to Your Mind (1966, Liberty LRP-3485 (mono), LST-7485 (stereo))

Mendes, Sergio (and Brasil '66)

Mendes was primarily a Brazilian jazz musician recording in Portuguese meeting with little success in the U.S. when he signed with Herb Alpert's A&M Records with a newly-formed band, Brasil '66. American Lani Hall was brought in to sing (although she had to learn the foreign lyrics phonetically) and the resulting sound came to fit the second half of the 1960's perfectly.

- The Beat of Brazil (1967, Atlantic 1480; as Sergio Mendes)
- Brasil '65 (1965, Capitol T-2294 (mono), ST-2294 (stereo); reissued as *In the Brazilian Bag*; with Wanda De Sah)
- Crystal Illusions (1969, A&M SP-4197)
- Equinox (1967, A&M LP-122 (mono), SP-4122 (stereo))
- Fool on the Hill (1968, A&M LP-160 (mono), SP-4160 (stereo))
- The Great Arrival (1966, Atlantic 1466 (mono), SD 1466 (stereo); as Sergio Mendes)

- *Herb Alpert Presents Sergio Mendes and Brazil '66* (1966, A&M LP-116 (mono), SP-4116 (stereo); there were various re-releases with different catalog numbers)

- In Person at El Matador (1965, Atlantic 8112 (mono), SD 8112 (stereo); as Sergio Mendes Brasil '65)

- In the Brazilian Bag (1966, Tower T-5052 (mono), ST-5052 (stereo); this was a re-issue of *Brasil '65*)

- Look Around (1968, A&M LP-137 (mono), SP-4137 (stereo))

- Quiet Nights (1968, Phillips PHS 600-263; as Sergio Mendes)

- Sergio Mendes' Favorite Things (1968, Atlantic 8177 (mono), SD 8177 (stereo); as Sergio Mendes)

- So Nice (1965, Sears SPS-474; re-released 1972, Pickwick/33 SPC-3149; as The Sergio Mendes Trio)

- Stillness (1970, A&M SP-4284)

- The Swinger from Rio (1965, Atlantic 1434 (mono), SD 1434 (stereo); as Sergio Mendes)

- Ye-Me-Le (1969, A&M SP-4236)

Merlin (aka **The Magic Fingers of Merlin**; **Merlin & His Trio**)

- More Organ Moods, Vol. 2 (Grand Prix Series K-136 (mono), KS-136 (stereo)) Note: Most, of not all, of these Grand Prix releases seem to also be available on the Bravo label.

- Music for Dancing (Grand Prix Series K-189 (mono), KS-189 (stereo))

- Organ Moods at Midnight (Grand Prix K-113 (mono), KS-113 (stereo))

- Pipe Organ in Hi-Fi (Grand Prix K-141 (mono), KS-141 (stereo))

- The Swinging Hi-Fi Organ (Grand Prix K-126 (mono), KS-126 (stereo))

- A Tribute to Ken Griffin (Grand Prix Series K-188 (mono), KS-188 (stereo))

- A Tribute to Ken Griffin: Sweetheart Songs (Grand Prix Series K-196 (mono), KS-196 (stereo))

Merrill, Buddy (see also **Lawrence Welk**)

Buddy Merrill is remembered for being the guitarist virtuoso on *The Lawrence Welk Show* for a couple of decades, as well as recording on Welk's albums.

- Beyond the Reef (1971, Accent ACS 5034)

- Buddy Merrill's World of Guitars (1972, Ranwood R-8096)

- Electro Sonic Guitars (1969, Accent ACS 5028)

- The Exciting World of Buddy Merrill and His Guitars (1966, Accent AC 5020 (mono), ACS 5020 (stereo))

- The Guitar Sounds of Buddy Merrill (1965, Accent AC 5010 MLP (mono), AC 5010 SLP (stereo))
- Guitar Sounds of the 70's (1970, Accent ACS 5032)
- Guitars On Fire (1967, Accent SQBO-91997) Two-record set.
- Holiday For Guitars (1965, Accent AC 5016 MLP (mono), AC 5016 SLP (stereo))
- Land of a Thousand Guitars (1968, Accent ACS 5026)
- Latin Festival (1966, Accent AC 5018 (mono), ACS 5018 (stereo); also released on GNP Crescendo CRL 1003)
- The Many Splendored Guitars of Buddy Merrill (1967, Accent ACS 5022)
- Sounds of Love (1968, Accent ACS 5024)

Mexicali Brass, The

This was another **Tijuana Brass** clone group, this time in service to the Crown budget record label.
- Downtown with the Mexicali Brass (1966, Crown CLP 5492 (mono), CST 492 (stereo))
- Mame & Hello Dolly (1967, Crown CLP 5542 (mono), CST 542 (stereo))
- Mexicali Brass featuring Songs from South of the Border (Longines Symphonette Society LWCP 2)
- Mexicali Brass Go South of the Border (1966, Crown CLP 5524 (mono), CST 524 (stereo))
- Mexicali Brass Treasury (Longines Symphonette Society LWS 290 through LWS 294) This was a multi-LP set that came in a premium package and was sold via mail order.
- The Mexicali Brass, Vol. 3: 30 Great Songs (ARA Records ST13; available in mono also?)
- Michelle (1966, Crown CL-5503 (mono), CST 503 (stereo))
- The Shadow of Your Smile (1967, Crown CLP-5544 (mono), CST 544 (stereo))
- Sold Out! (Contessa CON 15030)
- A Taste of Honey (1964, Crown CLP 5487 (mono), CST 487 (stereo))
- Theme from The Green Hornet (1967, Crown CLP 5546 (mono), CST 546 (stereo))
- Theme From Thunderball (1966, Crown CLP 5506 (mono), CST 506 (stereo))
- Tijuana Sounds (Hallmark MST-10357; as Teddy Phillips and the Mexicali Brass)
- Tijuana Sounds Plus Sax (Square Sounds SS-3601; as Teddy Phillips and the Mexicali Brass)

- Viva Mexicali Brass (1967, Crown CLP 5540 (mono), CST 540 (stereo))
- What Now My Love (1966, Crown CLP 5511 (mono), CST 511 (stereo))
- Whipped Cream & The Lonely Bull (1964, Crown CLP 5471 (mono), CST 471 (stereo)) Note that there are two versions of this album; the second one, titled simply *Whipped Cream*, replaces "The Lonely Bull" with "Espana Cani".
- The Work Song (1966, Crown CLP-5523 (mono), CST-523 (stereo))
- Zorba the Greek (1966, Crown CLP-5497 (mono), CST 497 (stereo))

Mexicali Singers, The (a pseudonym of **The Anita Kerr Singers**, or at least one of Kerr's vocal projcets)

- The Further Adventures of The Mexicali Singers (1966, Warner Brothers W 1651 (mono), WS 1651 (stereo))
- The Mexicali Singers Ride Again (1967, Warner Brothers (W 1677 (mono), WS 1677 (stereo))
- Voices in Instrumentation (1966, Warner Brothers W 1641 (mono), WS 1641 (stereo))

Mexican Brass

- Spanish Flea / What Now My Love (1966, Wyncote W-9145 (mono), SW-9145 (stereo))
- Taste of Honey / Lonely Bull (1966, Wyncote W-9129 (mono), SW-9129 (stereo))
- Whipped Cream – Zorba the Greek – Java (1966, Wyncote W-9136 (mono), SW-9136 (stereo))

Mexicani Marimba Band, The

Wow. This band's name indicates that they aren't even good enough to be a direct **Tijuana Brass** ripoff, but instead are a **Baja Marimba Band** ripoff, which are themselves a takeoff on the Tijuana Brass's quick popularity.

- Mexicani Marimba Band (1966, Wyncote W-9141 (mono), SW-9141 (stereo))

Meynard, Raoul and His Orchestra

- Carte Blanche/Continentale (1960, Warner Brothers B 1370 (mono), WS 1370 (stereo))
- Continental Host (1961, Warner Brothers W 1424 (mono), WS 1424 (stereo))
- Continental Visa (1958, Warner Brothers B 1215 (mono), BS 1215 (stereo))

- Continental Visa Renewed (1959, Warner Brothers B 1320 (mono), WST 1320 (stereo))
- Passport to Pleasure (1962, Warner Brothers W 1469 (mono), WS 1469 (stereo))
- Strolling Mandolins (1961, Warner Brothers W 1405 (mono), WS 1405 (stereo))
- Where Love is Everything (1959, Warner Brothers W 1286 (mono), WS 1286 (stereo))

MGM Singing Strings, The

- The Hits of 1966 (1967, MGM SE-4357)

Midnight String Quartet

- Goodnight My Love and Other Rhapsodies for Young Lovers (1969, Viva V-36019)
- The Look of Love and Other Rhapsodies for Young Lovers (1968, Viva V-36015)
- Love Rhapsodies (1968, Viva V-36013)
- Rhapsodies For Those in Love (Viva SQBO 91379) Two-record set.
- Rhapsodies For Young Lovers (1966, Viva V-6001 (mono), VS-6001 (stereo))
- Rhapsodies For Young Lovers, Vol. 2 (1967, Viva V-6008 (mono), V-36008 (stereo))
- Rhapsodies For Young Lovers, Vol. 3 (1968, Viva V-36022)
- Spanish Rhapsodies For Young Lovers (1967, Viva V-6004 (mono), V-36004 (stereo))

The Midnight Strings (see also **Bobby Hackett**)

- The Midnight Strings Play Rhapsodies For Romance (Somerset/Stereo Fidelity SF-29000) Apparently this was a completely different group from the Midnight String Quartet or the later Midnight Strings Orchestra.

Mills, Verlye and Billy May

- Harp With a Beat (1959, HiFi R-606)

Mineo, Attilio 'Art'

- Man In Space With Sounds: Music from the Seattle World's Fair (1962, World's Fair Records LP-66666) Experimental space-age music with the usual 'futuristic' sound effects.

Mods, The

'The Mods' were actually The Modernaires, whose musical careers dated back to the 1930's and included a time with Ozzie Nelson's band. This must have been their late-career attempt to appeal to the youths of the time.

- The "Mods" Salute Herb Alpert and the Tijuana Brass (1966, Columbia CL 2490 (mono), CS 9290 (stereo))

Montalba, Georges

- Fantasy in Pipe Organ and Percussion (1959, Somerset P-8400 (mono), SF-8400 (stereo))

Monte, Mark and the Continentals

- Dancing at the Habana Hilton (Jubilee JLP-1072)

The Monte Carlo Strings

- Music for Moonlight Madness (1959 Grand Award GA 247 SD)

Montenegro, Hugo and His Orchestra

Hugo Montenegro was a versatile composer and arranger comfortable with a wide variety of music, but he most remembered today for his film scores.

- Black Velvet (1964, Time 52196 (mono), S/2196 (stereo))
- Candy's Theme and Other Sweets (1965, RCA Victor LPM-3332 (mono), LSP-3332 (stereo))
- Cha Chas For Dancing (1962, Time 52018 (mono), S/2018 (stereo))
- Colours of Love (1970, RCA Victor LSP-4273)
- Come Spy With Me (1966, RCA Victor LPM-3540 (mono), LSP-3540 (stereo))
- Good Vibrations (1969, RCA Victor LSP-4104)
- Great Songs from Motion Pictures, Vol. 3: 1945-1960 (1961, Time 52046 (mono), S/2046 (stereo))
- Hurry Sundown (1967, RCA Victor LOC-1133 (mono), LSO-1133 (stereo))
- In a Sentimental Mood (1962, RCA Camden CAL-729 (mono), CAS-729 (stereo))
- Loves of My Life (1957, Vik LX-1089; as Montenegro)
- Montenegro in Italy (1961, Time 52051 (mono), S/2051 (stereo))
- Moog Power (1969, RCA Victor LSP-4170)
- More Music from The Man from U.N.C.L.E. (1966, RCA Victor LPM-3574 (mono), LSP-3574 (stereo))
- Original Music from The Man from U.N.C.L.E. (1965, RCA Victor LPM-3475 (mono), LSP-3475 (stereo))

- Russian Grandeur (1964, RCA Victor LPM-2902 (mono), LSP-2902 (stereo))
- The Young Beat of Rome (1964, RCA Victor LPM-2958 (mono), LSP-2958 (stereo))

Monterey Brass, The
- Blue Hawaii (Diplomat D-2394 (mono), DS-2394 (stereo))
- Great Songs from the Movies (Diplomat D-2383 (mono), DS-2383 (stereo))
- Isn't It Romantic (Diplomat D-2401 (mono), DS-2401 (stereo))
- South of the Border / The Lonely Bull (1966, Diplomat D-2379 (mono), DS-2379 (stereo))
- Standing Room Only (Diplomat D-2406 (mono), DS-2406 (stereo))
- Strangers in the Night (Diplomat D-2392 (mono), DS-2392 (stereo))
- A Taste of Honey / Million Seller Trumpet Hits (Diplomat D-2370 (mono), DS-2370 (stereo))
- What Now My Love (1966, Diplomat D-2377 (mono), DS-2377 (stereo))

Montevideo Singing Strings, The
- I Love Paris (1964, Clarion 616 (mono), SD 616 (stereo))
- Moonlight & Roses (1964, Clarion 618 (mono), SD 618 (stereo))
- Paradise (1964, Clarion 617 (mono), SD 617 (stereo))

Montez, Bobby
- Hollywood Themes in Cha Cha Cha (1959, GNP 38)
- Jungle Fantastique (1958, Jubilee JGM 1085; JGM 7001) JGM 1085's cover features a woman holding a parrot; JGM 7001 has a blonde woman in a bikini lying on a tiger skin rug; this second one lists the artist as 'The Bobby Montez Quintet'.
- The Music of Lerner and Loewe in Latin Fashion (1960, GNP 46; this appears to be the same album as *My Fair Lady Latin*)
- My Fair Lady Latin (1960, GNP 46; this was probably a retitling of *The Music of Lerner and Leowe in Latin Fashion*)
- Pachanga y Cha Cha Cha (1961, World Pacific 1804)
- Viva! Montez (1961, World Pacific 1803)

Mooney, Hal and His Orchestra
- An Affair to Remember (1959, Mercury MG 20420 (mono), SR 60093 (stereo))
- Dreamland... USA (1961, Mercury MG 20180 (mono), SR 60047 (stereo))

- Flutes and Percussion (1959, Time 52001 (mono), S/2001 (stereo))
- Musical Horoscope (1957, Mercury MG 20175; later re-released as *Any Time: Music for Every Month of the Year*)
- The Passion of Paris (1960, Time 52005 (mono), S/2005 (stereo))
- Voices in Song and Percussion (1961, Time 52008 (mono), S/2008 (stereo))
- Woodwinds and Percussion (1961, Mercury PPS 2013 (mono), PPS 6013 (stereo))

Moonlight Strings, The
- Love After Midnight (1969, Columbia DS 441)
- Moonlight Becomes You (1966, Columbia Record Club D 209 (mono), DS 209 (stereo))

Moore, Phil and His Orchestra
- Polynesian Paradise (1959, Strand SL 1004 (mono), SLS 1004 (stereo))

Morales, Lalo and His Latin Dance Orchestra
- Latin Dance Party (1970, Crown CST-605)

Morales, Noro (**and His Orchestra**)
- Adios Muchachos (Riverside RLP 7501)
- Cha Cha Cha's (1960, Design DCF 1008)
- Como Esta (1962, Tico SLP 1068)
- His Piano and Rhythm (1959, Ansonia SALP 1272)
- Holiday in Havana (1958, Design DLP 86 (mono), SDLP 86 (stereo))
- Latin American Dance Party (1966?, Design DLP 244)
- Latin American Rhythms (Tiara TST 7534)
- Latin Dance Party (International Award Series K-154 (mono), ASK-154 (stereo))
- Latin Dance Time (Grand Prix KS-154)
- Latin Favorites (1964, Wyncote W-9025 (mono), SW-9025 (stereo))
- Latin Hour with Noro Morales (1954, Royale 1345)
- Lecuona's Afro-Cuban Suite (1957, Vik LX-1100)
- Let's Go Latin American (1957, Vik LX-1072)
- Mambo With Morales (1957, Harmony HL 7039; with Humberto Morales) There was an earlier 10" disc from Columbia with this title, but the song selections are completely different.
- Merengue a la Noro (1956, RCA Victor LPM 1163)

Moreau, Pierre and His Orchestra

- Love is Blue (L'amour est Bleu) (Custom CS 1106)

Morgan, Tommy

Tommy Morgan was actually a celebrated harmonica player who could be heard in the themes of many classic TV shows. This great album has him backed by **Warren Barker** and his orchestra.

- Tropicale (1958, Warner Brothers 1214)

Morrow, Buddy (**and His Orchestra**; **and His Night Train Orchestra**) (see also **Eddie Layton and Buddy Morrow**)

- Big Band Beatlemania (1964, Epic BN 26095 (mono), LN 24095 (stereo))
- Big Band Guitar (1959, RCA Victor LPM-2018 (mono), LSP-2018 (stereo))
- The Bostella! (Epic BN 26148 (mono), LN 26148 (stereo))
- Dance Date (Mercury Wing MGW 12012 (mono), SRW 16102 (stereo))
- Double Impact (1960, RCA Victor LMP-2180 (mono), LSP-2180 (stereo))
- Impact (1959, RCA Victor LMP-2042 (mono), LSP-2042 (stereo))
- Let's Have a Dance Party! (RCA Camden CAL 381)
- Music For Dancing Feet (1955, Mercury MG 20210; Wing MGW 12006)
- Night Train Goes To Hollywood (1962, Mercury MG 20702 (mono), SR 60702 (stereo))
- New Blues Scene (1967, United Artists UAS 6639)
- Night Train (1957, RCA Victor LPM 1427; 1958, Mercury MG 20396 (mono), SR 60009 (stereo))
- Poe For Moderns (1960, RCA Victor LPM-2208 (mono), LSP-2208 (stereo)) One would assume this would be Poe's words recited to music; but instead it's a collection of music 'inspired by' the author's works, in a sort of Crime Jazz format.
- Shall We Dance (1954, Mercury MG 20062)
- Tribute to a Sentimental Gentleman (1957, Mercury MG 20290; Mercury Wing MGW 12105

Mottola, Tony

As a young man guitarist Tony Mottola found his way into a lucrative career writing and performing music for radio and television. He would later strike up a friendship with **Enoch Light** and record several albums for Light's labels Command and Project 3 Total Sound.

- Amor Mexico/S.A. (1966, Command RS 33 900 (mono), RS 900 SD (stereo))
- Close To You (1970, Project 3 Total Sound PR 5050 SD)
- Command Performances (1965, Command RS 33 885 (mono), RS 885 SD (stereo))
- Folk Songs (1961, Command RS 33 823 (mono), RS 823 SD (stereo))
- Guitar... Mottola (1963, Command RS 33 807 (mono), RS 807 SD (stereo); this was a re-release of *Mr. Big*, retaining the same catalog numbers)
- Guitar... Paris (1964, Command RS 33 877 (mono), RS 877 SD (stereo))
- Guitar U.S.A. (1966, Command RS 33 908 (mono), RS 908 SD (stereo))
- Heart & Soul (1966, Project 3 Total Sound PR 5003 SD)
- I Only Have Eyes For You (1975, Project 3 Total Sound PR 5094 SD)
- A Latin Love-In (1967, Project 3 Total Sound PR 5010 SD)
- Let's Put Out the Lights! (1956, RCA Camden CAL-305; as Tony Mottola and His All-Stars)
- Love Songs Mexico/S.A. (1965, Command RS 33 889 (mono), RS 889 SD (stereo))
- Lush, Latin, & Lovely (1967, Project 3 PR 5020 SD)
- Mr. Big (1959, Command RS 33 807 (mono), RS 807 SD (stereo); re-released in 1963 as *Guitar... Mottola* with the same catalog numbers)
- Mr. Guitar (1973, ABC ABCX-770/2) Two-record set.
- Roma Oggi: Rome Today (1968, Project 3 Total Sound PR 5032 SD)
- Roman Guitar (1960, Command RS 33 816 (mono), RS 816 SD (stereo))
- Roman Guitar, Vol. 2 (1962, Command RS 33 836 (mono), RS 836 SD (stereo))
- Romantic Guitar (1963, Command RS 33 847 (mono), RS 847 SD (stereo))
- Sentimental Guitar (1964, Command RS 33 864 (mono), RS 864 SD (stereo))
- Sixteen Great Performances (1971, ABC ABCS-738)

- Spanish Guitar (1962, Command RS 33 841 (mono), RS 841 SD (stereo))
- String Band Strum-Along (1961, Command RS 33 828 (mono), RS 828 SD (stereo))
- Superstar Guitar (1972, Project 3 Total Sound PR 5062 SD)
- Tony & Strings (1972, Project 3 Total Sound PR 5069 SD)
- Tony Mottola and the Brass Menagerie (1974, Project 3 Total Sound PR 5082 SD)
- Tony Mottola and the Quad Guitars (1973, Project 3 Total Sound PR 5078 SD)
- Tony Mottola Joins the Guitar Underground (1969, Project 3 Total Sound PR 5035 SD)
- Tony Mottola's Guitar Factory (1970, Project 3 Total Sound PR 5044 SD)
- Tony 'Mr. Guitar' Mottola, Vol. 2 (1973, Command RSSD 966-2) Two-record set.
- Two Guitars For Two in Love (1972, Project 3 Total Sound PR 5074 SD)
- Warm Feelings (1971, Project 3 Total Sound PR 5058 SD)
- Warm, Wild, and Wonderful (1968, Project 3 Total Sound PR 5025 SD)

Moulin, Subri and His Equatorial Rhythm Group (see also **Chief Bey and His Royal Household**; **Cawanda's Group**; **Sabu and His Jungle Percussionists**; **The Tahitian Percussionists and Exotic Voices**; *Taboo* (1959, Riviera) in Compilations)

- Jungle Beat: Authentic African Chants and Rhythms (1959, RKO-Unique ULP-141 (mono), SLP-1005 (stereo); re-released as *Jungle Percussion*, *Jungle Rhythms and Chants*, and *Taboo* – see next entries) Songs from this album would be re-used (and even re-recorded) on a variety of 'jungle-drums'-themed albums over the next decade. 12 songs.
- Jungle Percussion (1960, Tops/Mayfair L 1709 (mono), 9709 S (stereo); available in black and yellow vinyl) This was a re-release of *Jungle Beat* with all 12 songs intact.
- Jungle Rhythms and Chants (1978, Olympic OL-6150) This was another re-issue of *Jungle Beat*, with all 12 songs present.
- Taboo (1959, Riviera R 0028 (mono), STR 0028 (stereo)) Another re-release of *Jungle Beat*, with 10 of the original 12 songs; but the artist isn't listed on either the jacket or the record label.

Mozian, Roger King

- El Twist (1962, EX 5076 (mono), ES 1776 (stereo))
- Spectacular Brass (1960, MGM E3844 (mono), SE3844 (stereo))

- Spectacular Brass Goes Cha-Cha-Cha (1961, MGM E3920 (mono), SE3920 (stereo))
- Spectacular Percussion (1960, MGM E3845 (mono), SE3845 (stereo))
- Spectacular Percussion Goes Latin (1961, MGM E3921 (mono), SE3921 (stereo))

Muller, Werner and His Orchestra
- Cherry Blossom Time in Japan (Decca DL 8603)
- Hawaiian Swing (1963, London SP 44021)
- Italian Festival (1969, London SP 44132)

Mumm, Lloyd and His Starlight Roof Orchestra
- Pink Champagne For Dancing (1959, Omega OML-1001 (mono), OSL-1 (stereo))
- Pink Champagne For Dancing, Vol. 2 (1960?, Omega OSL-37) There is much confusion regarding these albums, which appear in at least 4 different cover versions. The most common cover features a young woman's face to the right with her eyes closed, while two glasses of champagne are poured nearby (although one version exists with this image reversed!). The other is of male and female hands, toasting each other holding champagne glasses. The important point is that the first collection of songs starts with "Bubbles in the Wine" and goes by the catalog number of OSL-1 (at least, for the stereo version); the second collection starts with "Blue Cocktails for a Pink Lady" and is listed as OSL-37. Despite the myriad cover variations, these appear to be the two basic collections of songs.

Mure, Billy (**His Guitar and Orchestra**)
- Around the World in Percussion (1961, Strand SL 1021 (mono), SLS 1021 (stereo))
- Blue Hawaii (Spin-O-Rama M-147 (mono), S-147 (stereo); with **Harry Kaapuni and His Royal Hawaiians**; side A featured five songs by Mure, side B had five songs by Kaapuni)
- Fireworks (1958, RCA Victor LPM-1694 (mono), LSP-1694 (stereo); as Billy Mure's Supersonic Guitars)
- Hawaiian Percussion (1961, Strand SL 1010 (mono), SLS 1010 (stereo))
- Strictly Cha Cha (1960, Everest LPBR 5120 (mono), SDBR 1120 (stereo))
- A String of Trumpets (1960, Everest LPBR 5067 (mono), SDBR 1067 (stereo))
- Super-Sonic Guitars in Hi-Fi (1957, RCA Victor LPM-1536)
- Supersonic Guitars (1959, MGM E-3780 (mono), SE-3780 (stereo))

- Supersonic Guitars, Vol. 2 (1960 MGM E-3807 (mono), SE-3807 (stereo))
- Supersonics in Flight (1959, RCA Victor LPM-1869 (mono), LSP-1869 (stereo))
- Teen Bossa Nova (1963, MGM E-4131 (mono), SE-4131 (stereo); as Billy Mure's Supersonic Guitars)
- Tough Strings (1961, Kapp KL-1253 (mono), KS-3253 (stereo); as Billy Mure and His Combo)

Mure, Billy and His Orchestra with Luke Leilani and His Orchestra
- Hawaiian Moods (Spin-O-Rama M-157 (mono), S-157 (stereo))

Mure, Billy and The Islanders
- Pink Hawaii (1962, Strand SL 1070 (mono), SLS 1070 (stereo))

Murphy, Chips and His Border Brass

Despite featuring country music songs, this one is included because it's basically a quickie **Tijuana Brass** cash-in.

- Tijuana Country (1966, Pickwick/33 PC-3051 (mono), SPC-3051 (stereo))

Mystic Moods Orchestra, The

The Mystic Moods Orchestra recordings were largely the work of a guy named Brad Miller, who experimented with mixing Easy Listening-style orchestral music with naturalistic sound effects (to produce the 'mood'), mixed using advanced studio techniques.

- Awakening (1973, Warner Brothers BS 2690)
- Clear Light (1973, Warner Brothers BS 2745)
- Emotions (1968, Phillips PHS 600-277)
- English Muffins (1971, Phillips PHS 600-349)
- Erogenous (1974, Warner Brothers BS 2786)
- Extensions (1969, Phillips PHS 600-301)
- Highway One (1972, Warner Brothers BS 2648)
- Love the One You're With (1972, Warner Brothers BS 2577)
- Love Token (1969, Phillips PHS 600-321)
- Mexican Trip (1967, Phillips PHM 200-250 (mono), PHS 600-250 (stereo))
- More Than Music (1967, Phillips PHM 200-231 (mono), PHS 600-231 (stereo))
- The Mystic Moods of Love (1968, Phillips PHS 600-260)
- Nighttide (1966, Phillips PHM 200-213 (mono), PHS 600-213 (stereo))
- One Stormy Night (1966, Phillips PHM 200-205 (mono), PHS 600-205 (stereo))

- Stormy Weekend (1972, Phillips PHS 600-342)

Namaro, Jimmy (aka **The Jimmy Namaro Trio**)

- Driftwood (1958, Dot DLP 3246 (mono), DLP 25246 (stereo))

Nash, Ted and His Orchestra

- Peter Gunn (1959, Crown CLP-5101 (mono), CST-138 (stereo))

Neel, John

- Blue Martini (1963, Ava A-24 (mono), AS-24 (stereo))

Nero, Peter

Peter Nero is a pianist who first studied classical music as a child, then discovered a love of jazz when a young man. He went on to produce several albums that combined a popular approach somewhere between the two musical styles.

- Career Girls (1965, RCA Victor LPM-3313 (mono), LSP-3313 (stereo))
- The Colorful Peter Nero (1962, RCA Victor LPM-2618 (mono), LSP-2618 (stereo))
- The First Time Ever (I Saw Your Face) (1972, Columbia C 31335)
- For the Nero-Minded (1962, RCA Victor LPM-2536 (mono), LSP-2536 (stereo))
- Hail the Conquering Nero (1963, RCA Victor LPM-2638 (mono), LSP-2638 (stereo))
- Hits from Hair to Hollywood (1969, Columbia CS 9907; re-issued as *Midnight Cowboy*, with the same catalog number and cover art)
- I'll Never Fall in Love Again (1970, Columbia CS 1009)
- In Person (1963, RCA Victor LPM-2710 (mono), LSP-2710 (stereo))
- I've Gotta Be Me (1969, Columbia CS 9800)
- Love Story (1971, Columbia C 30586)
- Love Trip (1969, RCA Victor LSP-4205)
- Midnight Cowboy (1969, Columbia CS 9907; this was a re-issue of *Hits from Hair to Hollywood* soon after its release, with the same catalog number and cover art)
- Nero-ing in On the Hits (1967, RCA Victor LPM-3871 (mono), LSP-3871 (stereo))
- New Piano in Town (1961, RCA Victor LPM-2383 (mono), LSP-2383 (stereo))
- Peter Nero On Tour (1966, RCA Victor LPM-3610 (mono), LSP-3610 (stereo))

- Peter Nero Plays a Salute to Herb Alpert and the Tijuana Brass (1967, RCA Victor LPM-3720 (mono), LSP-3720 (stereo))
- Peter Nero Plays Born Free and Others (1967, RCA Camden CAL-2139 (mono), CAS-2139 (stereo))
- Peter Nero Plays Songs You Won't Forget (1964, RCA Victor LPM-2935 (mono), LSP-2935 (stereo))
- Piano Forte (1961, RCA Victor LPM-2334 (mono), LSP-2334 (stereo))
- Reflections (1964, RCA Victor LPM-2853 (mono), LSP-2853 (stereo))
- The Screen Scene (1966, RCA Victor LPM-3496 (mono), LSP-3496 (stereo))
- Summer of '42 (1972, Columbia C 31105)
- Sunday in New York (1964, RCA Victor LPM-2827 (mono), LSP-2827 (stereo))
- Up Close (1966, RCA Victor LPM-3550 (mono), LSP-3550 (stereo))
- Xochimilco (1967, RCA Victor LPM-3814 (mono), LSP-3814 (stereo))
- Young and Warm and Wonderful (1961, RCA Victor LPM-2484 (mono), LSP-2484 (stereo))

Nero, Peter with Arthur Fiedler and The Boston Pops Orchestra

- Nero Goes "Pops" (1965, RCA Victor Red Seal LM-2821 (mono), LSC-2821 (stereo))

Nevins, Al and His Orchestra

- Dancing With the Blues (1958, RCA Victor LPM-1654 (mono), LSP-1654 (stereo))
- Escapade in Sound (1956, RCA Victor LPM-1166)
- Light and Shadows: Dinner Music (1958, RCA Victor LPM-1475 (mono), LSP-1475 (stereo))
- Smooth Listening... Smooth Sailing (1956, RCA Victor Custom NPT-1001) This was a special pressing for the North Pier Terminal Co. of Chicago; was it sold or given away?

Newman, Alfred and His Orchestra

- A Holiday for Strings (1954, Vocalion VL 73749)

Newman, Alfred and Ken Darby (aka **The Ken Darby Singers**)

- The Magic Islands (1957, Decca DL 9048 (mono), DL 79048 (stereo))
- Ports of Paradise (1960, Capitol TAO-1447 (mono), TAOS-1447 (stereo))

Newman, Lionel

- Exciting Hong Kong (1961, ABC-Paramount ABC 367 (mono), ABCS 367 (stereo)) Music from the television series *Hong Kong*, which starred Rod Taylor and lasted only one season.

- Let's Make Love (1960, Columbia CL 1527 (mono), CS 8327 (stereo)) Music from the film starring Marilyn Monroe.

- The Pleasure Seekers (1964, RCA Victor LOC-1011 (mono), LSO-1011 (stereo))

Night Strings, The

- Soulful: Instrumental Love Machine (1969, Evolution 2011)

Nimoy, Leonard

The multi-talented Mr. Nimoy loaned his voice to both sing and narrate on a series of albums starting in the year after *Star Trek* first appeared on television.

- Mr. Spock's Music from Outer Space (1967, Dot DLP 3794 (mono), DLP 25794 (stereo)) This well-known LP, actually better than one might expect, mixes instrumentals (the grooved-up *Star Trek* theme song) with Nimoy singing and narrating in his clear, distinctive voice.

- The New World of Leonard Nimoy (1970, Dot DLP 25966)

- The Touch of Leonard Nimoy (1969, Dot DLP 3910 (mono), DLP 25910 (stereo))

- The Two Sides of Leonard Nimoy (1967, Dot DLP 3835 (mono), DLP 25835 (stereo)) As good as *Mr. Spock's Music from Outer Space* is, this one is deliciously, cringe-worthily bad.

- The Way I Feel (1968, Dot DLP 3883 (mono), DLP 25883 (stereo))

Nitzsche, Jack (**and His Orchestra**)

- Dance to the Hits of the Beatles (1964, Reprise R-6115 (mono), RS-6115 (stereo))

- The Lonely Surfer (1963, Reprise R-6101 (mono), R9-6101 (stereo))

Nogueira, Paulinho

- Bossa Nova Guitar (1963, Hamilton HLP 157 (mono), HLP 12157 (stereo))

Norman, Jay (aka **The Jay Norman Quintet**)

- Dancing and Dreaming (1958, Concert-Disc CS-24)

Ogerman, Klaus and His Orchestra

- Latin Rock (1967, RCA Victor LPM-3813 (mono), LSP-3813 (stereo))

- Soul Searchin' (1965, RCA Victor LPM-3366 (mono), LSP-3366 (stereo))
- Sounds For Sick (?) People (1960, Shell 1711 (mono), S 1711 (stereo))
- Watusi Trumpets (1965, RCA Victor LPM-3455 (mono), LSP-3455 (stereo))

Orchestra Del Oro

- All Time Latin Dance Hits (1961, Sonodor MO-SON-102 (mono), ST-SON-102 (stereo))
- Hit Movie Themes Go Latin (1962, Somerset P-19100; Stereo-Fidelity SF-19100)
- Hits from Latin America (Dyna-Disc CH-807 (mono), SCH-807 (stereo); as Juan Del Oro and His Orchestra)
- Lolita (1962, Sonodor MO-SON-105 (mono), ST-SON-105 (stereo))
- The Pop Classics Go Latin (1961, Somerset P-19200; Stereo-Fidelity SF-19200)
- The Soul of Harlem (1961, Sonodor MO-SON-100 (mono), ST-SON-100 (stereo))

Osborn, Eddie

- Fabulous Eddie Osborn at the Baldwin Organ (1962, Audio Fidelity AFLP 1968 (mono), AFSD 5968 (stereo))
- Percussive Baldwin Organ and Bongos (1960, Audio Fidelity DFM 3004 (mono), DFS 7004 (stereo))

Osser, Glenn and His Orchestra (see also **Bobby Hackett**, the Compilations section)

- Be There At Five (1956, Mercury MG 20218)
- But Beautiful (Kapp KL-1022)
- In My Merry Oldsmobile (Dajon, DJ-88-98) Almost certainly done as a promotional item, this album features 26 different, very short versions of the old tune "My Merry Oldsmobile," done in various musical styles (Hawaiian, Viennese waltz, mambo, etc.).
- Love Songs from the Hollywood Screen and the Broadway Stage (1958, Kapp KL-1078)

Out Islanders, The

This group and album were a one-time project of **Billy May** with musicians he had previously worked with, including pianist Jimmy Rowles and drummer **Irv Cottler**.

- Polynesian Fantasy (1961, Capitol T-1595 (mono), ST-1595 (stereo))

Outriggers, The (see also **George Greeley**)

- Captivation: Hawaiian Moods (1959, Warner Brothers W 1314 (mono), WS 1314 (stereo))
- Golden Hits of Hawaii (1960, Warner Brothers W 1549 (mono), WS 1549 (stereo))
- Rapture: Hawaiian Moods (1958, Warner Brothers W 1224 (mono), WS 1224 (stereo))
- Surrender: The Hawaiian Spell of The Outriggers (1960, Warner Brothers W 1376 (mono), WS 1376 (stereo))

Owen, Reg and His Orchestra

- All I Do is Dream of You (1958, RCA Victor LPM-1580 (mono), LSP-1580 (stereo))
- Coffee Break (1958, RCA Victor LPM-1582 (mono), LSP-1582 (stereo))
- Cuddle Up a Little Closer (1959, RCA Victor LPM-1914 (mono), LSP-1914 (stereo))
- Deep in a Dream (1959, RCA Victor LPM-1970 (mono), LSP-1970 (stereo))
- Girls Were Made to Take Care of Boys (1959, RCA Victor LPM-1908 (mono), LSP-1908 (stereo))
- Under Paris Skies (Decca DL 8859 (mono), DL 78859 (stereo))

Owens, Harry and His Royal Hawaiians

- Great Songs of Hawaii (Hamilton HLP 141)
- Polynesian Holiday (1957, Capitol T-804)
- Voice of the Trade Winds (1957, Capitol T-333)

Page, Bill

- Sounds of the Sonic Sixties (1968, Tower ST 5084) Instrumental interpretations of hits using traditional and modern electronic instruments.

Pahinui, Gabby

- Gabby (1972, Panini PS-1002)
- Gabby Pahinui with the Sons of Hawaii (1960, Hula H 503; with **Eddie Kamae and The Sons of Hawaii**)
- Hawaiian Slack Key: Guitar With Singing, Vol. 1 (1962, Waikiki 119 (mono), 319 (stereo))
- Hawaiian Slack Key: Guitar Instrumental, Vol. 2 (1962, Waikiki 120 (mono), 320 (stereo))
- Pure Gabby (1978, Hula HS 567)
- Rabbit Island Music Festival (1973, Panini PS-1004)

Palmieri, Eddie and Cal Tjader – see **Cal Tjader and Eddie Palmieri**

Pan American Orchestra

- Star Dust Samba (1959, Musidisc MS 16002) Though advertised as 'South America's Greatest Dance Band,' the Pan American Orchestra sounds awfully middle-of-the-road American on this collection.

Pandit, Korla

Korla Pandit was actually John Rowland, an African-American from Missouri, but to television viewers and record buyers starting in the 1950's, he was an Indian mystic who weaved musical fantasies while gazing suggestively from beneath a jewel-pinned turban.

- An Evening With Korla Pandit: A Concert Performance (1960, Fantasy 3304 (mono), 8049 (stereo))
- Hypnotique (1961, Fantasy 3329 (mono), 8075 (stereo))
- Korla Pandit at the Pipe Organ (1960, Fantasy 3286 (mono), 8018 (stereo))
- Korla Pandit in Paris (1963, Fantasy 3347 (mono), 8347 (stereo))
- Korla Pandit Plays Music of the Exotic East (1958, Fantasy 3272 (mono), 8013 (stereo);note: all of Pandit's Fantasy-label records were issued in various colors of vinyl such as red and blue as well as black)
- Latin Holiday (1959, Fantasy 3284 (mono), 8027 (stereo))
- Love Letters (1961, Fantasy 3327 (mono), 8070 (stereo))
- Music for Meditation (1962, Fantasy 3342 (mono), 8342 (stereo))
- Music of Hollywood (1962, Fantasy 3334 (mono), 8086 (stereo))
- Music of Mystery and Romance (1961, Fantasy 3320 (mono), 8061 (stereo))
- Speak to Me of Love (1959, Fantasy 3293 (mono), 8039 (stereo))
- Tropical Magic (1959, Fantasy 3288 (mono), 8034 (stereo))
- The Universal Language of Music, Vol. 1 (1954, India 400)

Paramor, Norrie and His Orchestra (see also **Eddie Calvert**)

- Amor, Amor! (1961, Capitol T-10238 (mono), ST-10238 (stereo))
- Endearing Young Charms (1967, Capitol DT-10459)
- I Love... In London Again (1958?, Capitol T-2071 (mono), ST-2071 (stereo))
- Jet Flight (1958, Capitol T-10190 (mono), ST-10190 (stereo))
- Just We Two (1959, Capitol International Series T-10111)
- Moods (1958, Capitol T-10130)
- Music from My Fair Lady (1959, Capitol T-10100 (mono), ST-10100 (stereo))

- Strings! Staged for Stereo! (1959, Capitol STAC-1639)
- Warm & Willing (1965, Capitol T-2357 (mono), ST-2357 (stereo))

Parker, John (aka **The John Parker Orchestra**)
- The Sound of Conversations in Music (1960, Kapp Medallion ML-7504 (mono), MS-7504 (stereo))

Paulo, Rene (aka **The Rene Paulo Group**; **Trio**)
- Beyond Happiness (Mahalo M-3006 (mono), S-3006 (stereo))
- Black Coral (1960, Liberty LRP 3143 (mono), LST-7143 (stereo))
- Favorite Melodies of Japan (Mahalo M-3012)
- Forever More (1968, P&N PNS-1001) 'Featuring Akemi' – Akemi Paulo was Rene's wife.
- Heat Wave (1963, HiFi L-1012 (mono), SL-1012 (stereo); *Tropical Heat Wave* on the covers)
- Here is Happiness (Mahalo M-3001)
- Rene Paulo Plays in Person (1962, Mahalo M-3004)
- Whispering Sands (1964, HiFi L-1019 (mono), SL-1019 (stereo))

Peretti, Hugo and His Orchestra
- ...And So To Sleep: The Music of Harry Revel (1957, Mercury MG 20179)

Percussion All Stars, The
- Predominant Percussion (1960, Crown CLP-5193 (mono), CST-216 (stereo))

Percussion Unlimited
- My Fair Lady On Fire (1961, Kapp Medallion ML 7514 (mono), MS 7514 (stereo))
- New Shows in Town (1961, Kapp Medallion ML 7515 (mono), MS 7515 (stereo))

Perito, Nick and His Orchestra
- Blazing Latin Brass (1960, United Artists WW-7502 (mono), WWS-8502 (stereo))
- Latin Brass Goes to Italy (1961, United Artists WWR-3512 (mono), WWS-8512 (stereo))

Perkins, Frank
- Music for My Lady (1956, Decca DL 8395)
- Pictures in Music (1957, Decca DL 8467)

Perrey & Kingsley (aka **Jean-Jeaques Perrey** and **Gershon Kingsley**)

- The In Sound From Way Out! (1966, Vanguard VRS-9222 (mono), VSD-79222 (stereo); several re-releases) Early electronic music, influential to later practitioners.

- Kaleidoscopic Vibrations (1967, Vanguard VRS-9264 (mono), VSD-79264 (stereo); several re-releases)

Perry, Al Kealoha (see also **Webley Edwards**)

- Hawaiian Magic (1957, MacGregor MAC 1202; as Al Perry and His Singing Surf Riders) Pressed on red vinyl.

Peterson, Oscar

- In A Romantic Mood (1956, Verve MGV-2002; 1961, Verve V-2002)

- Nostalgic Memories (1956, Clef MG C-695)

- Pastel Moods (1956, Verve MGV-2004)

- Soft Sands (1957, Verve MGV-2079)

Peterson, Oscar and Nelson Riddle

- Oscar Peterson & Nelson Riddle (1963, Verve V-8562 (mono), V6-8562 (stereo))

Peterson, Oscar Trio and Singers Unlimited

- In Tune (1973, MPS MC 20905)

Phillips, Paul and His Band

- The Sound of Midnight: Naked City (1961, Medallion ML-7517 (mono), MS-7517 (stereo))

Phillips, Stu

Not to be confused with the Canadian-born country singer, this Stu Phillips was an industry veteran who created the Hollyridge Strings project and also did his share of soundtrack work.

- Feels Like Lovin' (1965, Capitol T-2356 (mono), ST-2356 (stereo); as Stu Phillips, His Orchestra and Chorus)

- Follow Me (1969, Uni 73056) Soundtrack to the film.

- The George, John, Paul, & Ringo Songbook (1971, Capitol ST-839; as Stu Phillips and **The Hollyridge Strings**)

- A Touch of Modern (1956, MGM E3391; as The Stu Phillips Sextet)

Pike, Dave

- Bossa Nova Carnival (1962, New Jazz NJ 8281 (mono), NJST 8281 (stereo))

- Limbo Carnival (1962, New Jazz NJ 8284 (mono), NJST 8284 (stereo))

- Manhattan Latin (1964, Decca DL 4568 (mono), DL 74568 (stereo))

Pineapple, Johnny

- Hawaii (1958, Audio Fidelity AFLP 1850 (mono), AFSD 5850 (stereo); as Johnny Pineapple and His Islanders)
- Hawaiian Holiday with Johnny Pineapple & His Orchestra (1965, Pickwick/33 PC-3018 (mono), SPC-3018 (stereo))
- Johnny Pineapple & Co. from Hawaii (1960, Design DCF-1034)

Pleis, Jack and His Orchestra

- All the Hits of 1962 (1962, Cameo C-1024 (mono), SC-1024 (stereo))
- Music for Two Sleepy People (1958, Decca DL-8763 (mono), DL-78763 (stereo))
- Serenades to Remember (1957, Decca DL 8586)

Plummer, Bill and The Cosmic Brotherhood

The Now Sound meets the sitar.

- Bill Plummer and The Cosmic Brotherhood (1968, Impulse! A-9164 (mono), AS-9164 (stereo))

Poliakin, Raoul and His Orchestra with the Stereochorale

- I'll Remember April... (1960, Everest LPBR-5001 (mono), SDBR-1001 (stereo))

Polynesians, The

- Aloha Hawaii (1958, Crown CLP-5044 (mono), CST-113 (stereo))
- Beautiful Blue Hawaii (1965, Crown CLP-5472 (mono), CST-472 (stereo))
- Beautiful Hawaii (1960, Crown CLP-5191 (mono), CST-214 (stereo))
- Beautiful Hawaii (1964, Crown CLP-5446 (mono), CST-446 (stereo)) This appears to be a completely different album from the previous listing.
- Blue Hawaii (1959, Crown CLP-5130 (mono), CST-163 (stereo))
- Hawaii Calling (1961, Crown CLP-5206 (mono), CST-223 (stereo))
- Hawaiian Love Songs (1966, Crown CLP-5519 (mono), CST-519 (stereo))
- Hawaiian Memories (1963, Crown CLP-5301 (mono), CST-301 (stereo); re-released 1970, CST-604)
- Hawaiian Paradise (1962, Crown CLP-5271 (mono), CST-271 (stereo))

- Hawaiian Wedding Song (1967, Crown CLP-5535 (mono), CST-535 (stereo))
- Lovely Hawaii (1962, Crown CLP-5265 (mono), CST-265 (stereo))
- Polynesia: The Music of Hawaii-Tahiti-Samoa (1959, Crown CLP-5136 (mono), CST-169 (stereo))
- Romantic Hawaii (1966, Crown CLP-5488 (mono), CST-488 (stereo))
- Sweet Leilani (1964, Crown CLP-5416 (mono), CST-416 (stereo))

Poole, George and His Orchestra (aka **Johnny Poole**)
- Hawaiian Enchantment for Dancing (Omega OSL-34; Clarion 620) Note: the Clarion release lists the artist as Johnny Poole, with the title simply *Hawaiian Enchantment*; the same list of songs is retained, but they are in a different order.

Pourcel, Franck (**and His French Strings**)
- Aquarius (1969, ATCO 33-299)
- Beautiful Obsession (1966, Imperial LP 12322; LP 9322)
- French Sax (1957, Capitol T-10126)
- The French Touch (1957, Capitol T-10103)
- French Wine Drinking Music (1959, Capitol T-10229 (mono), ST-10229 (stereo))
- Les Baxter's La Femme (1956, Capitol T-10015)
- Love is Blue (1968, Imperial LP-12383)
- Pourcel Portraits (1963, Capitol T-1855 (mono), ST-1855 (stereo))
- Pourcel's Pastels (1961, Capitol T-10260 (mono), ST-10260 (stereo))
- Rainy Night in Paris (1958, Capitol T-10151)

Powell, Baden (aka **Baden**)
- Fresh Winds (1969, UA International UNS 15559; with **Paul Mauriat and His Orchestra**)

Prado, Perez and His Orchestra

Perez Prado was one of the important pioneers in American acceptance of Afro-Cuban music, especially the mambo craze.
- Big Hits by Prado (1960, RCA Victor LPM-2104 (mono), LSP-2104 (stereo))
- Concierto Para Bongo (1967, United Artists UAL-3489 (mono), UAS-6489 (stereo))
- Dance Latino (1965, RCA Victor LPM-3330 (mono), LSP-3330 (stereo))
- Dilo (Ugh!) (1958, RCA Victor LPM-1883 (mono), LSP-1883 (stereo))

- "Estas Si Viven" ("The Living End") (1968, UA Latino L 31032 (mono), LS 61032 (stereo))
- Exotic Suite of the Americas (1962, RCA Victor LPM-2571 (mono), LSP-2571 (stereo))
- Great Mambos and Other Latin American Favorites (1958, Bell BLP-12)
- Havana, 3 a.m. (1956, RCA Victor LPM-1257)
- Latin Dance Rhythms (1961, Diplomat 2243 (mono), DS 2243 (stereo))
- Latin Satin (1957, RCA Victor LPM-1459)
- Latino! (1961, RCA Camden CAL-547 (mono), CAS-547 (stereo))
- Lights! Action! Prado! (1965, United Artists UAL-3394 (mono), UAS-6394 (stereo))
- Mambo by the King (1956, RCA Victor LPM-1196)
- Mambo Happy (1957, RCA Camden CAL-409)
- Mambo Mania (1955, RCA Victor LPM-1075)
- Now! Twist Goes Latin (1962, RCA Victor LPM-2524 (mono), LSP-2524 (stereo))
- Our Man in Latin America (1963, RCA Victor LPM-2610 (mono), LSP-2610 (stereo))
- Perez Prado A Go Go (1965, Orfeon ALP-1401)
- Perez Prado Features the New Dance La Chunga by the Arthur Murrays (1961, RCA Victor LPM-2379 (mono), LSP-2379 (stereo))
- Pops and Prado (1959, RCA Victor LPM-2028 (mono), LSP-2028 (stereo))
- "Prez" (1958, RCA Victor LPM-1556 (mono), LSP-1556 (stereo))
- Rockambo (1961, RCA Victor LPM-2308 (mono), LSP-2308 (stereo))

Prado, Perez and Carlos Molina

- In Mexico (1964, Spin-O-Rama M-156 (mono), S-156 (stereo); Prado's music takes up side A, Molina's side B)

Previn, Andre

- All Alone (1967, RCA Victor LPM-3806 (mono), LSP-3806 (stereo))
- Andre Previn Plays Music of the Young Hollywood Composers (1965, RCA Victor LPM-3491 (mono), LSP-3491 (stereo))
- Andre Previn Plays Songs by Jerome Kern (1959, Contemporary M-3567 (mono), S-3567 (stereo))
- But Beautiful (1963, Decca DL 4350 (mono), DL 74350 (stereo))

- Composer – Arranger – Conductor – Pianist (1964, MGM E-4186 (mono), SE-4186 (stereo))
- The Faraway Part of Town (1962, Columbia CL 1786 (mono), CS 8586 (stereo))
- Featuring the Magic Moods of Andre Previn (Coronet CXS-181) This was actually a 'split' album, with Previn's music on side A, and Mike Di Napoli & Trio on side B. Oddly, only Previn is mentioned on the front cover.
- Let's Get Away From It All (1955, Decca DL 8131)
- Like Love (1960, Columbia CL 1437 (mono), CS 8233 (stereo))
- Love Walked In (1964, RCA Camden CAL-792 (mono), CAS-792(e) (stereo))
- Mad About the Boy (1958, RCA Camden CAL-406)
- Misty (1965, Harmony HL 7348 (mono), HS 11148 (stereo))
- The Popular Previn (1965, Columbia CL 2294 (mono), CS 9094 (stereo))
- The Previn Scene (1961, MGM E-3908 (mono), SE-3908 (stereo))
- Previn With Voices (1966, RCA Victor LPM-3551 (mono), LSP-3551 (stereo))
- Soft and Swinging: The Music of Jimmy McHugh (1964, Columbia CL 2114 (mono), CS 8914 (stereo))
- Sound Stage! (1964, Columbia CL 2158 (mono), CS 8958 (stereo))
- Straight Piano (Harmony HS 11207)
- Thinking About You (1961, Columbia CL 1595 (mono), CS 8395 (stereo))
- Three Little Words (1956?, RCA Victor LPM-1356)

Previn, Andre and David Rose and His Orchestra (see also **David Rose and Andre Previn**)

- Like Blue (1960, MGM E-3811 (mono), SE-3811 (stereo))
- Secret Songs for Young Lovers (1958, MGM E-3716 (mono), SE-3716 (stereo))

Prudden, Bonnie

- Keep Fit and Be Happy (1959, Warner Brothers W 1358 (mono), WS 1358 (stereo))
- Keep Fit and Be Happy, Number 2 (Warner Brothers WS 1445; music by **Otto Cesana and His Orchestra**) These were records meant to be listened to while exercising, with different tracks meant to be paired with certain techniques.

Puente, Tito (see also **Woody Herman and Tito Puente**)

Tito Puente's career in Latin music spanned several decades, but he gained his earlier successes during the mambo and cha-cha crazes.

- Bailables (1963, Tico LP-1093 (mono), SLP-1093 (stereo))
- Cha Cha Cha's For Lovers (1956, Tico LP-1005)
- Cha Cha With Tito Puente at Grossinger's (1960, RCA Victor LPM-2187 (mono), LSP-2187 (stereo)
- Dance Mania (1958, RCA Victor LPM-1692 (mono), LSP-1692 (stereo))
- El Rey Bravo (1962, Tico LP-1086 (mono), SLP-1086 (stereo))
- The Exciting Tito Puente Band in Hollywood (1967 GNP Crescendo GNPS-1535)
- The Latin World of Tito Puente (1963, Tico SLP-1109)
- Mucho Puente, Plenty Puente (1964, Tico LP-1115 (mono), SLP-1115 (stereo)
- On the Bridge (1969, Tico LP-1191 (mono), SLP-1191 (stereo))
- Pachanga con Puente (1961, Tico LP-1083 (mono), SLP-1083 (stereo))
- Pa'Lante/Straight (1970, Tico LP-1214)
- Puente in Percussion (1956, Tico LP-1011)
- Tambo (1960, RCA Victor LPM-2257 (mono), LSP-2257 (stereo))
- Tito Puente in Puerto Rico, Recorded Live (1963, Tico LP-1088 (mono), SLP-1088 (stereo))
- Top Percussion (1958, RCA Victor LPM-1617 (mono), LSP-1617 (stereo))

Purcell, Pancho and His Bambuco Players

- Bambuco Moves In (1966, Columbia CL 2543 (mono), CL 9343 (stereo))

Radiant Velvet Orchestra, The

- Silk Satin & Strings (1963, Concert-Disc CS-36)

Rady, Simon (aka **Sy Rady**)

- This Thing Called Love (1962, Columbia CL 1911 (mono), CS 8711 (stereo); as The Sy Rady Singers)
- Voices in Motion (1961, Columbia CL 1665 (mono), CS 8465 (stereo))

Raim, Walter

- 12 String Guitar 12 Great Hits (1964, Liberty LRP-3347 (mono), LST-7347 (stereo))
- The Electrifying Guitar of Walter Raim (1965, Mercury MG 21021 (mono), SR 61021 (stereo))

- Endless Possibilities (1970, MTA MTS-5020)

Rains, Gene (aka **The Gene Rains Group**)

- Far Across the Sea (1961, Decca DL 4164 (mono), DL 74164 (stereo))
- Lotus Land (1960, Decca DL DL 4064 (mono), DL 74064 (stereo))
- Rains in the Tropics (1962, Decca DL 4348 (mono), DL 74348 (stereo))

Ralke, Don (see also **Johnny Gunn and Don Ralke**)

- Bourbon Street Beat (1959, Warner Brothers W 1321 (mono), WS 1321 (stereo))
- But You've Never Heard Gershwin With Bongos (1960, Warner Brothers W 1360 (mono), WS 1360 (stereo))
- The Savage and The Sensuous Bongos (1960, Warner Brothers W 1398 (mono), WS 1398 (stereo))
- Very Truly Yours (1957, Crown CLP 5018)

Ralke, Don and Buddy Collette

- Bongo Madness (1957, Crown CLP 5019) One of the classics of the bongo music genre.

Ralston, Bob (see also **Living Strings**)

- 22 All-Time Organ Favorites (1966, RCA Camden CAL-917 (mono), CAS-917 (stereo))
- All Time Organ Favorites (1972, RCA Camden) Five album set. OK, did this thing have its own primary catalog number? It was composed of five separate albums, most of which were previously released, and each of which sported its previous solo catalog number. The fifth disc was called *Make Someone Happy*, R-213727-1; this may not have been a previous release.
- Bob Ralston Playing the Great Movie & Show Themes (1968, Ranwood R-8031)
- Bob Ralston Plays His Most Requested Songs (1966, RCA Victor LPM-3598 (mono), LSP-3598 (stereo))
- I Left My Heart in San Francisco (1969, Ranwood R-8064; 'Lawrence Welk Presents'…)
- Music For Everyone (1964, RCA Camden CAL-845 (mono), CAS-845 (stereo))
- Red Roses for a Blue Lady (1965, RCA Camden CAL-896 (mono), CAS-896 (stereo))
- Tea for Two and Other Organ Favorites (1972, RCA Camden CXS-9021; also Pickwick)

Ramblers, The

- Tea Dansero (1959, Coral CRL 57253)

Raskin, Milt

It's a great loss to the world of music that Milt Raskin really only produced one album's worth of music that can be found on vinyl today, because the music he created for *Kapu/Exotic Percussion* can stand among the best in the Exotica genre.

- Exotic Percussion (1960, Crown CLP 5189 (mono), CST 212 (stereo); this was a re-release of *Kapu (Forbidden)* with the songs in a different order.

- Exotic Sounds of Hawaii (1970, Crown CST 616) This was another re-issue of *Kapu (Forbidden)* with the songs in the original order.

- *Kapu (Forbidden)* (1959, Crown CLP 5110 (mono), CST 142 (stereo); re-released as *Exotic* Percussion with the songs placed in a different order, then again laster as *Exotic Sounds of Hawaii* with the original song order restored; stereo version released on red vinyl as well as black with red apparently being the first release)

Raymond, Lew and His Orchestra

- The Best of Oklahoma & Carousel (1958, Tops L1620 (mono); Mayfair 9620S (stereo))

- Big Hits from the Fabulous 50's (1957, Tops L1592) Jayne Mansfield is featured on the cover.

- For Men Only (1957, Tops L1583) This cover also features Jayne Mansfield.

- Holiday in Spain (1957, Tops L1586)

- Million Sellers (1958, Tops L1647; with The Hollywood Studio Orchestra) This one has Mary Tyler Moore on the cover.

- Music from Michael Todd's Around the World in 80 Days (1957, Tops L1591)

- My Fair Lady (1957, Tops L1537)

- South Pacific (1958, Tops L1634 (mono); Mayfair 9634S (stereo))

- Themes from the Movies (1957, Tops L1519)

Reed, Les and His Orchestra

Pure Easy Listening. This Les Reed is not to be confused with the one who was apparently a Gospel musician/comedian.

- Fly Me to the Sun (1967, Deram DE-16007 (mono), DES-16007 (stereo))

- Love Is All (1969, London SP 44136; with The Eddie Lester Singers)

- New Dimensions (1968, Deram DE-16011 (mono), DES-16011 (stereo); as The Les Reed Sound)

Rehbein, Herbert and His Orchestra

- ...And So to Bed: The Love Music of Bert Kaempfert (1969, Decca DL 75107)
- Love After Midnight (1957, Decca DL 4847 (mono), DL 74847 (stereo))
- Music to Soothe That Tiger (1964, Decca DL 4584 (mono), DL 74584 (stereo))

Reisman, Joe and His Orchestra (see also **Eddie Haywood**)

- Door of Dreams (1957, RCA Victor LPM-1519)
- Instrumental Imports (1960, Roulette R 25114 (mono), SR 25114 (stereo))
- Walt Disney Songs for the Family (1955, RCA Victor LPM-1119; also released as *Walt Disney Song Carousel* with the same catalog number)

Rene, Henri and His Orchestra

- Compulsion to Swing (1959, RCA Victor LPM-1947 (mono), LSP-1947 (stereo))
- Dynamic Dimensions (1961, RCA Victor LSA-2396) (Stereo Action)
- In Love Again! (1956, RCA Camden CAL-312)
- Intermezzo (1954, RCA Victor LPM-1245)
- Melodic Magic (RCA Camden CAL-353; also released as *Melodies of Love in Hi-Fi*; was there a stereophonic release?)
- Music for Bachelors (1956, RCA Victor LPM-1046) Jayne Mansfield is featured on the cover.
- Music for the Weaker Sex (1958, RCA Victor LPM-1583 (mono), LSP-1583 (stereo))
- Paris Loves Lovers (1963, Decca DL 4269 (mono), DL 74269 (stereo))
- Portfolio for Easy Listening (RCA Camden CAL-130)
- Serenade to Love (1956, RCA Victor LPM-1194)
- Show Boat (1958, RCA Victor LOP-1505 (mono), LSO-1505 (stereo))
- The Swinging 59 (1960, Imperial LP-9096 (mono), LP-12040 (stereo))
- They're Playing Our Song (Decca DL 4574 (mono), DL 74574 (stereo))

Rene, Michael and His Orchestra

- Strings in the Enchanted Garden (Hollywood LPH 14)

Rey, Alvino

- As I Remember Hawaii (1962, Dot DLP 3448 (mono), DLP 25448 (stereo))

- That Lonely Feeling (1960, Capitol T-1395 (mono), ST-1395 (stereo))

Reyes, Emilio and His Orchestra

- An Occasional Cha Cha Cha (1958, Mardi-Gras LP-5004)

- Perfect Dance Tempos for Latin Lovers (1960, Decca DL 74021)

Richards, Emil (**and The Microtonal Blues Band**)

Emil Richards's musical jazz output, especially in these four albums, stray from straight jazz into such areas as Space Age Pop, exotica, Latin jazz, and others. Not for everyone, but much of it is interesting.

- Journey to Bliss (1968, ABC Impulse AS-9166)

- New Time Element (1967, Uni 3003 (mono), 73003 (stereo))

- New Sound Element: "Stones" (1967, Uni 3008 (mono), 73008 (stereo))

- Yazz Per Favore (1961, Del-Fi DFLP 1216 (mono), DFST 1216 (stereo); as Emil Richards's Yazz Band)

Richards, Johnny and His Orchestra

- My Fair Lady – My Way (1964, Roulette R 52114 (mono), SR 52114 (stereo))

- Something Else by Johnny Richards (1956, Bethlehem BCP 6011)

- Walk Softly/Run Wild! (1959, Coral CRL 57304 (mono), CRL 757304 (stereo))

Riddle, Nelson and His Orchestra (see also **101 Strings**)

Nelson Riddle had a hell of a musical career, from film scores and arrangements for popular singers like Sinatra and Dean Martin, to several albums' worth of Easy Listening-style orchestrated offerings.

- Batman (1966, 20th Century Fox TFM-3180 (mono), TFS-4180 (stereo)) Music from the TV series.

- Bridge Over Troubled Water (1971, Alshire S-5203; this was a re-release of the previous year's *Nelson Riddle Arranges and Conducts 101 Strings*; with **101 Strings**)

- The Bright and the Beautiful (1967, Liberty LRT-3508 (mono), LST-7508 (stereo))

- Can Can (1960, Capitol T-1365 (mono), ST-1365 (stereo)) Music from the film.

- Changing Colors (1971, MPS MB-20887)

- C'mon... Get Happy! (1958, Capitol T-893)
- Come Blow Your Horn (1963, Reprise R-6071 (mono), R9-6071 (stereo)) Music from the film.
- Communication (1973, MPS MB-20888)
- Contemporary Sound of Nelson Riddle (1968, United Artists UAS 6670)
- El Dorado (1967, Epic FLS 15114) Music from the film.
- Great Music, Great Films, Great Sounds (1964, Reprise R-6138 (mono), R9-6138 (stereo))
- Harlow (1965, Warner Brothers W-1599 (mono), WS-1599 (stereo)) Music from the film.
- Hey... Let Yourself Go! (1957, Capitol T-814)
- The Joy of Living (1959, Capitol T-1148 (mono), ST-1148 (stereo))
- Let's Face the Music & Dance! (1966, Pickwick/33 PC-3036 (mono), SPC-3036 (stereo))
- Lolita (1962, MGM E 4050 ST (mono), SE 4050 ST (stereo)) Music from the film.
- Love is a Game of Poker (1962, Capitol T-1817 (mono), ST-1817 (stereo))
- Love Tide (1961, Capitol T-1571 (mono), ST-1571 (stereo))
- Magic Moments from 'The Gay Life' (1962, Capitol T-1670 (mono), ST-1670 (stereo)) Music from the stage production.
- More Hit TV Themes (1963, Capitol T-1869 (mono), ST-1869 (stereo))
- Music For Wives and Lovers (1967, Solid State SS 18013)
- The Music from Oklahoma! (Capitol T-596)
- Nelson Riddle and His Orchestra Play the Wonderful Nat King Cole Songs (1969, Harmony H 11320)
- Nelson Riddle Arranges and Conducts 101 Strings (1970, Alshire S-5203; re-released as *Bridge Over Troubled Water* with the same catalog number; with **101 Strings**)
- Paint Your Wagon (1970, Forward ST-F-1016) Music from the film.
- Paris When it Sizzles (1964, Reprise R-6113 (mono), R9-6113 (stereo)) Music from the film.
- A Rage to Live (1965, United Artists UAL-4130 (mono), UAS-5130 (stereo); with **Ferrante & Teicher**) Music from the film.
- The Riddle of Today (1968, Liberty LRP-3532 (mono), LST-7532 (stereo))
- The Riddle Touch (Sunset SUS-5233)
- The Rogues (1964, RCA Victor LPM-2976 (mono), LSP-2976 (stereo)) Music from the film.

- Route 66 Theme and Other Great TV Themes (1962, Capitol T-1771 (mono), ST-1771 (stereo))
- Sea of Dreams (1958, Capitol T-915 (mono), ST-915 (stereo))
- Sing a Song With Riddle (Capitol TAO-1259 (mono), STAO-1259 (stereo) This record was apparently marketed to entice people to sing along with the songs; a little booklet with lyrics to each tune was included in the package.
- The Tender Touch (1956, Capitol T-753)
- The Untouchables (1959, Capitol T-1430 (mono), ST-1430 (stereo))
- What a Way to Go! (1964, 20th Century Fox TFM 3143 (mono), TFS 4143 (stereo)) Music from the film.
- 'White on White,' 'Shangri-La,' 'Charade,' and Other Hits of 1964 (1965, Reprise RS-6120)
- Witchcraft! (1965, Pickwick/33 PC-3007 (mono), SPC-3007 (stereo))

Rio Carnival Orchestra, The

- Caribbean Cruise (1959, Somerset P-5900 (mono), SF-5900 (stereo))
- Honeymoon in South America (1958, Somerset P-1900 (mono), SF-1900 (stereo))

Rivera, Manuel, and His Orchestra

- Dance Tempo: Cha Cha Cha (1959, Crown CLP 5138 (mono), CST 171 (stereo))
- Latin Dances and Rhythms (Crown CLP 5261 (mono), CST 261 (stereo))

Riviera Strings, The

- Love is Blue (1968, Mercury Wing SRW-16355)
- Music from Funny Girl and Other Movie Hits (1968, Mercury Wing SRW-16387)
- This Guy's In Love With You (1968, Mercury Wing SRW-16370)

Roberto and His Orchestra

Whoever was recording under the pseudonym 'Roberto and His Orchestra,' the recurring theme was an interesting one – orchestral albums with music devoted to a different famous beauty queen each time.

- Anita, My Love (1956, Coral CRL 57154) This disc was devoted to Swedish bombshell Anita Ekberg.
- I Love Gina (1956, Coral CRL 57152) This one was devoted to Italian beauty Gina Lollobrigida.

- My Love for Jane (1956, Coral CRL 57153) This record was dedicated to buxom American actress Jane Russell.

Rodriguez, Willie

- Anyone Can Play Bongos (Epic BN 583; with **Chuck Sagle and His Orchestra**) This was another bongo instructional record.
- A Bunch of Bongos (1960, Grand Award GA 33 421 (mono), GA 253 SD (stereo); as Willie Rodriguez and the International Stars)
- Willie Rodriguez Swings (1965, Man WR-1001)

Rogers, Milton and His Orchestra

- Jet Set: Ports of Call (1966, Time S/2202)
- The Ultimate in Percussion (1960, Dot DLP 3319 (mono), DLP 25319 (stereo))

Romero, Luis & His Satin Strings

- Latin Flight (Manhattan Man 509)

Ros, Edmundo and His Orchestra (see also **Ted Heath and Edmundo Ros**)

- Arriba (1966, London SP 44080)
- Bongos of the South (1961, London P 54003 (mono), SP 44003 (stereo))
- Calypso Mania (1969, Richmond/London B 20021)
- Dance Again (1962, London SP 44015)
- Hair Goes Latin (1970, London SP 44134)
- Heading South... Of The Border (1971, London SP 44153)
- Hi-Fiesta (1958, London LL 3000 (mono), PS 105 (stereo))
- Hollywood Cha Cha Cha (1959, London LL 3100 (mono), PS 152 (stereo))
- Latin Boss Senor Ros (1966, London SP 44073)
- Latin Hits I Missed (1967, London SP 44094)
- The Latin Kings (1971, London SP 44169)
- New Rhythms of the South (1964, London LL 3388 (mono), SP 44054 (stereo))
- Rhythms of the South (1958, London LL 1612 (mono), PS 114 (stereo)) The stereo version of this album was reputed to be one of the first really high-quality recordings in that new format.
- Ros on Broadway (1958, London LL 3048 (mono), PS 110 (stereo))
- Strings Latino (1968, London SP 44107)
- This is My World (1972, London SP 44189)

Rossani, Roberto and His Orchestra

- Soft and Warm (1959, Somerset P-12300 (mono), SF-12300 (stereo))

Rose, David and His Orchestra

David Rose had an adimarable career composing music for radio and television; this included his tune "The Stripper," which sold 2 million copies and still stands today as THE music to scat-sing whenever anybody starts taking their clothes off.

- 21 Channel Sound (1962, MGM E 4004 (mono), SE 4004 (stereo))
- Autumn Leaves (1958, MGM E 3592 (mono), SE 3592 (stereo))
- Beautiful Music to Love By (1953, MGM E 3067)
- The Bible (1966, Capitol T-2627 (mono), ST-2627 (stereo); re-issue of *Themes from the Great Screen Epics*)
- Butterfield 8 (1960, MGM E 3952 (mono), SE 3952 (stereo)) Music from the film.
- David Rose and His Orchestra (1962, Rondo-Lette 882)
- David Rose Plays David Rose (MGM E 3748 (mono), SE 3748 (stereo))
- Deep Purple (1965, Metro M-502 (mono), MS-502 (stereo))
- Exodus and Other Great Themes (1961, MGM E 3950 (mono), SE 3950 (stereo))
- Happy Heart (1970, Capitol ST-393)
- Holiday for Strings (1957, Crowell-Collier Record Guild G-146; last song on side B is "La Ronde")
- Holiday for Strings (1958, RCA Camden CAL-463; RCA Victor LPT-1011; a different selection of songs from the previous entry; last song on side B is "The Last Time I Saw Paris")
- Holiday for Strings (1967, Capitol T-2717 (mono), ST-2717 (stereo); this is a completely different collection of songs; the last song on side B is "Wig-Wam")
- In a Mellow Mood (1957, Masterseal ST-9000)
- Lovers' Serenade (1955, MGM E 3289)
- MGM Movie Hits (MGM SE 3988; with Leroy Holmes and His Orchestra)
- More! More! More! Music of The Stripper (1962, MGM E 4099 (mono), SE 4099 (stereo))
- Nostalgia (1954, MGM E 3134)
- Quick, Before It Melts (1964, MGM E 4285 (mono), SE 4285 (stereo)) Music from the film.
- Sentimental Journey (1955, MGM E 3255)
- Something Fresh (1969, Capitol ST-124)

- The Song is You: Melodies by Jerome Kern (1956, MGM E 3555)

- Spectacular Strings (1961, MGM E 3895 (mono), SE 3895 (stereo))

- Strings Alive (1962, Spin-O-Rama M-95 (mono), S-95 (stereo))

- The Stripper and Other Fun Songs for the Family (1962, MGM E 4062 (mono), SE 4062 (stereo))

- Themes from the Great Screen Epics (1966, Capitol T-2627 (mono), ST-2627 (stereo); re-issued as *The Bible* with the same catalog number)

- The Velvet Beat (1965, MGM E 4307 (mono), SE 4307 (stereo))

- The Wonderful World of the Brothers Grimm (1962, MGM E 4077 (mono), SE 4077 (stereo))

Rose, David and Andre Previn (see also **Andre Previn and David Rose**)

- Vibrant Strings/Enchanted Keys (1964, Spin-O-Rama M-132 (mono), S-132 (stereo); David Rose plays side A ("Vibrant Strings") while Andre Previn takes side B ("Enchanted Keys")

Rose, David and His Orchestra, and the Stradivari Strings

- Enchanted Strings (Spin-O-Rama M-103 (mono), S-103 (stereo); this is one of those 'split' albums – David Rose and his orchestra are featured on side A and the Stradivari Strings are featured on side B)

Rosengarden, Bob and Phil Kraus

- Hollywood Sound Stage (1961, Decca DL 4184 (mono), DL 74184 (stereo))

- Hot Line For Sound (1966, Project 3 Total Sound PR 5002-SD; as 'Bob & Phil and the Orchestra')

- Like Bongos (1960, Time 52025 (mono), S/2025 (stereo))

- Percussion Playful and Pretty (1965, RCA Victor CPM 113 (mono), CSP 113 (stereo))

Royal, Lani and the Diamond Head Band

- Hawaiian War Chant (1962, Kapp KL-1302 (mono), KS-3302 (stereo))

- The Sound of Hawaii: Percussive Pineapples (1961, Kapp/Medallion ML-7516 (mono), MS-7516 (stereo))

Royal Tahitians, The

- Melodies from the South Seas (1962, Hamilton HLP 123 (mono), HLP 12123 (stereo))

- Melodies from the South Seas, Vol. 2 (1963, Hamilton HLP 146 (mono), HLP 12146 (stereo))

- Soft Sounds from the South Seas (1960, Dot DLP 3305 (mono), DLP 25305 (stereo))
- Soft Sounds from the South Seas, Vol. 2 (Dot DLP 3411 (mono), DLP 25411 (stereo))

Rugolo, Pete and His Orchestra

- 10 Saxophones and 2 Basses (1961, Mercury PPS 2023 (mono), 6023 (stereo))
- 10 Trumpets and 2 Guitars (1961, Mercury PPS 2016 (mono), PPS 6016 (stereo))
- Adventures in Rhythm (1954, Columbia CL 604)
- An Adventure in Sound – Brass (1958, Mercury MG 20261 (mono), SR 60044 (stereo))
- An Adventure in Sound – Reeds (1958, Mercury MG 20260 (mono), SR 60039 (stereo))
- Behind Brigitte Bardot: Cool Sounds from Her Hot Scenes (1960, Warner Brothers B-1371 (mono), WS-1371 (stereo)) The actress is featured in a wide photo on the gatefold cover to this album.
- Brass At Work (1956, Blue Ribbon BRM 8001)
- Introducing Pete Rugolo and His Orchestra (1955, Columbia CL 635)
- Music for Hi-Fi Bugs (1956, EmArcy MG 36082)
- The Music from Richard Diamond (1959, Mercury MG 36162 (mono), SR 80045 (stereo)) Music from the TV series.
- Music from Out of Space (1957, Mercury MG 20118)
- New Sounds (1957, Harmony HL 7003)
- The Original Music of 'Thriller' (1961, Time 52034 (mono), S/2034 (stereo))
- Out on a Limb (1957, Emarcy MG 36115; as Pete Rugolo and His All Stars)
- Percussion at Work (1958, Mercury MG 36122 (mono), SR 80003 (stereo); Mercury Wing MGW 12229 (mono), SRW 16229 (stereo); the Mercury Wing version for whatever reason has the same songs in a different order)
- Rhythm Meets Rugolo (1959, Mercury MG 20551 (mono), SR 60119 (stereo))
- Rugolo Plays Kenton (1958, Mercury MG 36143 (mono), SR 80014 (stereo))
- Rugolomania (1955, Columbia CL 689; with 'The Rugolettes')
- The Sweet Ride (1968, 20th Century Fox S-4198) Music from the film.

- TV's Top Themes (1959, Mercury MG 20706 (mono), SR 60706 (stereo))

Russin, Babe

- To Soothe the Savage (1956, Dot DLP-3060)

Sabu (aka **Sabu Martinez**)

- Jungle Percussion (Clarity 812; as Sabu and His Jungle Percussionists) This was a budget-label re-release of *Jungle Beat* by **Subri Moulin and His Equatorial Rhythm Group** and probably *not* by Sabu Martinez, but it is included here for the sake of reference.
- Palo Congo (1957, Blue Note BLP 1561)
- Sabu's Jazz Espagnole (1960, Alegre LPA 802)
- Safari With Sabu (1958, Vik LX-1122)
- Sorcery! (1957, Columbia WL 101; as Sabu and His Percussion Ensemble)

Sagle, Chuck and His Orchestra (see also **Willie Rodriguez**)

- Ping Pong Percussion (1961, Epic LN-3696 (mono), BN-568 (stereo))
- Splendor in the Brass (1962, Reprise R 6047 (mono), RS 6047 (stereo))

San Remo Golden Strings, The

- Hungry For Love (1966, Ric-Tic MLP-901 (mono), SLP-901 (stereo); 1967, Gordy S-923)
- The San Remo Golden Strings Swing (1968, Gordy GLPS 928)

San Remo Orchestra, The

- Romantique (Surrey S-1017 (mono), SS-1017 (stereo))

Sandpipers, The

They started rather late in the game, but the Sandpipers were a harmonizing vocal trio whose music falls into the Easy Listening category with a hint of the Now Sound groove of the time.

- Come Saturday Morning (1970, A&M SP-4262)
- A Gift of Song (1971, A&M SP-4328)
- Guantanamera (1966, A&M LP-117 (mono), SP-4117 (stereo))
- Misty Roses (1967, A&M LP-135 (mono), SP-4135 (stereo))
- The Sandpipers (1967, A&M LP-125 (mono), SP-4125 (stereo))
- Softly (1968, A&M SP-4147)
- Spanish Album (1969, A&M SP-4159)
- The Wonder of You (1969, A&M SP-4180)

Santamaria, Mongo (and His Afro-Latin Group) (see also **Cal Tjader**)

Mongo Santamaria was a Cuban conga player who is best remembered for recording Chick Corea's "Watermelon Man" and for writing the jazz tune "Afro Blue."

- All Strung Out (1970, Columbia CS 9988)
- Arriba-La Pachanga (1961, Fantasy 3324 (mono), 8067 (stereo))
- Drums and Chants (1957, Tico LP-1037)
- El Bravo! (1964, Columbia CL 2411 (mono), CS 9211 (stereo))
- El Pussy Cat (1965, Columbia CL 2298 (mono), CS 9098 (stereo))
- Feelin' Alright (1970, Atlantic SD 8252)
- Go, Mongo! (1962, Riverside RLP 423 (mono), RLP 9423 (stereo))
- Hey! Let's Party (1966, Columbia CL 2473 (mono), CS 9273 (stereo))
- La Bamba (1965, Columbia CL 2375 (mono), CS 9175 (stereo))
- Mighty Mongo (1962, Fantasy 3351 (mono), 8351 (stereo))
- Mongo (1959, Fantasy 3291 (mono), 8032 (stereo); released in black, red, and blue vinyl)
- Mongo '70 (1970, Atlantic SD 1567)
- Mongo Explodes (1966, Riverside R 3530 (mono), RS 93530 (stereo))
- Mongo in Havana: Bembe (1960, Fantasy 3311 (mono), 8055 (stereo) ; released in black, red, and blue vinyl)
- Mongomania (1967, Columbia CL 2612 (mono), CS 9412 (stereo))
- Mongo's Way (1971, Atlantic SD 1581)
- Soul Bag (1968, Columbia CS 9653)
- Stone Soul (1969, Columbia CS 9780)
- Up From the Roots (1972, Atlantic SD 1621)
- Viva Mongo! (1962, Fantasy 3335 (mono), 8087 (stereo))
- Watermelon Man! (1963, Battle BM 6120 (mono), BS 96120 (stereo))
- Workin' on a Groovy Thing (1969, Columbia CS 9937)
- Yambu (1958, Fantasy 3267 (mono), 8012 (stereo); released in black, red, and blue vinyl)

Santiago and His Silver Strings

- Broadway Show Stoppers (Coronet CX-189 (mono), CXS-189 (stereo))
- Exodus and Other Great String Themes (Coronet CX-144 (mono), CXS-144 (stereo))
- Heart of Spain (Coronet CX-123 (mono), CXS-123 (stereo))
- Memories of You (Coronet CX-183 (mono), CXS-183 (stereo))

- Musical Holiday (Coronet CX-151 (mono), CXS-151 (stereo))
- Passionate Paris in Ping Pong Percussion (Coronet CX-142 (mono), CXS-142 (stereo))

Sarkissian, Buddy and His Mecca Four with Fred Elias

- Soul of the East (1962, Cameo C 1023 (mono), SC 1023 (stereo); re-released 1964, Wyncote W-9020 (mono), SW-9020 (stereo), with 2 songs removed)

Satin Strings

- The Sounds of the Satin Strings (Stereo Sounds SS-2) Three-record set.

Schifrin, Lalo

- Bossa Nova: New Brazilian Jazz (1962, Audio Fidelity AFLP 1981 (mono), AFSD 5981 (stereo))
- Bullitt (1968, Warner Brothers WS 1777) Music from the Steve McQueen film.
- Enter the Dragon (1973, Warner Brothers BS 2727) Music from the Bruce Lee film.
- The Fox (1967, Warner Brothers WS 1738) Music from the Peter Sellers film.
- Gone With the Wave (1965, Colpix CP 492 (mono), SCP 492 (stereo))
- Insensatez (1968, Verve V6-8785)
- The Liquidator (1965, MGM E-4413-ST (mono), SE-4413-ST (stereo)) Music from the film.
- Mannix (1968, Paramount PAS-5004) Music from the TV series starring Mike 'Touch' Connors.
- More Mission: Impossible (1969, Paramount PAM-5002 (mono), PAS-5002 (stereo))
- Music from Mission: Impossible (1967, Dot DLP 3831 (mono), DLP 25831 (stereo))
- Music from the Motion Picture Once A Thief and Other Themes (1965, Verve V-8624 (mono), V6-8624 (stereo))
- Piano, Strings, and Bossa Nova (1963, MGM E4110 (mono), SE4110 (stereo))
- There's a Whole Lalo Schifrin Goin' On (1968, Dot DLP 3852 (mono), DLP 25852 (stereo))

Schoen, Vic and His Orchestra

- Brass Laced with Strings (1961, RCA Victor LSA-2344) (Stereo Action)

- Girls With Brass (1966, Mainstream MMS 705; with 'The Girls from Ipanema')

Schory, Dick (aka **Dick Schory's Percussion Pops Orchestra**; **Dick Schory's Percussion and Brass Ensemble**; **Dick Schory and the Percussion Art Ensemble**)

- Carnegie Hall (1970, Ovation OV/14-10-2)
- Dick Schory On Tour (1964, RCA Victor LPM-2806 (mono), LSP-2806 (stereo))
- The Happy Hits (1964, RCA Victor LPM-2926 (mono), LSP-2926 (stereo))
- Holiday For Percussion (1962, RCA Victor LSA-2485) (Stereo Action)
- Movin' On (1971, Ovation 956C-1403)
- Music For Bang, Baaroom, and Harp (1958, RCA Victor LPM-1866 (mono), LSP-1866 (stereo))
- Music to Break Any Mood (1960, RCA Victor LPM-2125 (mono), LSP-2125 (stereo))
- Politely Percussive (1963, RCA Victor LPM-2738 (mono), LSP-2738 (stereo))
- Re-Percussion (1957, Concert-Disc M-1021 (mono), CS-21 (stereo))
- Runnin' Wild (1961, RCA Victor LSA-2306) (Stereo Action)
- Stereo Action Goes Broadway (1961, RCA Victor LSA-2382) (Stereo Action)
- Supercussion (1963, RCA Victor LPM-2613 (mono), LSP-2613 (stereo))
- Wild Percussion and Horns A'plenty (1960, RCA Victor LPM-2289 (mono), LSP-2289 (stereo))

Schumann, Walter (aka **The Voices of Walter Schumann**)

- Exploring the Unknown (1955, RCA Victor LPM 1025)
- Flirtation Walk (1956, RCA Victor LPM 1202)
- Scrapbook (1957, RCA Victor LPM 1465)
- Though Not a Word Was Spoken (1956, RCA Victor LPM 1266)
- The Voices of Walter Schumann (1955, Capitol T-297)
- Walter Schumann Presents the Voices (1958, RCA Victor LPM 1558 (mono), LSP 1558 (stereo))
- When We Were Young (1959, RCA Victor LPM 1477 (mono), LSP 1477 (stereo))

Scott, Frances and His Orchestra

- Moods for Candlelight (1955, Capitol T-304)
- Moods for Firelight (1955, Capitol W-552)
- Moods for Starlight (1953, Capitol H-446)

Scott, Raymond and His Orchestra

- Amor (1960, Everest SDBR 1080; as Raymond Scott and His Swinging Strings)
- At Home With Dorothy and Raymond (1957, Coral CRL-57105)
- Raymond Scott Conducts the Rock 'N Roll Symphony (1958, Everest LPBR 5007 (mono), SDBR 1007 (stereo))
- This Time With Strings (1957, Coral CRL-57174)
- The Unexpected (1960, Top Rank International RM 335; as Raymond Scott and the Secret 7)

Sebesky, Don

- The Distant Galaxy (1968, Verve V6-5063) Hippie-era sounds interpret others' songs as well as new ones. Very much a product of its time.

Senati, John and His Orchestra

- Music for Listening and Dancing (Bravo K 143)
- Stardust (International Award Series AK-143 (mono), AKS-143 (stereo))

Shaffer, Sy and His Orchestra

- Love Story (1958, Westminster WST 15023)
- Seems Like Old Times (1958, Westminster WST 15003)

Shank, Bud

- Brazil! Brazil! Brazil! (1966, World Pacific WP-1855 (mono), WS-21855 (stereo))
- Bud Shank & the Sax Section (1966, Pacific Jazz PJ-10110 (mono), ST-20110 (stereo))
- Bud Shank Plays Music from Today's Movies (1967, World Pacific WP-1864 (mono), WPS-21864 (stereo))
- California Dreamin' (1966, World Pacific WP-1845 (mono), WS-21845 (stereo))
- Girl in Love (1966, World Pacific WP-1853 (mono), WPS-21853 (stereo))
- I'll Take Romance (1958, World Pacific WP-1251; with The Len Mercer Strings)
- Magical Mystery (1968, World Pacific WPS-21873)

- Michelle (1966, World Pacific WP-1840 (mono), WPS-21840 (stereo))
- A Spoonful of Jazz (1967, World Pacific WP-1868 (mono), WPS-21868 (stereo))

Sharpe, Mike

- Mystic Light (1969, Liberty LRP-3615 (mono), LST-7615 (stereo))
- The Sharpest Sax (1968, Liberty LRP-3518 (mono), LST-7518 (stereo))
- The Spooky Sound of Mike Sharpe (1967, Liberty LRP-3507 (mono), LST-7507 (stereo))

Shaw, Roland and His Orchestra

- Mexico! (1963, London SP 44030)
- More Themes from the James Bond Thrillers (1965, London LL 3445 (mono), PS 445 (stereo))
- The Return of James Bond (1971, London 2BSP 24)
- Themes from the James Bond Thrillers (1964, London LL 3412 (mono), PS 412 (stereo))
- Themes from the James Bond Thrillers, Vol. 3 (1966, London LL 3514 (mono), PS 514 (stereo))
- Themes for Secret Agents (1966, London SP 44076)

Shearing, George (aka **The George Shearing Quartet/Quintet/and Strings**)

Keyboardist Shearing, blind since birth, was the author of the classic jazz tune "Lullaby of Birdland" and enjoyed a very long career in music.

- As Requested (1972, Sheba ST 105)
- Black Satin (1957, Capitol T-858)
- Blue Chiffon (1959, Capitol T-1124 (mono), ST-1124 (stereo))
- Burnished Brass (1958, Capitol T-1038 (mono), ST-1038 (stereo))
- Concerto For My Love (1962, Capitol T-1755 (mono), ST-1755 (stereo))
- Deep Velvet (1964, Capitol T-2143 (mono), ST-2143 (stereo))
- An Evening with the George Shearing Quintet (1954, MGM E3122)
- The Fool on the Hill (1969, Capitol ST-181)
- George Shearing Goes Hollywood (1959, Lion 70117)
- Here & Now! (1966, Capitol T-2372 (mono), ST-2372 (stereo))
- I Hear Music (1955, MGM E3266)
- Latin Affair (1960, Capitol T-1275 (mono), ST-1275 (stereo))
- Latin Escapade (1957, Capitol T-373)
- Latin Lace (1958, Capitol T-1082 (mono), ST-1082 (stereo))

- Latin Rendezvous (1963, Capitol T-2326 (mono), ST-2326 (stereo))
- Mood Latino (1961, Capitol T-1567 (mono), ST-1567 (stereo))
- Music to Hear (1972, Sheba ST 106)
- New Look! (1967, Capitol ST-2637)
- Night Mist (1957, Capitol T-943)
- On the Sunny Side of the Strip (1960, Capitol T-1416 (mono), ST-1416 (stereo))
- Out of This World (1971, Sheba ST 101)
- Rare Form! (1966, Capitol T-2447 (mono), ST-2447 (stereo))
- Satin Affair (1962, Capitol T-1628 (mono), ST-1628 (stereo))
- Satin Brass (1960, Capitol T-1326 (mono), ST-1326 (stereo)) Diane Webber is featured on the cover of this album.
- Satin Latin (1959, MGM E4041)
- Shearing Bossa Nova (1962, Capitol T-1873 (mono), ST-1873 (stereo))
- A Shearing Caravan (1955, MGM E3175)
- Shearing in Hi-Fi (1955, MGM E3293)
- Shearing On Stage! (1959, Capitol T-1187 (mono), ST-1187 (stereo))
- The Shearing Piano (1957, Capitol T-909)
- The Shearing Spell (1956, Capitol T-648)
- Shearing Today! (1968, Capitol ST-2699)
- The Shearing Touch (1960, Capitol T-1472 (mono), ST-1472 (stereo))
- Soft and Silky (1959, MGM E4042)
- That Fresh Feeling! (1966, Capitol T-2567 (mono), ST-2567 (stereo))
- Touch Me Softly (1963, Capitol T-1874 (mono), ST-1874 (stereo))
- Touch of Genius! (1955, MGM E3265)
- Velvet Carpet (1956, Capitol T-720)
- When Lights Are Low (1955, MGM E3264)
- White Satin (1960, Capitol T-1334 (mono), ST-1334 (stereo))

Shindo, Tak

- Accent on Bamboo (1960, Capitol T-1433 (mono), ST-1433 (stereo))
- Brass and Bamboo (1959, Capitol T-1345 (mono), ST-1345 (stereo))
- Far East Goes Western (1962, Mercury PPS 2031 (mono), PPS 6031 (stereo)) Traditional Western (as in cowboy) songs done in the Japanese manner.

- Mganga! (1958, Edison International CL-5000)
- Sea of Spring (1966, Grand Prix GPM-1)

Simpson, Mike and His Orchestra (see also **Eddie South**)
- Discussion in Percussion (1961, Mercury PPS 2004 (mono), PPS 6004 (stereo))
- Jungle Odyssey (1969, Evolution 2005) This is a good, interesting album that mixes the recorded sounds of African animals with lively, organ-led exotica numbers. Re-released in modern digital format, it is easy to find online.

Singers Unlimited, The (see also **The Oscar Peterson Trio and Singers Unlimited**; **Art Van Damme**)
- Four of Us (1974, MPS MB 21852)

Singing Strings, The (see also **Morty Craft and The Singing Strings**)
- Dream Along With the Singing Strings (1964, RCA Record Club CPM-108 (mono), CSP-108 (stereo))

Sir Julian

Space-age and Now Sound organ artistry.
- The 13 Fingers of Sir Julian (1962, RCA Victor LPM-2372 (mono), LSP-2372 (stereo))
- 50 Fabulous Organ Favorites (1965, United Artists UAL 3346 (mono), UAS 6346 (stereo))
- A Knight at the Organ (1962, RCA Victor LPM-2591 (mono), LSP-2591 (stereo))
- Love is Blue (1968, Unart MS 21029)
- Organ in Orbit (1965, United Artists UAL 3334 (mono), UAS 6334 (stereo))

Sizzling Brass, The
- The Sizzling Brass (Spin-O-Rama 2-186)

Slatkin, Felix
- Fantastic Percussion (1960, Liberty LRP-3150 (mono), LST-7150 (stereo))
- Fantastic Strings (1964, Liberty LRP-3376 (mono), LST-7376 (stereo))
- Fantastic Strings Play Fantastic Themes (1962, Liberty LMM-13021 (mono), LSS-14021 (stereo))
- Love Strings (1966, Sunset SUS-5016)
- The Magnificent XII (1961, Liberty LMM-13004 (mono), LSS-14004 (stereo))

- Many Splendored Themes (1961, Liberty LMM-13011 (mono), LSS-14011 (stereo))
- Our Winter Love (1963, Liberty LRP-3287 (mono), LST-7287 (stereo))
- Paradise Found (1960, Liberty LMM-13001 (mono), LSS-14001 (stereo))
- Street Scene (1961, Liberty LMM-13008 (mono), LSS-14008 (stereo))
- Tender Strings (1967, Sunset SUM-1170 (mono), SUS-5170 (stereo))

Smith, Ethel

Ethel Smith was a successful female organist whose theme song was "Tico Tico."

- At the End of a Perfect Day (1963?, Decca DL 4467 (mono), DL 74467 (stereo))
- Bright and Breezy (1958, Decca DL 8799)
- Dance to the Latin Rhythms of Ethel Smith (1955, Decca DL 8712)
- Ethel Smith Swings Sweetly (1961, Decca DL 4095 (mono), DL 74095 (stereo))
- Ethel Smith's Cha Cha Cha Album (1955, Decca DL 8164)
- Ethel Smith's Hit Party (1966, Decca DL 4803 (mono), DL 74803 (stereo))
- Galloping Fingers (1956, Decca DL 8456)
- Hollywood Favorites (1965, Decca DL 4618 (mono), DL 74618 (stereo))
- Lady Fingers (1958, Decca DL 8744)
- Lady of Spain (1962, Decca DL 4325 (mono), DL 74325 (stereo))
- Latin From Manhattan (1956, Decca DL 8457)
- Make Mine Hawaiian (1962, Decca DL 4236 (mono), DL 74236 (stereo))
- The Many Moods of Ethel Smith (1961, Decca DL 4145 (mono), DL 74145 (stereo))
- Miss Smith Goes to Paris (1957, Decca DL 8640)
- Organ Holiday (Vocalion VL 3778 (mono), VL 73778 (stereo))
- Organ Solos (Vocalion VL 3669 (mono), VL 73669 (stereo))
- Rhythm Antics! (1963, Decca DL 4414 (mono), DL 74414 (stereo))
- Seated One Day at the Organ (1959, Decca DL 8902 (mono), DL 78902 (stereo))

Smith, Paul (aka **The Paul Smith Quartet**)

- Slightly Latin (1963, MGM E4032 (mono), SE4032 (stereo))

Snyder, Bill and His Orchestra

- Bewitching Hour (1957, Decca DL 8405)
- Café Rendezvous (1957, Decca DL 8367)
- A Handful of Stars (1958, Decca DL 8734)
- Moonlight & Love (1966, Surrey S 1018 (mono), SS 1018 (stereo); as Bill Snyder and His Trio)
- Music for a Moonlight Rendezvous (1965, Surrey S 1016 (mono), SS 1016 (stereo))
- Music For Holding Hands (1956, Decca DL 8102)
- Treasure Chest (1957, Decca DL 8437)

Snyder, Terry and His All Stars

Snyder was a drummer and bandleader who worked with Enoch Light under the Command label for a time, before leaving to produce similar material at United Artists.

- Footlight Percussion (1967, United Artists Ultra Audio WWR 3508 (mono), WWS 8508 (stereo))
- Gentle Purr-Cussion (1962, United Artists Ultra Audio WWR 3521 (mono), WWS 8521 (stereo))
- Mister Percussion (1960, United Artists Ultra Audio WW 7500 (mono), WWS 8500 (stereo)) Note: This was re-released one year later as *Unique Percussion*, with the same catalog number and a similar cover (mostly colored dots and lines). Another cover also exists for the 1960 release, showing Snyder holding drumsticks.
- Persuasive Percussion (1959, Command RS 33 800 (mono), RS 800 SD (stereo))
- Persuasive Percussion, Vol. 2 (1959, Command RS 33 808 (mono), RS 808 SD (stereo))
- Terry Snyder's World of Sound (1963, Columbia CL 1944 (mono), CS 8744 (stereo))
- Unique Percussion (1961, United Artists Ultra Audio WW 7500 (mono), WWS 8500 (stereo); re-release of *Mister Percussion*)

Somerset Strings, The

- Look for the Silver Lining (1957, LN-3256)
- Music for Washing and Ironing (1958, Epic LG-3084)
- Wanting You (1958, Epic LG-3099)
- Will You Remember? (1957, Epic LN-3255)
- Young and Foolish (1957, Epic LN-3392; with Dick Willebrandts)

Sons of Hawaii, The – see **Eddie Kamae and The Sons of Hawaii**

Soulful Strings, The

- Another Exposure (1968, Cadet LPS-805)
- Back By Demand: The Soulful Strings In Concert (1969, Cadet LPS-820)
- Groovin' With the Soulful Strings (1967, Cadet LP-796 (mono), LPS-796 (stereo))
- Paint It Black (1966, Cadet LP-776 (mono), LPS-776 (stereo))
- The Soulful Strings Play Gamble-Huff (1970, Cadet LPS-846)
- String Fever (1969, Cadet LPS-834)

Sounds Galactic

- An Astromusical Odyssey (1971, London SP 44154) Songs done with (then-) modern electronic effects. Arrangements by **Johnny Keating**.
- Nova: Sounds of the Stars (1974, London SP 44199) More of the same, this time arranged by **Roland Shaw**.

Sounds of a Thousand Strings

- Cloud Nine (1960, Crown CLP-166 (mono), CST-194 (stereo))
- Hi-Fi Spectacular (1958, Crown CLP-5116 (mono); the stereo version is listed below as *Your Invitation to Stereo* with the same song list but different cover artwork)
- I Remember Paris (1960, Crown CLP-5152 (mono), CST-182 (stereo))
- Just For Listening (1962, Crown CLP-5260 (mono), CST-260 (stereo))
- The Magic of Hawaii (1960, Crown CLP-5163 (mono), CST-191 (stereo))
- Music for Big Dame Hunters (1960, Crown CLP-5173 (mono), CST-199 (stereo)) Actress and 50's bombshell Irish McCalla is shown on the cover for this LP.
- Musical Memories (1961, Crown CLP-5223 (mono), CST-236 (stereo))
- The Sound of Music (1959, Crown CLP-5135 (mono), CST-168 (stereo); some stereo copies pressed in red vinyl)
- Your Invitation to Stereo (1958, Crown CST-148 (stereo); the mono version is listed above as *Hi-Fi Spectacular*; they are otherwise the same album except for the cover artwork)

Sounds Orchestral

- Cast Your Fate to the Wind (1965, Parkway P-7046 (mono), SP-7046 (stereo))
- Impressions of James Bond (1965, Parkway P-7050 (mono), SP-7050 (stereo))

- One More Time (Janus JLS 3014)
- The Soul of Sounds Orchestral (1962, Parkway P-7047 (mono), SP-7047 (stereo))

South, Eddie and Mike Simpson

- Music For The Birds (1962, Mercury Wing SRW 16225) Violin, flute, electric guitar, bass, and drums play bird-themed songs with a jazzy swing. Not as bad as it sounds.

South Sea Serenaders, The

- Beachcomber Serenade (1955, Tahiti TR-200)
- Hawaii (1968, Pye NSPL 18250)
- Tradewinds Romance from Hawaii to Tahiti (Somerset S-251 (mono), SF-25100 (stereo)) This appears to be a song-for-song re-release of *The Sounds of Exotic Island* by **The Surfmen**.

Southern Tropical Harmony Steel Band, The

- Limbo Party (1962, Audio Fidelity AFLP 1967 (mono), AFSD 5967 (stereo))

Spencer, Johnny and the Kona Koasters

- s'Pacifica (1959, Imperial LP 9076)

Staples, Betty

- Organ Fantasy in Hi-Fi (1957, Crown CLP-5023) Note that this cover was re-used for a Riviera release with the same title but completely different songs, in 1959; see the Compilations section.

Stapleton, Cyril and His Orchestra

- Dim Lights and Blue Music (1957, MGM E 3351)
- I Wish You Love (1958, Lion L-70056)
- Just For You (1958, London PS 109)
- Top Pop Instrumental Hits (1961, Richmond B 20085 (mono), S 30085 (stereo))

Statler, Rudolph (aka **The Rudolph Statler Orchestra**)

- Cinema Holiday (1967, Wyncote W 9210 (mono and stereo))
- Henry Mancini Favorites (1964, Wyncote W 9046 (mono and stereo))
- Moods of Mancini (1967, Wyncote W 9158 (mono and stereo))
- More Mancini Favorites (1964, Wyncote W 9098 (mono and stereo))
- Music from My Fair Lady, Mary Poppins, The Sound of Music (1964, Wyncote W 9073 (mono and stereo))

- Songs from Hello Dolly and Funny Girl (1964, W 9019 (mono), SW 9019 (stereo))

Stefano, Al (and His Trio/Orchestra)

- Cha Cha Favorites (1963, Golden Tone C4050 (mono), 14050 (stereo))
- Latin Dance Party (1958, Decca DL 8646 (mono), DL 78646 (stereo))
- Rhumba Favorites (1960, Golden Tone C4049 (mono), 14049 (stereo))

Sterling, Jack (aka **The Jack Sterling Quintet**)

- Cocktail Swing (1959, Harmony HL 7202 (mono), HS 11015 (stereo))
- Music from 'Gypsy' (1960, Columbia HS 11016)

Stevens, Carl

- African Sounds (1962, Mercury PPS 2030 (mono), PPS 6030 (stereo))
- High Society Twist (1962, Mercury MG 20664 (mono), SR 60664 (stereo))
- Muted Memories (1959, Wing MGW 12138 (mono), SRW 12509 (stereo))
- "Skin" and Bones (1958, Mercury MG 20365 (mono), SR 60013 (stereo))

Stevens, Leith

- The James Dean Story (1957, Columbia W-881) Music from the film.
- Jazz Themes for Cops and Robbers (1958, Coral CRL 57283 (mono), CRL 757283 (stereo))
- Jazz Themes in 'The Wild One' (1953, Decca DL 8349)

Steward, Herb

- Herb Steward Plays So Pretty (1962, Choreo/Ava A9 (mono), AS9 (stereo))

Stordahl, Alex and His Orchestra

- Guitars Around the World! (1962, Decca DL 4337 (mono), DL 74337 (stereo))
- Jasmine & Jade (1960, Dot DLP 3282 (mono), DLP 25282 (stereo))
- The Lure of the Blue Mediterranean (1959, Decca DL 9073 (mono), DL 79073 (stereo))

- The Magic Islands Revisited (1967, Decca DL 9096 (mono), DL 79096 (stereo))

Stradivari Strings, The (see also **David Rose and The Stradivari Strings**)
- Accordion Fantasy (Pirouette FM-41; 'featuring Mario Kostellani and His Accordion')
- An Evening With Rodgers and Hammerstein (Spin-O-Rama MK-3070)
- "The Merry Widow" by Franz Lehar (Spin-O-Rama S-80)
- Music from the Films (Spin-O-Rama MK-3073; M-43 (mono), S-43 (stereo))
- The Music of Leroy Anderson (Spin-O-Rama MK 3087; this appears to be a re-release of *Ping Pong Percussion Sound of Leroy Anderson*)
- Music of Victor Herbert (Pirouette NFM 48)
- Ping Pong Percussion: Jerome Kern (1964, Spin-O-Rama M-66 (mono), S-66 (stereo); this is apparently a re-release of *Tribute to Jerome Kern*)
- Ping Pong Percussion: Lerner & Loewe (Spin-O-Rama M-33 (mono), S-33 (stereo))
- Ping Pong Percussion: Rodgers & Hammerstein (Spin-O-Rama S-42; Pirouette RFM-42; this is apparently a re-release of *An Evening with Rodgers & Hammerstein*)
- Ping Pong Percussion Sound of Leroy Anderson (Spin-O-Rama S-32; Pirouette RFM 32; also known as just *Sound of Leroy Anderson*)
- Relaxing With Leroy Anderson (Parade SPS-387)
- The Sound of Gershwin in Ping Pong Percussion (Spin-O-Rama M-50 (mono), S-50 (stereo))
- String Along With Me (Spin-O-Rama M-90 (mono), S-90 (stereo)) The cover for this album features a portrait photo of Jayne Mansfield.
- The Theme from Exodus and Other Great Themes (Spin-O-Rama MK-3112; Pirouette FM-69)
- Themes from the Films, Vol. 2 (Spin-O-Rama M-107 (mono), S-107 (stereo))
- Tribute to Jerome Kern (Spin-O-Rama MK 3049; also known called *Music of Jerome Kern* on the cover; apparently re-released as *Ping Pong Percussion: Jerome Kern*, with the same songs presented in a different order)

Strange, Billy
- 12 String Guitar (1963, GNP Crescendo GNP-94 (mono), GNPS-94 (stereo))

- Billy Strange & The Challengers (1966, GNP Crescendo GNP-2030 (mono), GNPS-2030 (stereo))
- Billy Strange Plays the Hits! (1964, GNP Crescendo GNP-2012 (mono), GNPS-2012 (stereo))
- Dyn-O-Mite Guitar (GNP Crescendo GNPS-2094)
- English Hits of '65 (1965, GNP Crescendo GNP-2009 (mono), GNPS-2009 (stereo))
- Folk Rock Hits (1965, GNP Crescendo GNP-2016 (mono), GNPS-2016 (stereo))
- Goldfinger (1965, GNP Crescendo GNP-2006 (mono), GNPS-2006 (stereo))
- In the Mexican Bag (1966, GNP Crescendo GNP-2022 (mono), GNPS-2022 (stereo); with The Mexicana Brass)
- James Bond Double Feature (1967, GNP Crescendo GNP-2039 (mono), GNPS-2039 (stereo))
- The James Bond Theme / Walk Don't Run '64 (1964, GNP Crescendo GNP-2004 (mono), GNPS-2004 (stereo))
- Mr. Guitar (1963, GNP Crescendo GNP-97 (mono), GNPS-97 (stereo))
- Secret Agent File (1965, GNP Crescendo GNP-2019 (mono), GNPS-2019 (stereo))

Strings Unlimited

- Award Hits (Oscar OS-114)
- The Fire and Romance of Spain (Oscar OS-128)
- Flirtation (1969, Tempo TS-1003)
- The Impossible Dream (Oscar OS-106)
- Introducing Strings Unlimited (Tempo TS-1001) This album's cover shares the same photo of a woman's face on *Award Hits*.
- Love Story Theme (Oscar OS-101)
- A Lover's Rhapsody (1972, Oscar OS-124)
- Martini Time (Tempo TS-1020)
- Million Seller Hits (1972, Oscar OS-103)
- Raindrops Keep Falling On My Head / Bridge Over Troubled Water (Oscar OS-109)
- Rendezvous With Strings (Tempo TS-1016)
- Romance (Tempo TS-1024)
- Romantic Moods (Oscar OS-108)
- Sad Roses (Tempo TS-1012)
- Scandal in Seville (Tempo TS-1022)
- The Sound of Music (Oscar OS-112)
- Strings For Lovers (1972, Oscar OS-119)

- A Toast to Broadway and Hollywood (Oscar OS-102)

Sumac, Yma

With her five-octave voice, elaborate stage outfits, and Peruvian good looks, Yma Sumac cut quite an exotic figure in the music world of the 1950's. Her recording career effectively lasted for only ten years, but her unique sound is still sought after today. Les Baxter was the godfather of exotica, and Yma Sumac was the fairy godmother.

- Fuego del Ande (1959, Capitol T-1169 (mono), ST-1169 (stereo))
- Legend of the Jivaro (1957, Capitol T-770)
- Legend of the Sun Virgin (1955, Capitol T-299)
- Mambo! (1955, Capitol T-564)
- Miracles (1972, London XPS 608)
- *Voice of the Xtabay* (Capitol SM-684) Re-release of the original 10" disc on 12". Orchestra conducted by **Les Baxter**.
- Voice of the Xtabay / Inca Taqui (Capitol T-684)

Sunset Strings, The (aka **The Sunset Strings and Voices**)

- American in Paris (Synthetic Plastics N 2518 (mono), NS 2518 (stereo))
- An Evening For Romance (Synthetic Plastics N 2514 (mono), NS 2514 (stereo))
- Film Music – Italian Style (1968, Sunset SUM-1188 (mono), SUS-5188 (stereo))
- Great Film Themes (1969, Sunset SUS-5272)
- Hello Young Lovers (Synthetic Plastics N 2502 (mono), NS 2502 (stereo))
- The Impossible Dream (1969, Sunset SUS-5208)
- Release Me (1967, Sunset SUM-1185 (mono), SUS-5185 (stereo))
- Showdown: Great Western Film Themes (1970, Sunset SUS-5275)
- Somewhere, My Love (1966, Liberty LRP-3469 (mono), LST-7469 (stereo))
- Stardust (Synthetic Plastics N 2519 (mono), NS 2519 (stereo))
- The Sunset Strings Play the Roy Orbison Songbook (1964, Liberty LRP-3395 (mono), LST-7395 (stereo))
- The Tender Touch (Synthetic Plastics N 2500 (mono), NS 2500 (stereo))

Surfmen, The

The Surfmen were basically an Exotica All-Stars group, consisting of **Jack Costanzo** (bongos), **Irv Cottler** (drums), Paul Horn (saxophone), **Alvino Rey** (lap steel guitar), Earl Richards (vibraphone), and Jimmy

Rowles (piano). It's unfortunate they recorded only two albums' worth of material.

- Hawaii (1963, Somerset P-17100 (mono), SF-17100 (stereo); aka *The Romantic Lure of Hawaii*)

- *The Sounds of Exotic Island* (1960, Somerset P-10500 (mono), SF-10500 (stereo))

Surrey Brass, The

Studio band put together for the Surrey label.

- Big! Fat! Brass! (Surrey S 1031 (mono), SS 1031 (stereo))
- Made in the 50's (Surrey S 1025 (mono), SS 1025 (stereo))

Surrey Strings, The (see also **Mat Mathews**)

Studio band put together for the Surrey label.

- Made in France (Surrey S 1012 (mono), SS 1012 (stereo))
- Made in Hollywood (Surrey S 1011 (mono), SS 1011 (stereo))
- Made in London (Surrey S 1036 (mono), SS 1036 (stereo))
- Made in Spain (Surrey S 1024 (mono), SS 1024 (stereo))

Swan, Don and His Orchestra

- All This and Cha Cha Too (1957, Liberty LRP 3068)
- Hot-Cha-Cha (1959, Liberty LRP-3114 (mono), LST-7114 (stereo))
- Latino (1959, Liberty LRP-3123 (mono), LST-7123 (stereo))
- Latino Vol. 2 (1960, Liberty LRP-3161 (mono), LST-7161 (stereo))
- Mucho Cha Cha Cha (1956, Liberty LRP 3001)

Swingle Singers, Les

While much of their catalog doesn't quite go in this volume, the Swingle Singers were such a unique vocal group, and did their thing so well, that the author would be remiss for not including them. The group was formed in France in 1962 by Ward Swingle.

- Anyone For Mozart? (1964, Phillips PHM 200-149 (mono), PHS 600-149 (stereo))

- Back to Bach (1969, Phillips PHS 600-288; released elsewhere as *Jazz Sebastien Bach, Vol. 2*)

- Encounter (1966, Phillips PHM 200-225 (mono), PHS 600-225 (stereo); with The Modern Jazz Quartet)

- Getting Romantic (1965, Phillips PHM 200-191 (mono), PHS 600-191 (stereo))

- Going Baroque (1964, Phillips PHM 200-126 (mono), PHS 600-126 (stereo))

- Jazz Sebastien Bach (1963, Phillips PHM 200-097 (mono), PHS 600-097 (stereo))

- The Joy of Singing (1972, Phillips PHS 700-004)

- Rococo A Go Go (1966, Phillips PHM 200-214 (mono), PHS 600-214 (stereo))
- Spanish Masters (1967, Phillips PHM 200-261 (mono), PHS 600-261 (stereo))

Syrene Quintet, The

- Moods of Rohde's (1960, AM3727) – This little curiosity was recorded especially for sale to customers of Rohde's Steak House in Madison, Wisconsin. 'Idea conceived and produced by Dick Hagen.' Tracks include versions of Moonlight in Vermont, Body and Soul, and Night and Day.

Tahitian Percussionists and Exotic Voices, The

- Tahitian Percussion (1961, Al-Fi C4075) This is yet another budget-label re-release (10 of the original 12 songs) of *Jungle Beat* by **Subri Moulin and His Equatorial Rhythm Group**.

Tampicos, The

- That Torrid Tampico Sound! (1965, Columbia CL 2347 (mono), CS 9147 (stereo))

Tanner, Paul and Andre Montero and His Orchestra

- Music for Heavenly Bodies (1959, Omega Disk OSL-4)

Tappen, Ashley

- Hammond Hits from Hollywood (1964, Somerset S-207 (mono), SF-20700 (stereo))
- Hammond Organ Hits in the Ken Griffin Style (1969, Somerset SF-33500)

Tarragano and His Orchestra

- The Sound of Latin Brass (1962, Kapp Medallion ML-7511 (mono), MS-7511 (stereo))

Taylor, Creed (aka **The Creed Taylor Orchestra**)

Creed Taylor must have been an interesting cat. *Shock: Music in Hi-Fi* and *Panic: The Son of Shock* both resemble nothing so much as horror films in musical form, while *Lonelyville* is an exercise in Crime Jazz. It's clear that Taylor wanted to use the recording medium to experiment with the popular music form.

- The Best of the Barrack Ballads (1960, ABC-Paramount ABC-317 (mono), ABCS-317 (stereo))
- Lonelyville: "The Nervous Beat" (1959, ABC-Paramount ABC-308 (mono), ABCS-308 (stereo))
- Panic: The Son of Shock (1960, ABC-Paramount ABC-314 (mono), ABCS-314 (stereo))

- Ping Pang Pong: The Swinging Ball (1960, ABC-Paramount ABC-325 (mono), ABCS-325 (stereo))
- Shock: Music in Hi-Fi (1958, ABC-Paramount ABC-259 (mono), ABCS-259 (stereo))

Taylor, Sam 'The Man'

- Blue Mist (1955, MGM E3292)
- It's a Blue World (1963, Decca DL 4417 (mono), DL 74417 (stereo))
- Mist of the Orient (1962, MGM E4066 (mono), SE4066 (stereo))
- Misty Mood (1962, Decca DL 4302 (mono), DL 74302 (stereo))
- More Blue Mist (1959, MGM E3783 (mono), SE3783 (stereo))
- Prelude to Blues (1957, MGM E3573)
- Sam The Man Taylor Plays Hollywood (1960, MGM E3967 (mono), SE3967 (stereo))
- Somewhere in the Night (1964, Decca DL 4573 (mono), DL 74573 (stereo))

Terrace, Pete (and His Orchestra)

- Baila La Pachanga (1961, Tico LP 1082 (mono), SLP 1082 (stereo))
- Dance Percussion (1961, Strand SL 1032 (mono), SLS 1032 (stereo))
- El Nuevo (1966, Scepter SRM-539 (mono), SPS-539 (stereo))
- Going Loco: Pete Terrace Plays Joe Loco Arrangements (1955, Fantasy 3-203; as The Pete Terrace Quintet; originally issued in red vinyl only)
- Invitation to the Mambo (1956, Fantasy 3-215; as 'The Pete Terrace Quintet with Arrangements by Joe Loco'; originally issued in red vinyl only)
- King of the Bugaloo (1967, AS Records ASR-101 (mono), SASR-101 (stereo))
- My One and Only Love (1959, Tico LP 1057 (mono), SLP 1057 (stereo))
- The Nearness of You (1956?, Tico LP 1028; as Pete Terrace and His Latin Jazz Quintet)
- A Night in Mambo-Jazzland (1956, Tico LP 1023)
- Pete with a Latin Beat (1958, Tico LP 1050)
- Sabrosa y Caliente (1962, Colpix CP 430 (mono), SCP 430 (stereo))
- Viejos pero Buenos: Oldies But Goodies (1962, Colpix CP 432 (mono), SCP 432 (stereo); as 'Latin Pete' Terrace)
- What a Night for the Cha Cha Cha (1957, Tico LP 1040)

Tedesco, Tommy

Tommy Tedesco was a multi-talented guitarist who was part of the Wrecking Crew, i.e., the loosely-associated group of musicians who were at the top of the list whenever a record company producer needed a hand to round out a record's sound. Dozens and dozens, possibly hundreds, of popular songs from the 1960's featured Tedesco playing the guitar, no matter whose name was on the cover.

- Calypso Soul (1966, Imperial LP-9321 (mono), LP-12321 (stereo))
- The Electric Twelve String Guitar (1964, Imperial LP-9263 (mono), LP-12263 (stereo))
- The Guitars of Tom Tedesco (1965, Imerial LP-9295 (mono), LP-12295 (stereo))

Textor, Keith (aka **The Chorus and Percussion of Keith Textor**)

- Dancing By the Firelight (1959, Warner Brothers WB-1345 (mono), WS-1345 (stereo); as The Keith Textor Singers)
- Hold Me (1971, A&R ARL-7100/006; as Keith Textor and Friends)
- Measure the Valleys (1970, A&R ARL-7100/001; as The Keith Textor Singers)
- Sounds Sensational! (1962, RCA Victor LSA-2425) (Stereo Action)
- Sounds Terrific! (1961, RCA Victor LSA-2365) (Stereo Action)

Thompson, Bob and His Orchestra and Chorus

- Just for Kicks (1959, RCA Victor LPM 2027 (mono), LSP 2027 (stereo))
- Mmm Nice! (1960, RCA Victor LPM 2117 (mono) LSP 2117 (stereo))
- Music from Wildcat (1961, RCA Victor LPM 2357 (mono), LSP 2357 (stereo))
- On the Rocks (1960, RCA Victor LPM 2145 (mono) LSP 2145 (stereo))
- The Sound of Speed (1959, Dot DLP 3123 (mono), 25123 (stereo))

Three Suns, The

Although ostensibly a trio, the Three Suns didn't let themselves be bound by their own musical limitations during their musical career, so that they felt free to hire extra musicians to help round out their sound as well as experiment in the studio.

- At the Candlelight Café (1959, RCA Camden CAL-513 (mono), CAS-513 (stereo))
- Continental Affair (1960, RCA Camden CAL-573 (mono), CAS-573 (stereo))

- Dancing on a Cloud (1961, RCA Victor LPM-2307 (mono), LSP-2307 (stereo))
- Easy Listening (1956, RCA Victor LPM-1316)
- Everything Under the Sun (1963, RCA Victor LPM-2715 (mono), LSP-2715 (stereo))
- Fever & Smoke (1961, RCA Victor LPM-2310 (mono), LSP-2310 (stereo))
- Fun in the Sun (1961, RCA Victor LPM-2437 (mono), LSP-2437 (stereo))
- The Happy-Go-Lucky Sound (1958, RCA Camden CAL-454)
- Having a Ball with the Three Suns (1958, RCA Victor LPM-1734 (mono), LSP-1734 (stereo))
- High Fi and Wide (1956, RCA Victor LPM-1249)
- In Orbit (1962, Rondo L-1756 (mono), L-9756 (stereo); Golden Tone 4094 (mono), 14094 (stereo))
- Let's Dance with the Three Suns (1958, RCA Victor LPM-1578 (mono), LSP-1578 (- tereo))
- Love in the Afternoon (1959, RCA Victor LPM-1669 (mono), LSP-1669 (stereo))
- Malaguena (1956, RCA Victor LPM-1220)
- Mean to Me (1973, RCA Camden ACL1-0085)
- Midnight For Two (1957, RCA Victor LPM-1333)
- Midnight Time (Rondo-Lette A36)
- Movin' 'N' Groovin' (1962, RCA Victor LPM-2532 (mono), LSA-2532 (stereo)) (Stereo Action)
- My Reverie (1956, RCA Victor LPM-1173)
- On A Magic Carpet (1960, RCA Victor LPM-2235 (mono), LSP-2235 (stereo))
- One Enchanted Evening (1964, RCA Victor LPM-2904 (mono), LSP-2904 (stereo))
- Slumbertime (1956, RCA Victor LPM-1219)
- Soft and Sweet (1955, RCA Victor LPM-1041)
- Swingin' on a Star (1959, RCA Victor LPM-1964 (mono), LSP-1964 (stereo))
- A Swingin' Thing (1964, RCA Victor LPM-2963 (mono), LSP-2963 (stereo))
- The Things in Love in Hi-Fi (1958, RCA Victor LPM-1543 (mono), LSP-1543 (stereo))
- This is the Three Suns (1972, RCA Victor VPS-6075) Two-record set. Gatefold cover offers a large photo of a young lady in a yellow bikini making up the covers.
- The Three Suns (1959, Rondo-Lette 844)

- The Three Suns Play... (Evon 328)
- Twilight Memories (1960, RCA Victor LPM-2120 (mono), LSP-2120 (stereo))
- Twilight Time (1956, RCA Victor LPM-1171)
- Twilight Time (1958, Rondo-Lette A14; 1966, Pickwick PC-3037 (mono), SPC-3037 (stereo)) This is a completely different album from the previous entry, with an entirely different song list.
- Warm and Tender (1962, RCA Victor LPM-2617 (mono), LSP-2617 (stereo))

Three Tops, The
- Mood Rhapsody (1957, Crown CLP-5017)

Tiare, Don (**and His Orchestra Exotique**; **and The Alohas**)
- The Music of Les Baxter (1963, Mercury MG 20845 (mono), SR 60845 (stereo))
- Soft Hawaiian Sounds (Dot DLP 3784 (mono), 25784 (stereo))
- Strings Over Hawaii (1961, Warner Brothers W-1420 (mono), WS-1420 (stereo))
- Strings Over Tahiti (1962, Warner Brothers W-1434 (mono), WS-1434 (stereo))
- Strings Over the South Seas (Dot DLP 3483 (mono), DLP 25483 (stereo))

Tijuana Brass – see **Herb Alpert and The Tijuana Brass**

Tiki Gardens
- Exotic Sounds of Tiki Gardens (1967, H&H Productions) This difficult-to-find LP was apparently created to promote the exotica-themed Tiki Gardens theme park located in Indian Shores, Florida, for two decades starting in 1964.

Tiny and His Hawaiian Bubbles
- Hawaiian Luau Party (Tifton International T 61 (mono), TS 61 (stereo))

Tjader, Cal (too many combos to list – Quartet, Quintet, Trio, etc.)
One of the giants of Latin jazz, Cal Tjader played drums before switching to his trademark vibraphone.
- Agua Dulce (1971, Fantasy 8416)
- Along Comes Cal (1967, Verve V-8671 (mono), V6-8671 (stereo))
- Breeze from the East (1964, Verve V-8575 (mono), V6-8575 (stereo))

- Cal Tjader (1958, Fantasy 3253 (mono, red vinyl only?); 1961, Fantasy 3313 (mono, red vinyl only?), 8084 (stereo, red and blue vinyl?))

- Cal Tjader Plays Harold Arlen (1961, Fantasy 3330 (mono, black or red vinyl); 8072 (stereo, in black, red, or blue vinyl))

- Cal Tjader Plays Latin for Dancers (1960, Fantasy 8019) This was the stereo version of *Tjader Plays Mambo*, with some songs substituted for others.

- Cal Tjader Plays the Contemporary Music of Mexico and Brazil (1962, Verve V-8470 (mono), V6-8470 (stereo))

- Cal Tjader Plugs In (1969, Skye SK-10)

- Cal Tjader Quartet (1956, Fantasy 3-227 (black or red vinyl); 1960, Fantasy 3307 (mono), 8083 (stereo) – black and red vinyl?)

- Cal Tjader Quintet (1956, Fantasy 3-232 (mono, black or red vinyl); 1962, 8085 (stereo, black or blue vinyl))

- Cal Tjader Sounds Out Burt Bacharach (1968, Skye SK-6)

- Cal Tjader's Latin Concert (1959, Fantasy 3275 (mono, black or red vinyl); 8014 (stereo, in black, red, or blue vinyl))

- Demasiado Caliente (1960, Fantasy 3309 (mono, black or red vinyl); 8053 (stereo, in black, red, or blue vinyl))

- Hip Vibrations(1967, Verve V-8730 (mono), V6-8730 (stereo))

- In A Latin Bag (1961, Verve V-8419 (mono), V6-8419 (stereo))

- Jazz at the Blackhawk (1957, Fantasy 3241 (mono, black or red vinyl); 1962, Fantasy 8096 (stereo, black or blue vinyl))

- Last Bolero in Berkeley (1973, Fantasy F-9446)

- Latin For Lovers (1959, Fantasy 3279 (mono, black or red vinyl), 8016 (stereo, in black or blue vinyl))

- Latin Kick (1958, Fantasy 3250 (mono, black or red vinyl); 1959, Fantasy 8033 (stereo, in black or blue vinyl))

- Latino Con Cal Tjader (1962, Fantasy 3339 (mono, black or red vinyl); 8079 (stereo, in black, red, or blue vinyl); with **Mongo Santamaria**)

- Live at the Funky Quarters (1972, Fantasy 9409)

- Mambo With Tjader (1955, Fantasy 3-202 (black or red vinyl); 1961, Fantasy 3326 (mono, black or red vinyl), 8057 (stereo, in black, red, or blue vinyl))

- Mas Ritmo Caliente (1958, Fantasy 3262 (mono, black or red vinyl), 8003 (stereo, in black or blue vinyl))

- Primo (1973, Fantasy F-9422)

- The Prophet (1968, Verve V6-8769)

- Ritmo Caliente! (1956, Fantasy 3216 (mono, black or red vinyl); 1962, Fantasy 8077 (stereo, in black, red, or blue vinyl))

- Several Shades of Jade (1963, Verve V-8507 (mono), V6-8507 (stereo))
- Solar Heat (1968, Skye MK-1 (mono), SK-1 (stereo))
- Sona Libre (1963, Verve V-8531 (mono), V6-8531 (stereo))
- Soul Bird: Whippenpoof (1965, Verve V-8626 (mono), V6-8626 (stereo))
- Soul Burst (1966, Verve V-8637 (mono), V6-8637 (stereo))
- Soul Sauce (1965, Verve V-8614 (mono), V6-8614 (stereo))
- Tjader (1971, Fantasy 8406)
- Tjader Goes Latin (1959, Fantasy 3289 (mono, black or red vinyl), 8030 (stereo, in black or blue vinyl))
- Tjader Plays Mambo (1956, Fantasy 3-221; stereo version was released as *Cal Tjader Plays Latin for Dancers*) Pressed in both black and red vinyl.
- Warm Wave (1964, Verve V-8585 (mono), V6-8585 (stereo))
- West Side Story (1960, Fantasy 3310 (mono, black and red vinyl); 8054 (stereo, in black, red, or blue vinyl))

Tjader, Cal and Don Elliott
- Vib-Rations (1956, Savoy MG-12054)

Tjader, Cal and Eddie Palmieri
- Bamboleate (1967, Tico LP 1150 (mono), SLP 1150 (stereo))
- El Sonido Nuevo (1966, Verve V-8651 (mono), V6-8651 (stereo))

Todd, Peter and His Orchestra
- Strings With A Beat (1956, MGM E-3326)
- Till We Meet Again (1958, RCA Camden CAL-418)

Tokyo Serenaders, The
- Holiday in Japan (49th State Hawaii LP-3452)

Tornadoes, The
- Taste of Honey / Tijuana Style (1966, Design DLP-248 (mono), SDLP-248 (stereo)) There were several different bands calling themselves The Tornadoes around that time, but this was probably a house band put together to crank out **Tijuana Brass**-inspired tunes for the Design label.

Touzet, Rene (**and His Orchestra**)
- Blue Bongo (1959, Fiesta FLP-1224; with **The Cha-Cha Rhythm Boys**)

- Bossa Nova! Brazil to Hollywood (1963, GNP Crescendo GNP-87 (mono), GNP-87S (stereo)) This album came with a sheet of dance instructions.
- The Cha Cha Cha and the Mambo (1954, GNP GNP-14; this is the same album as *The Charm of the Cha Cha Cha*, with the same song list and catalog number)
- Cha Cha Cha for Lovers (1958?, GNP GNP-29)
- Cha Cha Cha, Mambo, Merengue (1960, Fiesta FLP-1263; with **The Cha-Cha Rhythm Boys**)
- The Charm of the Cha Cha Cha (GNP GNP-14; this is the same album (probably a re-release) as *The Cha Cha Cha and the Mambo*, with the same song list and catalog number)
- Dinner in Havana (1954, RCA Victor LPM-1016)
- From Broadway to Havana (1957?, GNP GNP-22)
- Greatest Latin Hits!!!!! (GNP Crescendo GNP-74 (mono), GNP-74S (stereo))
- La Pachanga (1961, GNP GNP-57)
- Latin American Tempos (1956, MGM E3305)
- Latin Beat (Sunset SUS-5213)
- Learn to Dance the Cha Cha Cha (1959, Fiesta FLP-1244; with **The Cha-Cha Rhythm Boys**)
- Mr. Cha Cha Cha (1959, GNP GNP-36)
- Rene Touzet at The Crescendo (1959, GNP GNP-40)
- The Timeless Ones a la Touzet (1961, GNP GNP-52)
- Too Much! (1961, GNP GNP-49)
- Touzet Goes to the Movies (1962, GNP GNP-81 (mono), GNP-81S (stereo))

Trevanni, Jon and His Continental Orchestra

- I'm in the Nude for Love (1957, Crown CLP-5046)

Trombones Unlimited

Apparently a house band for Liberty, this group pushed out Easy Listening versions of popular songs very much in the **Tijuana Brass** style.

- Big Boss Bones (1967, Liberty LRP-3494 (mono), LST-7494 (stereo))
- Grazing in the Grass (1968, Liberty LST-7591)
- Holiday For Trombones (1967, Liberty LRP-3527 (mono), LST-7527 (stereo))
- One of Those Songs (1968, Liberty LST-7549)
- These Bones Are Made For Walkin' (1966, Liberty LRP-3449 (mono), LST-7449 (stereo))

- You're Gonna Hear From Me (Us)! (1966, Liberty LRP-3472 (mono), LST-7472 (stereo))

Trotter, John Scott

- Escape to the Magic Mediterranean (1956, Warner Brothers W 1266)
- A Thousand and One Notes (1958, Warner Brothers WS 1223)

Trovajoli, Armando and His Orchestra

- Musical Nightcap (1961, RCA Camden CAL 598 (mono), CAS 598 (stereo))
- One Night in Naples (1958, RCA Victor LPM-1755)
- One Night in Venice (1956, RCA Victor LPM-1278; as 'Armando and His Orchestra')
- One Night in Rome (1959, RCA Victor LPM-1920 (mono), LSP-1920 (stereo))
- Seven Golden Men (1969, United Artists UAS 5193) Music from the film.
- Yesterday, Today, and Tomorrow (1964, Warner Brothers W 1552 (mono), WS 1552 (stereo)) Music from the film.

Trumpets Ole

A Tijuana Brass knockoff project.

- Con Mucho Gusto (1967, Decca DL 4911 (mono), DL 74911 (stereo))
- The Trumpets Ole Play (1966, Decca DL 4821 (mono), DL 74821 (stereo))

Trumpets Unlimited, The

A **Tijuana Brass** clone, this was the only album produced.

- Sounds Tijuana! (1967, Design DLP-275 (mono), SDLP-275 (stereo))

Turez, Felipo

This was probably a fake name for another Surrey label studio effort.

- Spanish Saxes of Sonora (Surrey S 1021 (mono), SS 1021 (stereo)) 'Now Sound' easy listening music in the **Tijuana Brass** mode.

Tutmarc, Bud

Though he played Hawaiian music on the guitar, the bulk of Bud Tutmarc's recordings are of religious music, or at least Hawaiian-themed religious music. This LP for Dot seems to be the exception.

- Rainbows Over Paradise (1966?, Dot DLP 3759 (mono), DLP 25759 (stereo))

Tutti's Trumpets (aka Tutti Camarata; see also **Camarata**)

- Camarata (1963, Time 52106 (mono), S/2106 (stereo); previously released as *Tutti's Trumpets*)
- Tutti's Trumpets (1957, Disneyland WDL-3011 (mono), STER-3011 (stereo); re-released as *Camarata*)

Tyler, Jim and His Orchestra

- The Game of Love (Time S/2197)
- Pin Point Percussion (Time S/2106)

Valdes, Bebo

- Hot Cha Chas (1958, Decca DL 8660)

Van Damme, Art (aka **The Art Van Damme Quartet**; **Quintet**)

- Accordion a la Mode (1960, Columbia CL 1563 (mono), CS 8363 (stereo))
- The Art of Van Damme (1956, Columbia CL 876)
- Art Van Damme Swings Sweetly (1962, Columbia CL 1794 (mono), CS 8594 (stereo))
- Cocktail Capers (1954, Capitol T-178)
- Everything's Coming Up Music (1959, Columbia CL 1382 (mono), CS 8177 (stereo))
- Invitation (1974, MPS MC 22016; with **The Singers Unlimited**)
- Lover Man! (1965, Pickwick PC-3009 (mono), SPC-3009 (stereo))
- Manhattan Time (1956, Columbia CL 801)
- The Many Moods of Art (1972, MPS MC 25113)
- Martini Time (1955, Columbia CL 630)
- More Cocktail Capers (1954, Capitol T-300)
- A Perfect Match (1963, Columbia CL 2013 (mono), CS 8813 (stereo); with Johnny Smith)
- They're Playing Our Song (1958, Columbia C2L-7) Two-record set.
- The Van Damme Sound (1954, Columbia CL 544)

Vaughn, Billy (**and His Orchestra**; **The Billy Vaughn Singers**; etc.)

Billy Vaughn made a career out of quickly and efficiently interpreting hit songs and musical styles in the Easy Listening manner for the Dot record label.

- 12 Golden Hits from Latin America (1965, Dot DLP 3625 (mono), DLP 25625 (stereo))
- 1962's Greatest Hits (1963, Dot DLP 3497 (mono), DLP 25497 (stereo))
- Alfie (1966, Dot DLP 3751 (mono), DLP 25751 (stereo))

- Alone With Today (1968, Dot DLP 25897)
- Another Hit Album! (1964, Dot DLP 3593 (mono), DLP 25593 (stereo))
- As Requested (1968, Dot DLP 25841)
- Berlin Melody (1961, Dot DLP 3396 (mono), DLP 25396 (stereo))
- The Big 100 (1959, Dot DLP 10500 (mono), DLP 30500 (stereo)) Two-record set.
- Billy Vaughn Plays (1958, Dot DLP 3156 (mono); 1959, Dot DLP 25156 (stereo))
- Billy Vaughn Plays the Million Sellers (1958, Dot DLP 3119 (mono); 1959, Dot DLP 25119 (stereo))
- Blue Hawaii (1959, Dot DLP 3165 (mono), DLP 25165 (stereo))
- Blue Velvet & 1963's Great Hits (1964, Dot DLP 3559 (mono), DLP 25559 (stereo))
- Body & Soul (1968, Pickwick/33 SPC-3138)
- Chapel By The Sea (1962, Dot DLP 3424 (mono), DLP 25424 (stereo))
- A Current Set of Standards (1968, Dot DLP 25882)
- Electrified! (1974, Paramount PAS-1033)
- Embraceable You! (1967, Pickwick PC-3093 (mono), SPC-3093 (stereo))
- Everything is Beautiful (1970, Dot DLP 25985)
- Forever (1964, Dot DLP 3578 (mono), DLP 25578 (stereo))
- The Girl from Ipanema (1968, Pickwick SPC-3166)
- Golden Gems (1964, Hamilton HLP-113 (mono), HLP-12113 (stereo))
- Golden Hits (1959, Dot DLP 3201 (mono), DLP 25201 (stereo))
- The Golden Instrumentals (1957, Dot DLP 3016 (mono); 1959, Dot DLP 25016 (stereo))
- Golden Saxophones (1959, Dot DLP 3205 (mono), DLP 25205 (stereo))
- Great Golden Hits (1960, Dot DLP 3288 (mono), DLP 25288 (stereo))
- Guantamera (1968, Pickwick/33 SPC-3195)
- The Hit Sound of Billy Vaughn (Sears SP-411 (mono), SPS-411 (stereo))
- I Don't Know How to Love Him (1970, Paramount PAS-5037)
- I Love You (1967, Dot DLP 3813 (mono), DLP 25813 (stereo))
- Instrumental Souvenirs (1957, Dot DLP 3045)
- Josephine (1967, Dot DLP 3796 (mono), DLP 25796 (stereo))
- La Paloma (1958, Dot DLP 3140 (mono), DLP 25140 (stereo))
- Linger Awhile (1960, Dot DLP 3275 (mono), DLP 25275 (stereo))

- Look For A Star (1960, Dot DLP 3322 (mono), DLP 25322 (stereo))
- Melodies in Gold (1957, Dot DLP 3064 (mono); 1959, Dot DLP 25064 (stereo))
- Mexican Pearls (1965, Dot DLP 3628 (mono), DLP 25628 (stereo))
- Michelle (1966, Dot DLP 3679 (mono), DLP 25679 (stereo))
- Moon Over Naples (1965, Dot DLP 3654 (mono), DLP 25654 (stereo))
- Moon River (1969, Pickwick/33 SPC-3213)
- More (1967, Pickwick PC-3074 (mono), SPC-3074 (stereo))
- Music for the Golden Hours (1957, Dot DLP 3086 (mono); 1959, Dot DLP 25086 (stereo))
- Number 1 Hits, Vol. 1 (1963, Dot DLP 3540 (mono), DLP 25540 (stereo))
- An Old Fashioned Love Song (1972, Paramount PAS-6025)
- Pearly Shells (1965, Dot DLP 3605 (mono), DLP 25605 (stereo))
- Quietly Wild (1968, Dot DLP 25867)
- Sail Along Silv'ry Moon (1958, Dot DLP 3100 (mono); 1959, Dot DLP 25100 (stereo))
- The Shifting Whispering Sands (1962, Dot DLP 3442 (mono), DLP 25442 (stereo))
- Songs I Wrote (Hamilton HLP-162)
- Soundstage! (1972, Paramount PAS-6035)
- Sukiyaka (1961, Dot DLP 3523 (mono), DLP 25523 (stereo))
- The Sundowners (1960, Dot DLP 3349 (mono), DLP 25349 (stereo))
- Sweet Maria (1967, Dot DLP 3782 (mono), DLP 25782 (stereo))
- Sweet Music and Memories (1956, Dot DLP 3001)
- A Swingin' Safari (1962, Dot DLP 3458 (mono), DLP 25458 (stereo))
- That's Life (1967, Dot DLP 3788 (mono), DLP 25788 (stereo))
- Theme From A Summer Place (1960, Dot DLP 3276 (mono), DLP 25276 (stereo))
- This Is My Song (Sears SPS-468)
- Up Up & Away (1968, Pickwick/33 SPC-3146)
- The Windmills of Your Mind (1969, Dot DLP 25937)
- Winter World of Love (1970, Dot DLP 25975)

Video All Stars, The (see also **Skip Martin**)

- TV Jazz Themes (1958, Somerset P-8800 (mono), SF-8800 (stereo))

Voices in Latin

Eponymously titled *Voices in Latin* in England where it originated, the songs on this album were arranged by the cruelly-underrated Barbara Moore. This is one of the coolest and smoothest of mid-to-late 60's Now Sound collections.

- Something Cool (1968, Pulsar AR-10601)

Waikiki Beach Boys

- Breeze of Hawaii (1967?, Fiesta FLPS 1629)

Waikiki Boys, The

Is this the same group as the previous entry?

- Hawaiian Holiday (1958, Tops CL-1636)

Waikiki Hula Boys, The

- Hula (1954, Columbia CL 565)

Waikikis, The

The Waikikis weren't from Hawaii; heck, they weren't even from the United States. Originating in Belgium, this group of musicians gained more of their success in the German-speaking record market than in the U.S.

- Hawaii Beach Party (1965, Kapp KL 1437 (mono), KS 3437 (stereo))
- Hawaii Honeymoon (1965, Kapp KL 1432 (mono), KS 3432 (stereo))
- Hawaii Tattoo (1964, Kapp KL 1366 (mono), KS 3366 (stereo))
- Lollipops and Roses from Hawaii (1966, Kapp KL 1473 (mono), KS 3473 (stereo))
- Moonlight Luau (1968, Kapp KS 3575)
- Moonlight on Diamond Head (1969, Kapp KS 3593)
- Pearly Shells from Hawaii (1968, Kapp KS 3555)
- A Taste of Hawaii (1966, Kapp KL 1484 (mono), KS 3484 (stereo))

Waldo, Elisabeth

Ms. Waldo was an ethnomusicologist, and incorporated authentic instruments into the recordings she did during her brief career.

- Maracatu (1959, Barbary Coast BC 33022 (mono), BC 33022 S (stereo))
- Realm of the Incas (1960, GNP Crescendo GNP 603 (mono), GNPS 603 (stereo))
- Rites of the Pagan (1960, GNP Crescendo GNP 601 (mono), GNPS 601 (stereo))

Waldron, Mal (aka **The Mal Waldron Trio**)

These two records feature jazz pianist Mal Waldron and two bandmates playing what are essential backing tracks for the record owner to sing along with. Both releases carried inserts with sheet music and lyrics.

- For Singers 'N Swingers (1960, Music Minus One MMO 1018)
- Moonglow & Stardust: Backgrounds to Your Favorite Songs for Singing and Playing (1960, Music Minus One MMO 1012)

Wanderley, Walter (aka **The Walter Wanderley Set**; **Trio**) (see also **Astrud Gilberto and Walter Wanderley**)

Originally from Brazil organist Walter Wanderley was most associated with the musical style of Bossa Nova.

- Batucada (1967, Verve V-8706 (mono), V6-8706 (stereo))
- Brazilian Blend (1967, Phillips PHM 200-227 (mono), PHS 600-227 (stereo))
- Cheganca (1966, Verve V-8676 (mono), V6-8676 (stereo))
- From Rio With Love (1966, Tower T 5047 (mono), ST 5047 (stereo))
- Kee-Ka-Roo (1967, Verve V-8739 (mono), V6-8739 (stereo))
- Moondreams (1969, A&M SP 3022)
- Murmurio (1967, Tower T 5058 (mono), ST 5058 (stereo))
- Organ-ized (1964, Phillips PHM 200-233 (mono), PHS 600-233 (stereo))
- Quarteto Bossamba (1967, World Pacific WP-1866 (mono), WPS-21866 (stereo))
- Rain Forest (1966, Verve V-8658 (mono), V6-8658 (stereo))
- Samba So! (1967, World Pacific WP-1856 (mono), WPS-21856 (stereo))
- When It Was Done (1969, A&M LP-2018 (mono), SP-3018 (stereo))

Warren, Guy

Guy Warren came by his exotica credentials honestly: he was from Ghana, and eventually made his way to Chicago where he worked with various jazz artists. By the time the exotica fad arrived, he was ready to take advantage of it, but his popularity never took off the way it did with other artists.

- Africa Speaks – America Answers (1956, Decca DL 8446) (with The Red Saunders Orchestra)
- African Rhythms: The Exciting Soundz of Guy Warren and His Talking Drum (1962, Decca DL 4243 (mono), DL 74243 (stereo))

- The African Soundz of Guy Warren of Ghana (1972, Fiesta FLPS 1646)
- Themes For African Drums (1959, RCA Victor LPM-1864 (mono), LSP-1864 (stereo); as The Guy Warren Sounds)

Webb, Jack

- You're My Girl (1958, Warner Brothers B 1207; 'Romantic Reflections by Jack Webb, Music Arranged and Conducted by **Billy May**'). This little curiosity belongs in the Spoken Word category, with vocal stylings by TV's Sgt. Joe Friday, Jack Webb himself. Webb's delivery isn't bad, but Billy May's orchestration is lush and gorgeous.

Welcome, Ruth

- At a Sidewalk Café (1959, Capitol T-1209 (mono), ST-1209 (stereo))
- Continental Zither (1966, Capitol T-2472 (mono), ST-2472 (stereo))
- Hi-Fi Zither (1957, Capitol T-942)
- Latin Zither (1963, Capitol T-1863 (mono), ST-1863 (stereo))
- Romantic Zither (1961, Capitol T-1527 (mono), ST-1527 (stereo))
- Welcome to Zitherland (1960, Capitol T-1471 (mono), ST-1471 (stereo))
- Zither Goes Hollywood (1963, Capitol T-1986 (mono), ST-1986 (stereo))
- Zither Goes West (1962, Capitol T-1672 (mono), ST-1672 (stereo))
- Zither in ¾ Time (1960, Capitol T-1318 (mono), ST-1318 (stereo))
- Zither Magic (1959, Capitol T-1279 (mono), ST-1279 (stereo))
- Zither South of the Border (1960, Capitol T-1397 (mono), ST-1397 (stereo))

Welk, Lawrence

Those of us who are old enough remember Lawrence Welk's TV series, devoted to smooth, unthreatening popular music as well as a nostalgia for a white-bread, all-American viewpoint. His recorded music doesn't go quite that far, but for good or ill, Welk's image still stands as what many think of as the public face of Easy Listening.

- 1963's Early Hits (1963, Dot DLP 3510 (mono), DLP 25510 (stereo))
- Apples and Bananas (1965, Dot DLP 3629 (mono), DLP 25629 (stereo))
- Aragon Trianon Memories (Mercury Wing MGW 12214 (mono), SRW 16214 (stereo))
- As Time Goes By (Pickwick/33 SPC 3157)

- Baby Elephant Walk and Theme from The Brothers Grimm (1962, Dot DLP 3457 (mono), DLP 25457 (stereo))
- The Big Band Sound of Lawrence Welk (1973, Ranwood R-8114)
- Blue Hawaii (1969, Pickwick/33 SPC-3212)
- Bubbles in the Wine (1962, Dot DLP 3489 (mono), DLP 25489 (stereo))
- Calcutta! (1961, Dot DLP 3359 (mono), DLP 25359 (stereo))
- Candida (1970, Ranwood R-8083)
- Champagne and Roses (1957, Coral CRL 57148)
- Champagne Dance Party (1969, Harmony HS 11301)
- The Champagne Music of Lawrence Welk (1960, Vocalion VL 3671 (mono), VL 73671 (stereo); first song is "Stompin' at the Savoy")
- The Champagne Music of Lawrence Welk (1961, Dot DLP 3342 (mono), DLP 25342 (stereo); first song is a medley starting with "I'm Thru With Love") This is a completely different set of songs from the previous entry with the same title.
- The Champagne Music of Lawrence Welk (1956, Epic LN 3247; first song is "Bubbles in the Wine") This is a third collection with the same title.
- Champagne on Broadway (1966, Dot DLP 3688 (mono), DLP 25688 (stereo))
- Dance Party (Mercury Wing MGW 12119 (mono), SRW 16119 (stereo))
- Dance With Lawrence Welk (1959, Dot DLP 3224 (mono), DLP 25224 (stereo))
- Diamond Jubilee: 75 Years of Great American Music (Dot DLP 3395 (mono), DLP 25395 (stereo))
- Everybody's Music (Hamilton HLP 12125)
- Favorites (1957, Coral CRL 57139)
- Favorites from the Golden 60's (1970, Ranwood R-8068)
- Galveston (1969, Ranwood RLP-8049)
- Go Away Little Girl (1971, Ranwood R-8091)
- The Golden Millions (1964, Dot DLP 3611 (mono), DLP 25611 (stereo))
- Great American Composers (1960, Dot DLP 3238 (mono), DLP 25238 (stereo))
- The Happy Wanderer (1965, Dot DLP 3653 (mono), DLP 25653 (stereo))
- Hits of Our Time (1967, Dot DLP 3790 (mono), DLP 25790 (stereo))

- I Love You Truly (1969, Ranwood R-8053)
- If You Were the Only Girl in the World (1969, Pickwick SPC-3143)
- I'll See You Again (1967, Pickwick SPC-3070)
- I'm Forever Blowing Bubbles (1960, Dot DLP 3248 (mono), DLP 25248 (stereo))
- Jean (1969, Ranwood R-8060)
- Keyboard Kapers (1958, Coral CRL 57214)
- Lawrence Welk and His Sparkling Strings (1955, Coral CRL 57011)
- Lawrence Welk Plays Jerome Kern and Other Great Composers (Ranwood R-8077)
- Lawrence Welk Presents Jerry Burke's Greatest Organ Hits (Ranwood RLP-8009)
- The Lawrence Welk Television Show 10th Anniversary (1964, Dot DLP 3591 (mono), DLP 25591 (stereo))
- Lawrence Welk's Champagne Strings (1970, Ranwood R-8079)
- Love is a Many Splendored Thing (1962, Pickwick/33 SPC-3196)
- Love is Blue (1968, Ranwood RLP-8003)
- Mary Poppins (Dot HLP 152 (mono), HLP 12152 (stereo))
- Memories (1968, Ranwood R 8044; RLP 8044 (both stereo))
- Moon River (1961, Dot DLP 3412 (mono), DLP 25412 (stereo))
- Mr. Music Maker (Dot DLP 3164 (mono), DLP 25164 (stereo))
- Music to Dance By (Pickwick/33 PTP 2005) Two-record set.
- A Musical Trip to Latin America (1957, Coral CRL 57187)
- Reminiscing (1972, Ranwood R-5001) Two-disc set.
- Save the Last Dance for Me (1967, Pickwick SPC-3070)
- Say It With Music (1956, Coral CRL 57041 (mono), CRL 757041 (stereo))
- Scarlett O'Hara (1963, Dot DLP 3528 (mono), DLP 25528 (stereo))
- Sing-A-Long Party (1962, Dot DLP 3432 (mono), DLP 25432 (stereo))
- Snuggled On Your Shoulder (1967?, Hamilton HLP 177)
- Songs of the Islands (1960, Dot DLP 3251 (mono), DLP 25251 (stereo); with **Buddy Merrill**)
- The Starlit Hour (Harmony HS 11413)
- Strictly For Dancing (1960, Dot DLP 3274 (mono), DLP 25274 (stereo))
- Sweet and Lovely (Dot DLP 3296 (mono), DLP 25296 (stereo))

- Today's Great Hits (1965, Dot DLP 3663 (mono), DLP 25663 (stereo))
- A Tribute to the All-Time Greats (1963, Dot DLP 3544 (mono), DLP 25544 (stereo))
- TV Favorites (1955, Coral CRL 57025)
- TV Western Theme Songs (1959, Coral CRL 57267 (mono), CRL 757267 (stereo))
- The Voices and Strings of Lawrence Welk (1959, Dot DLP 3200 (mono), DLP 25200 (stereo))
- Welktime (1956, Decca DL 8324)
- Winchester Cathedral (1966, Dot DLP 3774 (mono), DLP 25774 (stereo))
- Wonderful! Wonderful! (1963, Dot DLP 3552 (mono), DLP 25552 (stereo))
- The World's Finest Music (1957, Coral 57113)
- Yellow Bird (1961, Dot DLP 3389 (mono), DLP 25389 (stereo))
- Young World (1962, Dot DLP 3428 (mono), DLP 25428 (stereo))
- Your TV Dance Party (1963, Golden Tone C4095 (mono), 14095 (stereo))

Welk, Lawrence and Johnny Hodges

- Lawrence Welk & Johnny Hodges (1965, Dot DLP 3682 (mono), DLP 25682 (stereo))

West Coast All Stars, The

- TV Jazz Themes (1958, Somerset P-8800 (mono), SF-8800 (stereo))

Weston, Paul (and His Orchestra)

Easy Listening probably would have existed without Paul Weston, but it might have taken a while longer to come into being. Starting in the 1940's, Weston began recording slower, more string-heavy orchestral pieces that pointed to a more romantic style of music, something that could be played in the background during a candlelight dinner. Dubbed 'Mood Music' at the time, the genre would stick around for another two decades or so, coinciding nicely with the coming of 12" records and stereo hi-fis, and providing an alternative to the increasingly loud and raucous music of the younger generation.

- Among My Souvenirs (Columbia CB-6; this was a record club premium)
- The Bells of Santa Ynez (1963, Capitol T-1849 (mono), ST-1849 (stereo))
- Carefree (1959, Capitol T-1261)
- Caribbean Cruise (1955, Columbia CL 572)

- Dream Time Music (1953, Columbia CL 528)
- Floatin' Like A Feather (1959, Columbia T-1153 (mono), ST-1153 (stereo))
- Hollywood (1958, Columbia CL 1112 (mono), CS 8042 (stereo))
- Love Music from Hollywood (1956, Columbia CL 794)
- Mood for 12 (1955, Columbia CL 693)
- Mood Music (1955, Columbia CL 527)
- Moonlight Becomes You (1956, Capitol T-909)
- Music for a Rainy Night (1954, Columbia CL 574)
- Music for Dreaming (1955, Capitol T-222; this was a re-release of a 10" disc with the addition of more songs)
- Music for Dreaming (1959, Capitol T-1154 (mono), ST-1154 (stereo)) This features a slightly different selection of songs from the previous entry.
- Music for Memories (1955, Capitol T-225; this was a re-release of a 10" disc with the addition of more songs)
- Music for Memories (1958, Capitol T-1222 (mono), ST-1222 (stereo)) This features a slightly different selection of songs from the previous entry.
- Music for Romancing (1955, Capitol T-153; this was a re-release of a 10" disc with the addition of more songs)
- Music for Romancing (1959, Capitol T-1223 (mono), ST-1223 (stereo)) This features a slightly different selection of songs from the previous entry.
- Music for the Fireside (1955, Capitol T-245; this was a re-release of a 10" disc with the addition of more songs)
- Music for the Fireside (1959, Capitol T-1192 (mono), ST-1192 (stereo)) This features the same song selection as the previous entry, just in a different order.
- Our Love (Pickwick/33 PTP-2037)
- Romantic Reflections (1967, Capitol SW 91212; record club edition)
- Solo Mood (1956, Columbia CL 879)
- Sound Stage: Hi-Fi Music from Hollywood (1955, Columbia CL 612)
- The Sweet and the Swingin' (1960, Capitol T-1361 (mono), ST-1361 (stereo))

Whitaker, David (aka **The David Whitaker Orchestra**)
- Latin in the Night (1967, Deram SML 703)

Whittemore & Lowe
- Exotique (1961, Capitol P-8550 (mono), SP-8550 (stereo))

- Immortal Music from the Movies (1961, Capitol T-1599 (mono), ST-1599 (stereo))

Wilkins, Ernie and His Orchestra

- Hard Mother Blues (1970, Mainstream MRL 305)
- Here Comes the Swingin' Mr. Wilkins! (1960, Everest LPBR 5077 (mono), SDBR 1077 (stereo))

Williams, George and His Orchestra

- We Could Make Such Beautiful Music (1956, RCA Victor LPM-1205)

Williams, Griff and His Society Orchestra

- America's Most Danceable Music For Any Party (1958, Mercury MG 20288 (mono), SR 60007 (stereo))
- Let's Dance Awhile to the Griff Williams Style (1960, Mercury MG 20494 (mono), SR 60173 (stereo))
- Oldies But Goodies (1959, Mercury MG 20393 (mono), SR 60068 (stereo))
- The Sound of Griff Williams (1961, Mercury MG 20608 (mono), SR 60608 (stereo))
- We Could Have Danced All Night (1958, Mercury MG 20334 (mono), SR 60021 (stereo))

Williams, Johnny

Years before he became famous for the music for *Jaws* and *Star Wars*, Johnny Williams was a Los Angeles composer whose work was in demand for TV series soundtracks.

- Checkmate (1961, Columbia CL 1591 (mono), CS 8391 (stereo)) Music from the TV series.
- Rhythm in Motion (1961, Columbia CL 1667 (mono), CS 8467 (stereo))
- World on a String (1958, Bethlehem BCP-6025)

Williams, Roger (see also the Compilations section)

- Academy Award Winners (1964, Kapp KL-1406 (mono), KS-3406 (stereo))
- Academy Award Winners, Vol. 2 (1966, Kapp KL-1483 (mono), KS-3483 (stereo))
- Almost Paradise (1957, Kapp KL-1063)
- Always (1960, Kapp KL-1172 (mono), KS-3056 (stereo))
- Autumn Leaves – 1965 (1965, Kapp KL-1452 (mono), KS-3452 (stereo))
- Born Free (1966, Kapp KL-1501 (mono), KS-3501 (stereo))

- The Boy Next Door (1955, Kapp KL-1003)
- By Special Request (1964, Kapp KL-3 (mono), KS-3 (stereo))
- By Special Request, Vol. 2 (1967, Kapp KL-4 (mono), KS-4 (stereo))
- Daydreams (1956, Kapp KL-1031)
- For You (1963, Kapp KL-1336 (mono), KS-3336 (stereo))
- Golden Hits (1967, Kapp KL-1530 (mono), KS-3530 (stereo); 1973, MCA MCA-64)
- Happy Heart (1969, Kapp KS-3595)
- I'll Remember You (1967, Kapp KL-1470 (mono), KS-3470 (stereo))
- The Impossible Dream (1968, Kapp KS-3550)
- In a Latin Mood: Amor (1968, Kapp KS-3549)
- It's a Big Wide Wonderful World (1955, Kapp KL-1008)
- Love Story (1971, Kapp KS-3645)
- Love Theme from 'Romeo and Juliet' (1969, Kapp KS-3610)
- Love Theme from 'The Godfather' (1972, Kapp KS-3665)
- Maria (1962, Kapp KL-1266 (mono), KS-3266 (stereo))
- Moments to Remember (1971, Vocalion VL-73918)
- More Songs of the Fabulous Fifties (1959, Kapp KL-1130 (mono), KS-3013 (stereo))
- Mr. Piano (1962, Kapp KL-1290 (mono), KS-3290 (stereo))
- Near You (1959, Kapp KL-1112 (mono), K-1112-S (stereo))
- Only For Lovers (1968, Kapp KS-3565)
- Play Me (1972, Kapp KS-3671)
- Roger! (1967, Kapp KL-1512 (mono), KS-3512 (stereo))
- Roger Williams (1956, Kapp KL-1012)
- Roger Williams Invites You to Dance (1961, Kapp KL-1222 (mono), KS-3222 (stereo))
- Roger Williams Plays Gershwin (1958, Kapp KL-1088 (mono), K-1088-S (stereo))
- Roger Williams Plays the Hits (1965, Kapp KL-1414 (mono), KS-3414 (stereo))
- The Solid Gold Steinway (1964, Kapp KL-1354 (mono), KS-3354 (stereo))
- Songs of the Fabulous Fifties (1959, Kapp KXL-5000 (mono), KX-5000-S (stereo)) Two-record set.
- Songs of the Fabulous Forties (1957, Kapp KXL-5003) Two-record set.
- Songs of the Fabulous Forties, Vol. 1 (1960, Kapp KL-1207 (mono), KS-3207 (stereo)) This album offers the first disc of the 5003 release, sold separately.

- Songs of the Fabulous Forties, Vol. 2 (1960, Kapp KL-1208 (mono), KS-3208 (stereo)) This album offers the second disc of the 5003 release, sold separately.

- Songs of the Fabulous Century (1958, Kapp KXL-5005 (mono), KX-5005-S (stereo)) Two-record set.

- Songs of the Fabulous Century, Vol. 1 (1960, Kapp KL-1211 (mono), KS-3211 (stereo)) This album offers the first disc of the 5005 release, sold separately.

- Songs of the Fabulous Century, Vol. 2 (1960, Kapp KL-1212 (mono), KS-3212 (stereo)) This album offers the second disc of the 5005 release, sold separately.

- Songs of the Soaring '60's, Vol. 1 (1961, Kapp KL-1251 (mono), KS-3251 (stereo))

- Summer of '42 [The Summer Knows] (1971, Kapp KS-3650)

- Summer Wind and Your Special Requests (1965, Kapp KL-1434 (mono), KS-3434 (stereo))

- Temptation (1960, Kapp KL-1217 (mono), KS-3217 (stereo))

- Themes from Great Movies (1970, Kapp KS-3629)

- Till (1958, Kapp KL-1081 (mono), K-1081-S (stereo))

- Tonight! Roger Williams at Town Hall (1961, Kapp KXL-5008 (mono), KX-5008-S (stereo))

- Twilight Themes (1971, Longines Symphonette Society LWS 640)

- With These Hands (1959, Kapp KL-1147 (mono), KS-3030 (stereo))

- Yellow Bird (1961, Kapp KL-1244 (mono), KS-3244 (stereo))

Williams, Roger and Ferrante & Teicher

- Roger Williams & Ferrante and Teicher (1966, Metro M-584) This featured Williams on side A and Ferrante & Teicher on side B.

Wilson, Marty and His Orchestra

- *Jun'gala* (1959, Warner Brothers B 1326 (mono), WS 1326 (stereo)) An exotica classic.

Wilson, Murray

- The Many Moods of Murray Wilson (1967, Capitol T-2819 (mono), ST-2819 (stereo)) Yes, this is the solo album put out by the infamous father of Brian, Carl, and Dennis Wilson of the Beach Boys. Brian produced, uncredited.

Wilson, Stanley

- The Mating Urge (1958, International LP 7777) Music from the film.

- The Music from M Squad (1959, RCA Victor LPM-2062 (mono), LSP-2062 (stereo))

- Pagan Love (1961, Capitol T-1552 (mono), ST-1552 (stereo)) An Exotica album that isn't all that exotic.

- Themes to Remember (1963, Decca DL 4481 (mono), DL 74481 (stereo))

Winding, Kai

- The In Instrumentals (1965, Verve V-8639 (mono), V6-8639 (stereo))

- Mondo Cane #2 (1964, Verve V-8573 (mono), V6-8573 (stereo))

- More (1963, Verve V-8551 (mono), V6-8551 (stereo) also released as *Soul Surfin'* with the same catalog number and song list)

- More Brass (1966, Verve V-8657 (mono), V6-8657 (stereo))

- Penny Lane & Time (1967, Verve V-8691 (mono), V6-8691 (stereo))

- Rainy Day (1965, Verve V-8620 (mono), V6-8620 (stereo))

- Solo (1963, Verve V-8525 (mono), V6-8525 (stereo))

- Soul Surfin' (1963, Verve V-8551 (mono), V6-8551 (stereo); also released as *More* with the same catalog number and song list; this version probably came out first)

- Suspense Themes in Jazz (1962, Verve V-8493 (mono), V6-8493 (stereo))

Winterhalter, Hugo and His Orchestra

- Airport Love Theme (1971, MusicO MDS-1036)

- All Time Movie Greats (Musicor M2S-3160) Two-disc set.

- Always (1955, RCA Victor LPM-1179)

- Applause (1970, Musicor MS-3190)

- The Best of '64 (1964, Kapp KL-1407 (mono), KS-3407 (stereo))

- The Best of the Motion Picture Hits (Musicor MDS-1042)

- Big and Sweet With a Beat (1958, RCA Camden CAL-443)

- The Big Hits of 1965 (1965, Kapp KL-1429 (mono), KS-3429 (stereo))

- The Eyes of Love… (1957, RCA Victor LPM-1338)

- The Great Music Themes of Television (1956, RCA Victor LPM-1020)

- Happy Hunting (1957, RCA Victor LPM-1400)

- Hawaiian Wedding Song (1969, RCA Camden CAS-2309; re-issue of *Hugo Winterhalter Goes… Hawaiian*)

- Hugo Winterhalter Goes… Continental (1962, RCA Victor LPM-2482 (mono), LSP-2482 (stereo))

- Hugo Winterhalter Goes Gypsy (1960, RCA Victor LPM-2167 (mono), LSP-2167 (stereo))
- Hugo Winterhalter Goes... Hawaiian (1961, RCA Victor LPM-2417 (mono), LSP-2417 (stereo); re-issued as *Hawaiian Wedding Song*)
- Hugo Winterhalter Goes... Latin (1959, RCA Victor LPM-1677 (mono), LSP-1677 (stereo))
- Hugo Winterhalter Goes... South of the Border (1961, RCA Victor LPM-2271 (mono), LSP-2271 (stereo))
- I Only Have Eyes For You (1964, RCA Victor LPM-2645 (mono), LSP-2645 (stereo))
- In a Sentimental Mood (RCA Camden CAL-729 (mono), CAS-729 (stereo))
- Latin Gold (1972, RCA Camden CAS-2546)
- The Magic Touch (RCA Camden CAL-379)
- Midnight Cowboy (1970, MusicO MDS-1029)
- Motion Picture Hit Themes (1971, MusicO MDS-1040)
- Music By Starlight (1956, RCA Victor LPM-1185)
- My Favorite Broadway & Hollywood Music (Musicor MS-3184)
- "Pop" Parade (1969, MusicO MDS-1013)
- Romanceable and Danceable (Musicor M2S-3168) Two-disc set.
- A Season For My Beloved (1963, ABC-Paramount ABC-447 (mono), ABCS-447 (stereo))
- Two Sides of Winterhalter (1958, RCA Victor LPM-1905 (mono), LPS-1905 (stereo))
- Wish You Were Here (1959, RCA Victor LPM-1904 (mono), LSP-1904 (stereo))
- Your Favorite Motion Picture Music (1969, Musicor M2S-3178) Two-disc set.

Winterhalter, Hugo and Eddie Heywood

- Classical Gas (1968, Musicor MS 3170)

Wrightson, Frank

- Hi-Fi Organ Moods (1957, Palace M-611; 1957, Masterseal MSLP 5015)
- Magical Pipe Organ (1958, Palace M-627 (mono), PST-627 (stereo))

Wyncote Orchestra, The

- Theme for Candy and Other Hits (1965, Wyncote W-9101 (mono), SW-9101 (stereo))

Wyncote Singers, The
- Love Me With All Your Heart (1964, Wyncote W-9018 (mono), SW-9018 (stereo))

Young, Victor (**and His Singing Strings**)
- After Dinner Music (1957, Decca DL-8350)
- April in Paris (1956, Decca DL-8243)
- Cinema Rhapsodies (1953, Decca DL-8051)
- Gypsy Magic (1953, Decca DL-8052)
- Hollywood Rhapsodies (1954, Decca DL-8060)
- Imagination (1956, Decca DL-8278)
- Love Themes from Hollywood (1957, Decca DL-8364)
- Night Music (1955, Decca DL-8085)
- Pearls on Velvet (1956, Decca DL-8285; 'featuring Ray Turner at the Piano')
- Sugar and Spice and Melodies Nice (1955, Decca DL-8466)

Zabach, Florian
- Golden Strings (1957, Mercury MG 20176; Mercury Wing MGW 12172)
- It's Easy to Dance with Florian Zabach (1959, Mercury MG 20436 (mono), SR 60107 (stereo))
- String Along (1963, Vocalion VL 3701 (mono), VL 73701 (stereo))
- 'Till the End of Time (1959, Mercury MG 20305 (mono), SR 60084 (stereo))

Zaccarias and His Orchestra
- Dance the Bossa Nova (1962, RCA Camden CAL-749 (mono), CAS-749 (stereo))

Zacharias, Helmut (**and His Magic Violins**)
- 2,000,000 Strings (1959, Decca DL-8926 (mono), DL-78926 (stereo))
- Magic Violins (Decca DL-8431)
- Romantic Strings (1959, Decca DL-8949 (mono), DL-78949 (stereo))
- Themes (1960, Decca DL-4083 (mono), DL-74083 (stereo))

Zapater, Carlos (aka **The Carlos Zapater Orchestra**)
- Romantic Spain (1964, Wyncote W 9002 (mono), SW 9002 (stereo))

Zentner, Si (**and His Big Band**; **Orchestra**) (see also **Martin Denny and Si Zentner**)

- ...A Thinking Man's Band (1959, Liberty LRP-3133 (mono), LST-7133 (stereo))
- Big Band Brilliance! (1966, Sunset SUM-1110 (mono), SUS-5110 (stereo))
- Big Band Plays the Big Hits (1961, Liberty LRP-3197 (mono), LST-7197 (stereo))
- Desafinado (1962, Liberty LRP-3273 (mono), LST-7273 (stereo))
- From Russia With Love (1964, Liberty LRP-3353 (mono), LST-7353 (stereo))
- It's Nice to Go Trav'ling (1965, RCA Victor LPM-3388 (mono), LSP-3388 (stereo))
- More (1963, Liberty LRP-3326 (mono), LST-7326 (stereo))
- Music That's Going Places (1963, Liberty RC-1) An RC Cola promotional release. How was this distributed?
- My Cup of Tea (1965, RCA Victor LPM-2992 (mono), LSP-2992 (stereo))
- Presenting Si Zentner (1962, Smash MGS 27007 (mono), SRS 67007 (stereo))
- Put Your Head On My Shoulder (1966, RCA Victor LPM-3484 (mono), LSP-2484 (stereo))
- Right Here! Right Now! The Big Mod Sound Of... (1967, Liberty LRP-3531 (mono), LST-7531 (stereo))
- Rhythm Plus Blues (1963, Liberty LRP-3290 (mono), LST-7290 (stereo))
- Si Zentner in Full Swing! (1965, Liberty LRP-3397 (mono), LST-7397 (stereo))
- Si Zentner Plays the Big Big-Band Hits (1964, Liberty LRP-3350 (mono), LST-7350 (stereo))
- Sleepy Lagoon (1957, Liberty LRP 3055; with **Russ Garcia and His Orchestra**)
- The Stripper and Other Big Band Hits (1962, Liberty LRP-3247 (mono), LST-7247 (stereo))
- Suddenly It's Swing (1960, Liberty LRP-3139 (mono), LST-7139 (stereo))
- Swing Fever (1959, Bel Canto SR-1014)
- The Swingin' Eye (1960, Liberty LRP-3166 (mono), LST-7166 (stereo))
- Up a Lazy River (Big Band Plays the Big Hits, Vol. 2) (1961, Liberty LRP-3216 (mono), LST-7216 (stereo))
- Warning Shot (1966, Liberty LRP-3498 (mono), LST-7498 (stereo))

Zentner, Si and The Johnny Mann Singers

- Great Band With Great Voices (1961, Liberty LMM-13009 (mono), LSS-14009 (stereo))

- Great Band With Great Voices Swing the Great Voices of Great Bands (1961, Liberty LMM-13017 (mono), LSS-14017 (stereo))

- A Perfect Blend (1966, Liberty LRP-3483 (mono), LST-7483 (stereo))

Compilations

Again, this is just a scraping of the surface of what's out there, a sampling of what collectors may find out in the wild.

- 3 Great Pianos (1963, RCA Victor LPM 2721 (mono), LSP 2721 (stereo))

- 80 Minutes in Lovers' Lane (Columbia XTV28701 thru XTV8704) This 4-album compilation set was given away with the purchase of a Lane Cedar Chest.

- Afro-Cubano (1956, Norgran M GN-1067; features **Jack Costanzo and His Orchestra** (side A) and **Andre's Cuban All-Stars** (side B))

- All-Time Favorites (1957, Tops L1514; **Tops All-Star Orchestra**)

- American Caravan (Columbia Musical Treasuries PS 5048) 10-record set.

- As You Remember Them: Great Instrumentals, Vol. 2 (1972, Time-Life STL-242)

- At Home with the Munsters (1964, Golden LP-139) Music from the TV series.

- Be There at 5 (1956, Mercury MG 20218)

- Bel Canto Stereo Demonstration Record (1959, Bel Canto SR-2000) Side 1 was a 'stereophonic tour of the city of Los Angeles.' Side 2 was music.

- Beyond the Reef (Waikiki LP 110 (mono), LP 310 (stereo))

- Broadway & Hollywood Sound Spectacular (Command 16102-SD)

- Bossa Nova (1963, Crown CLP-5302 (mono), CST-302 (stereo)) This album features **Buddy Collette**, Leo Acosta, and other jazz musicians.

- Command Popular Preview '67 (1967, Command COM 17 SD)

- Cool Sounds (1956, Hollywood LPH-16)

- Dancing Discotheque (1964, Mercury SR 60964)

- Dancing in the Dark (aka Romantic Strings Play Dancing in the Dark) (1969, Reader's Digest RD28B-MRCA; **Hill Bowen**)

- Demonstration Record (1962, London PD 4)

- A Dream of Love (1957, Hollywood LPH-111)

- East of Suez (Broadway P 1027) This was an apparent song-by-song re-release of *The Music of Port Said* by **Mohammed El-Sulieman and His Oriental Ensemble**.

- Fabulous Ping Pong Bongo Percussion (1960, Coronet, CX 141 (mono), CSX 141 (stereo)) The musicians for this album were listed as 'Kaino and His Afro-Percussion Group.'

- Fiji (Isla Lei): Enchanting Music of the South Pacific (Capitol T-10216)

- For All We Know and Other Academy Award Winners (1972, RCA Camden CAS-2493)

- Galaxy (1961, Mercury MGD 9 (mono), SRD 9 (stereo))

- Galaxy 30 (1962, Mercury MGD 2-13 (mono), SRD 2-13 (stereo))

- The Girl That I Marry – Vol. 9 for Hi-Fi Living (1957, RCA Custom RAL 1009; **Jack Say and His Orchestra**)

- The Greatest Music Available Today (Time TSD-4)

- Guitars in Italy (1961, Time S/2047)

- Hands Across the Table – Vol. 2 for Hi-Fi Living (1957, RCA Camden RAL 1002; **Tony Osborne and His Orchestra**)

- Hank Mancini Favorites and Others (1964, Crown CLP-5459 (mono), CST-459 (stereo))

- Hawaii Goes Percussion (Coronet CXS 162 (stereo); the mono version was released as *Hawaiian Moonbeams*; the label actually says *Hawaiian Percussion*)

- Hawaiian Favorites (1957, Tops L 1517 (mono), 9517 S (stereo)) Akoni Lani and His Islanders take Side A of this album, while Side B features Danny K. Stewart and His Aloha Boys.

- Hawaiian Holiday (Wyncote, SW-9006)

- Hawaiian Luau (1960, Riviera R0043 (mono), STR0043 (stereo))

- Hawaiian Moonbeams (Coronet CX 162 (mono); stereo version released as *Hawaii Goes Percussion*)

- Hey! Let's Go Latin (1967, Wyncote W-9197 (mono), SW-9197 (stereo))

- Hi-Fi Internationale: Music to Read Road Maps By (ca. 1950's, Mercury PVM-002)

- Hit Motion Picture Themes (1963, Mercury MG 20810)

- Hits From Hollywood – Vol. 3 for Hi-Fi Living (1957, RCA Camden RAL 1003; **Ronnie Ogden and His Orchestra**)

- Holiday in Hawaii: Exotic Songs of the Islands (Cosmic HH-100, HH-101, & HH-102; 3-record boxed set. Music by **The Hawaiian Strings**, The Islanders, and The Polynesians.)

- The Hollywood Scene (Columbia Special Products CSP 339)

- How to Get the Most Out Of Your Stereo (1960, Warner Brothers XS 1400)

- How to Save a Marriage and Ruin Your Life (1968, Columbia Masterworks OS 3140) Music from the motion picture by Ray Conniff's Singers and Michael Legrand.

- I Could Have Danced All Night – Vol. 1 for Hi-Fi Living (1957, RCA Custom RAL 1001; **Hill Bowen and His Orchestra**)

- I Married An Angel – Vol. 4 for Hi-Fi Living (1957, RCA Custom RAL 1004; **Hill Bowen and His Orchestra**)

- Invitation to Listening (1960, Decca DL 4020)

- Latin Holiday – Vol. 6 for Hi-Fi Living (1957, RCA Custom RAL 1006; **Don Amore and His Orchestra**)

- A Lazy Afternoon – Vol. 8 for Hi-Fi Living (1957, RCA Custom RAL 1008; **Malcolm Lockyer and His Orchestra**)

- Love On Broadway – Vol. 5 for Hi-Fi Living (1957, RCA Custom RAL 1005; **Hill Bowen and His Orchestra**)

- Luau at Waikiki (1964, RCA Victor LPM-2885 (mono), LSP-2885 (stereo)) **Ray Kinney** is listed as Master of Ceremonies for three other acts. 'Recorded live at the Long House at the Hilton Hawaiian Village, the Fun Resort.'

- Lure of Hawaii (Sutton SSU-220) This was apparently a re-release of **Willie Alunuai and His Band**'s *Hawaiian Holiday*.

- Magic Moods (1970, MCA Special Markets DL 734729) This features **Roger Williams** (side A) and **Bert Kaempfert** (side B).

- Mambo Cha Cha Cha (1959, Riviera R0023 (mono), STR0023 (stereo))

- Mambo in Havana (1959, Riviera R0010 (mono), STR0010 (stereo))

- Melodies from the South Seas, Vol. 2 (Hamilton HLP 12146)

- Mid-Night in Mexico (1957, Hollywood LPH 108)

- Moods 2: One Hour and Twelve Minutes (1960, Ampex RSL 408)

- Moon Music (1959, Janus FST-2010; The Blair-Smythe Society Orchestra)

- Mucho Calor (Much Heat) (1958, Andex A 3002) Latin jazz.

- Music for Gracious Living: After the Dance (1955, Columbia CL-697; all of this series by **Peter Barclay and His Orchestra**)

- Music for Gracious Living: Barbecue (1955, Columbia CL-695)

- Music for Gracious Living: Buffet (1955, Columbia CL-694)

- Music for Gracious Living: Do It Yourself (1955, Columbia CL-698)

- Music for Gracious Living: Foursome (1955, Columbia CL-696) Were any more of these done?

- Music For Heavenly Bodies (1959, Omega Disk)

- Music to Dream By (Columbia Special Products; XTV 82085 (side A) & XTV 82086 (side B) on labels) This was a special album given away as a premium for purchasers of General Electric Sleep-Guard blankets.

- *Music to Read James Bond By, Vol. 2* (1966, United Artists, UAS 6541)

- Music to Relax By in Your Barcalounger (Columbia) Produced as a premium for purchasers of Barcalounger chairs.

- Musical Memories (1964, International Award Series AK-240)

- The New Sound of Music: Percussive Stereo on Medallion (1961, Kapp Medallion MS 1)

- Organ Fantasy in Hi-Fi (1959, Riviera R0036 (mono), STR036 (stereo)). Note that this used the same cover as **Betty Staples**'s *Organ Fantasy in Hi-Fi* from 1957; but the song selection is completely different.

- Organ Goes South of the Border (Custom Records)

- Perfect For Dancing: Rumbas (1955, RCA Victor LPM-1069)

- Perspectives in Percussion, Vol. 1 (1961, Somerset, SFP-132)

- Port of Suez: Exotic Music of the Middle East (1958, Crown CLP-5085 (mono), CST-119 (stereo))

- Romantic Strings Play Dancing in the Dark (Reader's Digest) (1963, RCA Custom RD28B-M; **Hill Bowen and His Orchestra**)

- Sears Silvertone Demonstration Album (Command SR 1 SD)

- Serenade For Lovers (1969, RCA Custom/Reader's Digest RDA 61-A) 9-record set.

- Showcase – Phase 4 (1962, Decca PFS 34001)

- Silk Stockings (1957, MGM E 3542 ST)

- Songs of the South Seas (Waldorf Music Hall MHK 33-1201)

- Sound of Sitar (1966, Deram SML 1002)

- Sound Off... Softly (Columbia Special Products CSP 244) Promotional record produced for the makers of Gold Bond ceiling tile.

- Sounds Fantastic! (1966, RCA Victor PRS-210)

- Sounds In Space (1958, RCA Victor SP-33-13) Stereo action test record.

- Spectacular is the Sound For It (1960, MGM E3883 (mono), SE3883 (stereo))

- Squirt Does Its Thing: Semi-Soft Music in Tijuana Style (1970, Mark 56 570) This was another album of recycled songs similar to the company's *Tijuana Taxi* and related releases. Squirt was a brand of soda, so this might have been offered as a premium.

- Stereo Action Unlimited! (1962, RCA Victor LSA-2489) (Stereo Action)

- Stereo Sampler, Vol. 1 (Mercury SRD-1)

- A Stereo Sound Spectacular (Command 16101-SD)

- Such Brass! (1969, Mark 56 564) This was the usual Mark 56 collection of unthreatening Easy Listening songs produced by George Garabedian, many of which had already appeared on such albums as *Tijuana Taxi*.

- Suddenly It's Spring! (1965, Columbia Special Products CSP 281) 'Collector's album limited edition – created exclusively for Hammond Organ.'

- Taboo (1959, Riviera R 0028 (mono), STR 0028 (stereo)) This is another re-release of *Jungle Beat* by **Subri Moulin and His Equatorial Rhythm Group**, with 10 of the original 12 songs; but the artist isn't listed on either the jacket or the record label.

- Tahiti: Dream Island (Capitol TAO-10281 (mono), STAO-10281 (stereo))

- Tahiti Fete! (1958, Tiare Tahiti TT-1800)

- Tamure Tahiti (Dot DLP 3494 (mono), DLP 25494 (stereo))

- Tango Time (1954, Columbia CL 597) This features **Xavier Cugat and His Orchestra** (side A) and **Marek Webber and His Orchestra** (side B).

- Taste of Drums (1964, Time S/2140)

- Theme from Goldfinger and Others (1964, Crown CLP-5440 (mono), CST-440 (stereo))

- These Foolish Things – Vol. 7 for Hi-Fi Living (1957, RCA Custom RAL 1007; **Jack Say and His Orchestra**)

- This Could Lead to Love (1955, Riverside RLP 12-808)

- Thunderball, The Man From UNCLE, and Other Secret Agent Themes (1966, Design Records, DLP-206)

- Tijuana One More Time (Mark 56 545; aka *Alpha Beta Presents Tijuana One More Time*) This was another of Mark 56's mostly-anonymous collections of **Tijuana Brass**-influenced songs, this time co-branded with Alpha Beta supermarkets and probably sold there as a premium. This has the same catalog number as the next entry, but a different configuration of songs and different cover artwork.

- Tijuana Party (Mark 56 545; aka *Pizza Inn Presents Tijuana Party*) This was a collection of unassuming **Tijuana Brass**-influenced music that was recycled by the company for various album projects. This one was obviously co-branded with Pizza Inn restaurants and was probably sold as a premium in their locations.

- Tijuana Picnic (1968, Mark 56 543; aka *Colonel Sanders' Tijuana Picnic*) Col. Harlan Sanders apparently gave us his impressions of each song on this album, which was a premium sold or given away through Kentucky Fried Chicken franchisees.

- Tijuana Taxi (Mark 56 535) This album might have been sold in stores, but some copies bear a co-branding with Pepsi and so must also have been a premium. Different cover variations exist. Note that this shares almost the exact same playlist as the previous entry, *Tijuana Picnic*, except with "Zorba the Greek" replacing "Our Day Will Come." A different version replaces "Chile Verde" and "El Toro" with "El Burrito" and "Hot Tamale," and is branded with Acme markets (which explains the stockboy on the cover handing the bags of groceries to the musicians in the car). Another variation, co-branded with Spudnuts markets, keeps the original songlist but features different cover artwork, of the musicians parked in front of the market.

- Tijuana Taxi (1968, Mark 56 544) Also known as *Taco Bell Presents Tijuana Taxi*, this album shares the title of the previous entry, and similar cover artwork by the same artist, but mostly a different set of songs. This was almost certainly a premium sold at Taco Bell restaurants at the time.

- Toragee: The Romantic Music of Asia (1966, Epic LF 18042 (mono), BF 19042 (stereo))

- A Trip to Romance – Vol. 11 for Hi-Fi Living (1957, RCA Custom RAL 1011; **Tony Osborne and His Orchestra**)

- Up-Up and Away in My Beautiful Balloon (Mark 56 545; aka *Der Wienerschnitzel Presents...*) This album features the same catalog number as the company's *Tijuana Party*, and has mostly the same song lineup (the varying ones might just be instruments given new titles).

- Vitaphonic Stereo: Extra Sensory Perception in Sound (1958, Warner Brothers WS 1241)

- Walt Disney's The Enchanted Tiki Room (1968, Disneyland ST-3966)

- We're Having a Party – Vol. 12 for Hi-Fi Living (1957, RCA Custom RAL 1012; **Malcolm Lockyer and His Orchestra**)

- When We're Together... Remembering (Columbia Special Products CSP-279) Promotional record produced for Philco, a subsidiary of Ford.

- Williams, Roger and Ferrante & Teicher (1966 Metro M-584 (mono), MS-584 (stereo))

- The World of Phase 4 Stereo, Vol. 2 (1970, Decca SPA 114)

To purchase additional copies of this book directly from the author, send $24.95 (with free Media Mail shipping in the continental U.S.) to:

Todd Frye
PO Box 577
Harrogate TN 37752

Personal checks and money orders accepted.
To purchase via Paypal, or to make other shipping or special arrangements, please email the author at *toddfrye@yahoo.com*.

You might also be interested in some of my other books! All of them can be previewed by simply visiting

toddfrye.org

I Was a Teenage Monster Magazine Fiend is a visual guide to collecting monster and horror magazines from the years 1950 to 1979. Every published title is covered, from *3D Monsters* to *World Famous Creatures*, along with cover illustrations. That's 1,200 covers, all in full color, along with information on each title. 227 pages.

$24.95 with free shipping in the U.S.

Passion and Peril: The Complete Men's Magazines, Volume 1 features 601 covers from 35 different men's magazines from the 1950's and 60's; each large (no more than 4 to a page) and in full color, and is printed on heavy 70-lb. paper for better reproduction.

8-1/2 by 11". 195 pages.
$29.95 with free shipping in the U.S.

Fantastic Planets: The Complete Pulp Magazine Covers, Volume 1 reproduces 604 covers from 18 different classic pulp titles, ranging from the 1920's to the 1950's. Each image is given in full color and no more than 4 to a page; printed on heavy 70-lb. paper.

8-1/2 by 11:, 208 pages.
$29.95 with free shipping in the U.S.

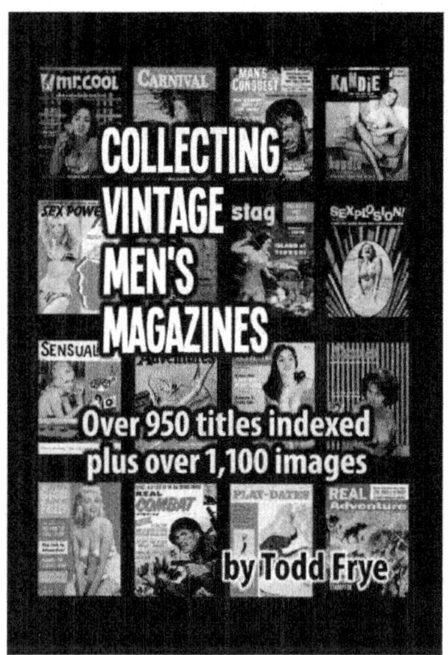

Collecting Vintage Men's Magazines is the first comprehensive guide to one of the hottest new collectibles categories. Adventure, girlie, humor, and 'sophisticates' magazines from 1950 to 1969 are covered. Over 950 titles are listed, with over 1,100 black and white illustrations. No other book like this currently exists. 265 pages.

$24.95 with free shipping in the U.S.

Marvelous Mythology tells the story of how the Marvel Comics superheroes were created, with a comprehensive history of the company during the 1960's and 70's. The work of men like Jack Kirby and Stan Lee, and their creation of Spider-Man, the Fantastic Four, the Avengers, the Hulk, and all of Marvel's other classic characters is detailed in this volume. 224 pages.

$19.95 with free shipping in the U.S.

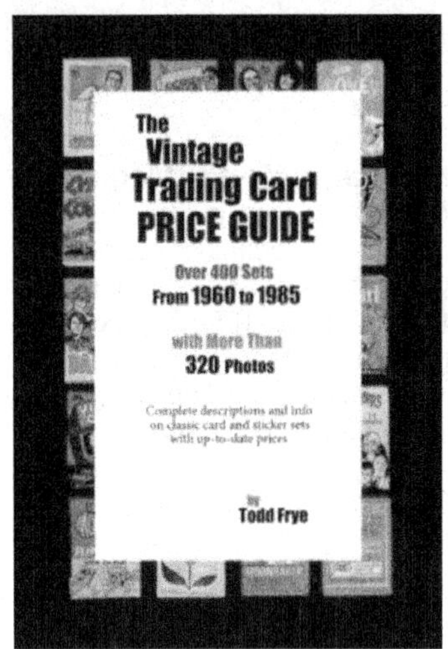

The Vintage Trading Card Price Guide gives detailed value information on over 400 vintage card and sticker sets from the years 1960 to 1985. Illustrated with over 320 black and white photos, this is the first major trading card price guide released to the mass market in nearly 30 years. It is essential reading for collectors who want to discover the fascinating world of cards that existed long before any of the modern issues. 271 pages.

$24.95 with free shipping in the U.S.

The Complete Marvel Comics Visual Checklist, Vol. 1: A-L features thumbnail cover images for every Marvel comic book published between 1939 and 1980 (whose titles begin with letters A through J); that's over 4,800 color images, plus additional information on each title. 272 pages.

$29.95 with free shipping in the U.S.

CPSIA information can be obtained
at www.ICGtesting.com
Printed in the USA
FSOW03n2119170816
23898FS